More Praise for *Understanding Mass Incarceration*

"Both comprehensive and wonderfully detailed, this book provides a key resource for anyone concerned with the injustices that ground the criminal 'justice' system. Through history, analysis, thorough research, and fresh ideas, Kilgore masterfully draws together the threads of this sprawling system." —Maya Schenwar, author of *Locked Down, Locked Out*

"As an organizer, I have been waiting for this book." —Mariame Kaba, founder of Project NIA, Chicago

"James Kilgore lays out everything the reader needs to gain a picture of the history, dynamics, and reality of mass incarceration and who is affected by it. Well written, documented, and illustrated, this is a must-read for anyone who wants to quickly get up to speed on what mass incarceration means in America today." —Paul Wright, editor of *Prison Legal News*

"James Kilgore untangles the threads of bureaucracy and misunderstandings to probe deeply into this human catastrophe, rendering a highly readable and compelling book, convincingly arguing that dismantling mass incarceration is the key civil rights struggle of our time." —Roxanne Dunbar-Ortiz, author of *An Indigenous Peoples' History of the United States*

"Written in a lively, accessible style, this book offers an introduction to those who are new to the topic as well as insights for the expert. . . . For anyone wanting a single book to paint a complete picture of the horrors of mass incarceration as well as the heroic resistance to this system of oppression, this would be my first choice." —Frank B. Wilderson III, winner of the 2008 American Book Award for *Incognegro: A Memoir of Exile and Apartheid*

Also by James Kilgore

Prudence Couldn't Swim

Freedom Never Rests

We Are All Zimbabweans Now

UNDERSTANDING
MASS
INCARCERATION

A PEOPLE'S GUIDE TO THE KEY CIVIL RIGHTS
STRUGGLE OF OUR TIME

JAMES KILGORE

THE NEW PRESS

NEW YORK
LONDON

Requests for permission to reproduce selections from this book should be mailed to:
Permissions Department, The New Press, 120 Wall Street, 31st floor, New York, NY 10005.

Excerpt from "Drug Warz" by The Coup on page 71 used by permission.

Published in the United States by The New Press, New York, 2015
Distributed by Perseus Distribution

LIBRARY OF CONGRESS CATALOGING-IN-PUBLICATION DATA

Kilgore, James William, 1947–
Understanding mass incarceration : a people's guide to the key civil rights struggle of our time / James Kilgore.
pages cm
Includes bibliographical references and index.
ISBN 978-1-62097-067-6 (paperback)—ISBN 978-1-62097-122-2 (e-book) 1. Imprisonment—United States—History.
2. Criminal justice, Administration of—United States—History. 3. Alternatives to imprisonment—United States.
4. Civil rights—United States. 5. Criminals—Rehabilitation—United States. I. Title.
HV9466.K55 2015
365'.973—dc23
2015008899

The New Press publishes books that promote and enrich public discussion and understanding of the issues vital to our democracy and to a more equitable world. These books are made possible by the enthusiasm of our readers; the support of a committed group of donors, large and small; the collaboration of our many partners in the independent media and the not-for-profit sector; booksellers, who often hand-sell New Press books; librarians; and above all by our authors.

www.thenewpress.com

Book design and composition by Bookbright Media
This book was set in Bembo and DIN

Printed in the United States of America

2 4 6 8 10 9 7 5 3 1

CONTENTS

UNDERSTANDING MASS INCARCERATION

Courtesy of Mary Sutton

INTRODUCTION

In writing *Understanding Mass Incarceration*, I am attempting to do two things. First and most important, I aim to provide a comprehensive, accessible text on a complex and important topic. For many people, mass incarceration simply refers to the United States' excessive use of imprisonment—we have 25 percent of the world's prisoners with just 5 percent of the world's population. It's a tragedy of the first order, but mass incarceration is not just about the number of people behind bars—there are lots of dots to connect.

Mass incarceration is actually one of this country's key strategies for addressing problems of poverty, inequality, unemployment, racial conflict, citizenship, sexuality, and gender, as well as crime. Hence, when we talk about mass incarceration, we are not speaking only of prison cells or the War on Drugs. A philosophy, a history, and a trail of profit and investment lurk behind the statistics.

Ultimately, mass incarceration is about opportunity—new opportunities for profit and political power for some and the denial of opportunity to others, largely poor people of color. During the past three decades, the urge to punish and incapacitate the most vulnerable sectors of the population has replaced the desire to nurture and develop. As a placard in the photo on page 166 says, JAIL EMBODIES OUR FAILURE TO CARE.

Understanding mass incarceration means getting at the root of it, focusing on the fundamental reasons why many states spend more on corrections than on higher education, why nearly 6 million people are denied the right to vote because of their criminal record, why law enforcement cracks down on petty crime in impoverished African American and Latino communities while letting those who loot the economy and commit war crimes go free, and why billions are spent on bailing out Bank of America and General Motors while poor people remain in jail because they can't raise $500 to bail themselves out.

Second, in this book I offer an introduction to the types of actions people are taking throughout the country to oppose mass incarceration. These help bring to life the dynamics of the key civil rights struggle of our time. The actions highlighted herein—campaigns against draconian drug prosecutions, mobilizations to "ban the box" on employment applications for those with felony convictions, efforts to block jail construction in large urban centers and small Midwestern towns, and lobbying to overturn repressive sentencing and immigration laws—all represent paths to undermining or fundamentally altering mass incarceration.

DIALOGUES, NOT DIATRIBES

Having spent many years of my life both inside and outside prison as an educator, I've approached each topic in this book by trying to create dialogues for the reader among the various opinions, rather than attempting to offer all the answers (as if anyone really has them). Achieving success in this key civil rights struggle will rest on the capacity of activists and community members to think and act critically. A social movement in opposition to mass incarceration must engage in action but also must promote serious reflection and rigorous debate.

Obviously, I must rely on my own understanding to frame the debates, but I've tried to offer many perspectives on important issues. The book makes use of multiple sidebars and extracts to highlight the voices of those who are rarely heard in mainstream sources, particularly the formerly incarcerated, their loved ones, and members of their communities. But I also include the words of those who have written or commented on mass incarceration from a variety of other viewpoints, including CEOs of private prison corporations and corrections officials. My intent is to facilitate a process wherein readers can critically analyze the controversy and develop their own perspectives. This type of critical thought is crucial for building a movement based on democracy, not on authoritarian models. We can't afford to create a social movement in opposition to mass incarceration that develops into another structure of oppression.

A NOTE ON LANGUAGE

I have made every effort to avoid the use of stigmatizing language. Words such as *convict*, *inmate*, *felon*, *probationer*, and *parolee* do not appear in this text. Neither do I refer to anyone as an ex-offender, an ex-prisoner, or an ex-anything. Instead, I use terms that humanize: formerly incarcerated person, people with sex offense convictions, individuals on parole, et cetera. In making this choice, I salute the late Eddie Ellis, who reminded us that words "are of fundamental importance to the process of public opinion formulation, positive media images, effective social service delivery and, most importantly, progressive policy change."[1] Similarly, I have tried to avoid succumbing to the gender binary, especially in discussing the population of men's and women's prisons. Transgender and gender-nonconforming people suffer incredible discrimination in excessive incarceration and inappropriate categorization and treatment after arrest. Their position in this system needs to be recognized and properly depicted.

THE STRUCTURE OF THE BOOK

The book contains five parts. The first part, "The Basics," provides the historical background of the process that has quadrupled the prison population in the past four decades. Chapter 1 presents a snapshot of mass incarceration, the essential facts and figures of who is locked up and why. In chapter 2, I turn to the history—explaining the political forces that made mass incarceration possible and detailing the ways in which pro-imprisonment leaders, such as President Ronald Reagan and researcher John DiIulio Jr., used the media to build popular support for prison expansion. Here we will also unearth the racial roots of mass incarceration, showing how the construction of the young Black male as criminal was essential to convince voters and politicians that cluttering our landscape with prisons and jails was a necessary stage in U.S. history. Chapter 3 will detail the rise of harsh sentences and the legal vehicles, such as truth-in-sentencing and three strikes, that enabled prosecutors to lock people up for decades with impunity. Part 1 also depicts the philosophical changes that have accompanied mass incarceration—the shifting of the ethos of criminal justice from an emphasis on providing people in prison an opportunity to rehabilitate themselves through job training, education, and treatment to a system that warehouses human beings as though they were out-of-date products, setting them up for failure when they do finally exit the prison gates.

Part 2, "The Many Faces of 'Tough on Crime,'" describes the policies and processes that have enabled mass incarceration. Chapter 4 describes the racially based War on Drugs that has devastated African American communities, normalizing the presence of militarized police forces and the constant harassment of stop-and-frisk policing. Chapter 5 depicts the attack on immigrants that some refer to as the New Operation Wetback. It has led to drastic rises in the incarceration and deportation of the undocumented, especially since the late 1990s. Chapter 6 looks at the increasingly harsh post-incarceration regimes of parole and probation that have made prison release a revolving door rather than a permanent exit.

Chapter 7 examines the local face of mass incarceration—jail. Municipal "tough on crime" laws have criminalized poverty. A host of common ordinances now outlaw daily activities of the poor, such as sleeping in public and "aggressive" panhandling. Even feeding people in public places is forbidden in some jurisdictions. The tightening of law enforcement at the local level has sparked a massive increase in jail populations from coast to coast, housing not only those in transit to longer prison sentences but people locked up simply because they lack the money to pay a few dollars in fines or bail.

The final chapter of Part 2 addresses the school-to-prison pipeline—the ways in which education in low-income communities of color has increasingly been infused with the discipline-and-punishment ethos of prison, from lockdowns to the campus cops known as Student Resource Officers, who frequently bring criminal charges against pupils for petty offenses such as truancy or tardiness. Schools throughout the country have become places where young people are prepared to be under the control of the state rather than directed toward success and community building.

The two chapters of Part 3 unravel the "gendered threads" of mass incarceration, particularly its impact on women. While men make up roughly 90 percent of those behind bars, chapter 9 explores how those left behind in the communities hit hardest by mass incarceration also carry extra burdens. In the absence of incarcerated loved ones, this cohort, mostly women and children, must shoulder extra financial, parenting, emotional, and community responsibilities.

The gender impact does not end there, however. Chapter 10 explains why in recent years the incarceration rate of women has escalated far faster than that of men. When women land in prison, they face extra punishment, such as sexual harassment from prison staff and a lack of suitable clothing and medical programs. Moreover, one woman in thirty who lands behind bars is pregnant. In many states, women who give birth in prison still must do so in shackles. Men may be the main targets of incarceration, but women have their own burdens as a result of this process.

Part 4, "Prison Profiteers," surveys those who benefit from mass incarceration. Chapter 11 focuses on the most famous of the profiteers, the private prison corporations. We'll see how the Corrections Corporation of America and the GEO Group use a combination of lobbying and negotiating skills to redirect taxpayer money into their coffers and rise to the top of the prison industry. In chapter 12 we will look at other companies that rely on prison business to secure their bottom lines. From large-scale construction firms to finance houses to Bob Barker Industries, which supplies prison toiletries and shower shoes, businesses have found ways to make money off of prisoners.

Part 5, "Ending Mass Incarceration," highlights the current efforts at carving a path away from excessive imprisonment, at charting strategy for the new civil rights struggle. Chapter 13 examines new philosophical approaches to justice, genuine alternatives to "lock 'em up and throw away the key." We'll meet practitioners and proponents of restorative justice, transformative justice, and prison abolition.

In the final chapter, we will consider organizations and communities that have taken some successful steps along the road of change. We will become acquainted with the work of activist groups, such as All of Us or None, which champions the rights of the formerly incarcerated, and the Drug Policy Alliance, which has led the effort to reduce drug offense prosecutions in New York. We will also look at campaigns outside the major centers, in places such as Bloomington, Indiana, and my own hometown, Champaign, Illinois, where activists have blocked efforts to build new prisons and jails.

MY NETWORK OF SUPPORT

As is true for all such volumes, researching and writing *Understanding Mass Incarceration* was not a solitary journey. Along the road to completion, I had the benefit of support from a number of friends, colleagues, and fellow activists in the struggle for social justice. I am particularly grateful to the many people who read chapters or offered helpful information and sources for this work. These include Francisco Baires, Holly Cooper, Alex Friedman, Judy Greene, Alexes Harris, Emily Harris, Tracy Huling, Mariame Kaba, Manuel Lafontaine, Jason Lydon, Claude Marks, Miguel Saucedo, Peter Wagner, Paul Wright, and Diana Zuñiga.

I owe special thanks to Craig Gilmore, who read and gave wonderful comments on several chapters; to Brian Dolinar, who offered a host of his pictures and his own incredible insights as a journalist to this process; and to Mary Sutton for her longtime friendship and political solidarity as well as for her magnificent photographs.

In the midst of writing this book, two personal political struggles emerged, one against attempts to build a county jail in my Illinois hometown and another against an attempt by right-wing critics to strip me of my employment at the University of Illinois due to my "criminal background." Keeping my head above water during these struggles required the solidarity of a huge number of people. I owe special gratitude to Jim Barrett, Diana Block, Merle Bowen, Danielle Chynoweth, Al Davis, Susan Davis, Roxanne Dunbar-Ortiz, Mark Enslin, Chris Evans, Dianne Feeley, Behrooz Ghamari-Tabrizi, Rebecca Ginsburg, Terri

Gitler, Charlotte Greene, Patsy Howell, Scott Humphrey, Amanda Hwu, Allen and Bobbie Isaacman, Stephen Kaufman, Barbara Kessel, Sophia Lewis, Claude Marks, Martel Miller, Faranak Miraftab, Marlon Mitchell, Nathaniel Moore, Natalie Prochaska, Bruce Reznick, Dede Ruggles, Ken Salo, Bill Sullivan, Rafter Sass Ferguson, Heather Thompson, Bobbi Trist, Dottie Vura-Weis, David Wilson, and Laura Worby. I have also had wonderful support in these situations from my longstanding international friends, especially those from southern Africa, who have taught me so much about how to persevere. Special acknowledgments are due to Patrick Bond, Laura Czerniewicz, Rick DeSatge, Roger and Kordula Dunscombe, Mondli Hlatshwayo, Stephen Morrow, Trevor Ngwane, Ighsaan Schroeder, Salim Vally, and Everjoice Win.

I also need to pay special thanks to the wonderful and supportive editorial team at The New Press, Ellen Adler, Diane Wachtell, Jed Bickman, and Sarah Fan, as well as copy editor Gary Stimeling. From day one, Ellen and Diane's enthusiasm for this project was effusive, helping me know that I had stumbled onto something useful and much needed. Once production started, Jed Bickman was the hands-on commentator, carefully steering me back onto the main argument when I strayed and inserting helpful comments and carefully placed question marks when the logic of my argument defied easy comprehension.

Most important of all has been the constant presence of my family members, who have ceaselessly stuck by me through good times and bad with love and solidarity—the two things a person cannot live without. I am especially grateful to my mother, Barbara Kilgore, who at 101 still manages to kick along with a smile and a proclamation of pride in and love for her son. I also could not have stayed on track without the undying support of my in-laws, Dave and Pat Barnes-McConnell, who have always stood nearby with the required doses of love and carefully crafted intellectual critique. Equally critical to the success of this project were my two sons, Lewis and Lonnie, whose rock-solid determination to succeed in life and not be deterred by whatever obstacles have been placed in their way has given me the peace of mind to remain focused on this work. Finally, the one person who knows me and this work best is Terri Barnes, lifelong partner and comrade, intellectual inspiration, a woman who fears not to articulate either devastating and insightful criticism or unflinching expressions of love and support. And she can top it all off with a goose-bump-producing version of "Redemption Song" or "Where Do Broken Hearts Go?" with her magic soprano. Without her, neither this book nor its author would be anything close to complete.

PART ONE

THE BASICS OF MASS INCARCERATION

Courtesy of WISDOM

1

A SNAPSHOT OF THE SYSTEM

Since the 1980s, the United States has embarked on the most extensive campaign of prison building and incarceration in modern history. Lawyer Bryan Stevenson, winner of the 2012 Smithsonian American Ingenuity Award, argues that "mass incarceration defines us as a society the way slavery once did."[1] Former New York and Pennsylvania state prison administrator Martin Horn sums it up: "We are on a prison binge. We're addicted to incarceration in this country."[2] To begin to understand why, we'll need some background on the system.

INCARCERATION NATION

Our prison binge can be assessed in several ways. *The total number of people imprisoned is growing rapidly.* From 1980 to 2013, the number of people in U.S. prisons and jails rose from just over five hundred thousand to more than 2 million, reaching a peak in 2009 at about 2.5 million. With only 5 percent of the world's population, the United States holds 25 percent of the world's prisoners.[3]

Compared to other countries, America's gone stir crazy. Among industrialized nations, the United States is an outlier, incarcerating at more than four times the rate of Britain and China and more than fourteen times the rate of Japan.[4]

Prisons lock up more and more money. Prison and jail expenditures in America jumped from

$7 billion in 1980 to $57 billion in 2000 and have exceeded $70 billion every year since 2007. During that period, crime rates first remained steady and then declined after 1993.[5] Those figures don't include the downstream costs to society or the opportunity costs, the things we can't do because we spend so much money on prisons.

Besides locking up millions of people, the United States has expanded the ranks of those under some form of community oversight, usually called parole, probation, or supervised release. In 1980 about 1.3 million people were under such supervision; by 2011, their numbers had grown to 4.8 million—about 2.9 percent of American adults.[6] *The burdens of the after-prison system have grown in proportion to the prison system itself.*

Here are seven key facts about mass incarceration to chart some of the symptoms of our prison addiction:

1. The U.S. incarceration rate in 2013 was 702 per 100,000 people, topping all nations with a population of more than 100,000. Russia was second among industrialized nations at 470 per 100,000. The rate for the United Kingdom was 149; for China, 124; and for Sweden, just 60.[7]

2. Annual admissions to U.S. prisons and jails rose from 171,884 in 1980 to a peak of 747,031 in 2006.[8]

3. In 2012 incarceration rates for Blacks stood at 2,805 per 100,000—about six times higher than that of whites and almost three times that of Hispanics.[9]

4. Although women make up only 8 percent of the U.S. incarcerated population, their rate of 67 per 100,000 is higher than that of more than three dozen countries, including Japan, Nigeria, India, Yemen, and Pakistan.[10]

5. In 2012 New York spent more than $60,000 a year to incarcerate one person. By comparison, the total 2011–2012 annual cost of attending Harvard was $52,652 for tuition, room, board, and fees combined.[11]

6. In 2012 some 5.8 million people were denied the right to vote because of a felony conviction.[12]

7. At least 2,500 people in the United States are serving life sentences for crimes

they committed as juveniles. Many serve time in adult prisons even while they are juveniles.[13]

These basic facts show the scale of U.S. mass incarceration, but to understand it we must address two critical questions: who gets locked up? and why has incarceration increased so dramatically?

WHO GETS LOCKED UP?

The overall number of people behind bars has skyrocketed, but the selection is not random. The incarcerated population has been largely determined by factors of race, class, and gender.

Mass Incarceration Pro and Con

Political scientist John Dilulio Jr. explained his support for mass incarceration in 1996: "On average it costs about $25,000 a year to keep a convicted criminal in prison. For that money society gets four benefits: Imprisonment punishes offenders and expresses society's moral disapproval. It teaches felons and would-be felons a lesson: Do crime, do time. Prisoners get drug treatment and education. And, as the columnist Ben Wattenberg has noted, 'a thug in prison can't shoot your sister.'"[14]

In her 2010 book *The New Jim Crow: Mass Incarceration in the Age of Colorblindness*, Michelle Alexander offers a different view:

> We could choose to be a nation that extends care, compassion, and concern to those who are locked up and locked out or headed for prison before they are old enough to vote. We could seek for them the same opportunities we seek for our own children; we could treat them like one of "us." We could do that. Or we can choose to be a nation that shames and blames its most vulnerable, affixes badges of dishonor upon them at young ages, and then relegates them to a permanent second-class status for life. That is the path we have chosen, and it leads to a familiar place.[15]

PEOPLE OF COLOR, PARTICULARLY AFRICAN AMERICANS, ARE DISPROPORTIONATELY INCARCERATED

While African Americans make up only about 13 percent of the U.S. population, by 2012 Blacks[16] constituted nearly 40 percent of those in prisons and jails. Hispanics are about a 14 percent of the general population, yet they are about 22 percent of those incarcerated. The prison population has changed from about 30 percent people of color in the 1970s to roughly 70 percent in 2012.[17] Transgender people also have extremely high rates of incarceration, with one in six experiencing some form of incarceration during their lifetime.[18]

POOR PEOPLE, REGARDLESS OF RACE, ARE THE MOST LIKELY TO BE INCARCERATED

People in prisons and jails have lower average incomes on the outside than the general population, are more likely to be unemployed, and less likely to have completed high school or college. They represent the poorest, most marginalized members of the U.S. working class. Wealthy people who commit white-collar crimes that lead to losses that go into the millions often avoid prosecution or receive lighter sentences than those responsible for theft, robbery, or drug sales involving far smaller amounts of money. Paul Wright, editor of *Prison Legal News*, refers to this "two-tier nature of the American criminal justice system, where you have one system of justice for the poor and politically unconnected and another system of justice for the wealthy and politically connected."[19]

One of the most egregious instances of special justice for the rich was the 2014 case of a young white Texan named Ethan Crouch. He drove while under the influence of alcohol and caused a crash that killed four people. During the trial, his lawyer called a witness who claimed Crouch suffered from "affluenza," an affliction of privileged children whose wealthy parents never set limits on their behavior. In passing sentence, presiding Judge Jean Boyd acknowledged the affluenza issue, sentenced Crouch to ten years' probation, and mandated that he live in an upmarket treatment facility at a cost of about a quarter of a million dollars per year.[20] Crouch's parents were required to pay only about $13,000 of those annual fees. The remainder was covered by taxpayers.[21]

The Structure of the U.S. Criminal Legal System

When a person is arrested, he or she is generally sent to a county jail. In minor cases, individuals may be released shortly thereafter and will remain in the community until their cases are resolved. This is called release on own recognizance (ROR). Others will have to pay bail or bonds to the court in order to be released until resolution of their cases. In more serious matters, the accused will usually remain in jail until the case is resolved in court. If convicted of a serious charge, a felony, a person will be sentenced to more than a year and typically will go to a prison. After completing the sentence, one is normally under a form of community supervision called parole. People who serve less than a year, usually convicted of misdemeanors, complete their sentence in a county jail. When they are released, they usually go on probation, which is like parole but under the authority of the county rather than the state. More details about parole and probation are discussed in chapter 6.

Prisons are divided into federal, state, and county systems. Violators of federal law are processed in federal courts and, if convicted, serve time in a facility run by the Federal Bureau of Prisons. Federal prisons hold about 10 percent of the incarcerated population. Each state has its own laws, and most states have their own prison systems run by their departments of corrections. State prisons hold about 60 percent of the nation's prisoners. Most counties have their own jails, which range in size from a few beds to facilities in big cities that hold thousands. On a given day, county jails hold about 20 percent of the imprisoned population.

In addition, the federal government is responsible for immigration detention centers, which hold people charged under immigration law violations, which are civil, not criminal violations. They make up about 1.5 percent of those behind bars. Some Native American nations also have their own courts and jails, which account for fewer than 1 percent of those in custody. See Figure 1.1 for more details.

The Thirteenth Amendment Allows Slavery for the "Convicted"

Neither slavery nor involuntary servitude, *except as a punishment for crime whereof the party shall have been duly convicted*, shall exist within the United States, or any place subject to their jurisdiction. (Emphasis added.)

PEOPLE'S CHANCES OF ENDING UP IN PRISON RISE DRAMATICALLY IN TARGETED NEIGHBORHOODS

Large sectors of the incarcerated population come from low-income urban communities, usually either predominantly African American or Latino. In certain parts of the United States, Native American communities in reservations, urban areas, and poor rural towns with largely white populations also suffer disproportionate levels of incarceration.

THE BURDENS OF MASS INCARCERATION ARE APPORTIONED BY GENDER

The overwhelming majority of those in prisons and jails are men. Overall, men's prisons and jails hold more than 90 percent of all those behind bars. Although men suffer the actual imprisonment, their removal has important effects on those left behind in their communities, mostly women and children. The absence of men shifts a host of tasks onto the largely female group that remains behind—financial support for the family, care of children and other loved ones, and civic and community duties. In addition, women often have to lend financial and emotional support to the incarcerated men, contributing money toward basic necessities for loved ones on the inside and organizing visits to often distant prisons and jails. When men finally gain release from custody, women frequently must provide housing, food, supervision, and assistance with the emotional transition to life on the outside.

INCARCERATION RATES FOR HISPANICS AND WOMEN HAVE RISEN SHARPLY SINCE 2001

Although African Americans have the highest incarceration rate per capita, since 2001 the absolute number of Hispanics behind bars has been growing at a much faster pace than that of any other racial group. In fact, from 2000 to 2013, the number of Blacks in prison declined slightly, whereas the number of Hispanics increased by more than 50 percent.

Music of the Incarceration Experience

The collective experience of mass incarceration has sparked a vast array of music depicting the reality of communities that have been directly affected by it. A number of hip-hop artists have crafted numbers that chronicle police victimization and life behind bars. Perhaps the most well known is Akon's "Locked Up," which grabbed nearly 50 million YouTube views. Other high-profile numbers include Public Enemy, "Black Steel in the Hour of Chaos"; Nas, "Last Words"; Jah Cure, "Prison Walls"; Beanie Sigel, "What Ya Life Like"; and Ludacris and friends, "Do Your Time." Nate Dogg performed his "One More Day" in an orange jumpsuit surrounded by his crew in the same prison attire. California artist Tiny Doo was actually charged with criminal conspiracy based on the content of his 2014 album *No Safety*. The prison theme has not been limited to men, with several songs by female artists focusing on the experience of women whose partner is incarcerated, such as "Gotta Man" by Eve, with more than 2 million YouTube views.

We have also seen a rapid growth in the number of women in prisons and jails. From 2000 to 2010, the population of women in prison grew at a far faster rate than that of men, and the absolute numbers for white and Hispanic women rose faster than those for African American women.

Finally, from 2009 to 2011, the total number of people in prisons throughout the United States declined slightly for the first time since the 1970s. The figure rose slightly in 2012, then fell by 0.6 percent for 2013. The reasons for these recent trends are economic as well as political. We will explore shifts toward "decarceration" in chapter 14.

This brief profile of mass incarceration raises many disturbing issues. The key question, however, is *why* this major transformation in U.S. society has taken place. A number of researchers and activists have offered explanations. Here we will look at several.

WHY HAS INCARCERATION INCREASED SO DRAMATICALLY?

Mass incarceration has its roots in a time when crime rates were rising. Throughout the 1970s, crime, especially violent crime, steadily increased. Once mass incarceration began in the early 1980s, however, crime rates varied. During the 1980s, crime rates increased, then declined, then increased again, hitting a peak in the early 1990s. From 1993 onward, violent and property crime decreased year after year. Yet the number of people incarcerated rose every year from the late 1970s to 2009. Author and legal scholar Michelle Alexander maintains that "violent crime rates have fluctuated over the years and bear little relationship to incarceration rates—which have soared during the past three decades regardless of whether violent crime was going up or down."[22]

Supporters of expanded imprisonment argue that locking people up is necessary to reduce crime. President Richard Nixon articulated this view quite succinctly in 1968 when he said, "Doubling the conviction rate in this country would do more to cure crime in America than quadrupling the funds for . . . war on poverty."[23]

Some social scientists, such as James Q. Wilson and Steve Levitt, contend that putting a "criminal" behind bars prevents a significant number of crimes. Wilson and Levitt maintain that the United States had a serious crime problem in the late 1970s and early 1980s and that mass incarceration has made a major impact by reducing crime rates and making cities safer.[24]

Critics of mass incarceration have responded to these arguments and pointed out other explanations for fluctuating crime rates and the rise of mass imprisonment. Here we will summarize three perspectives.

ECONOMIC REASONS

In her renowned book *The Golden Gulag*, scholar-activist Ruth Wilson Gilmore linked the rise of mass incarceration to globalization. She described the late 1970s as a moment of crisis for the U.S. economy, highlighted by falling corporate profits.[25] Sociologist Loïc Wacquant echoed Gilmore's perspective in *Punishing the Poor: The Neoliberal Government of Social Insecu-*

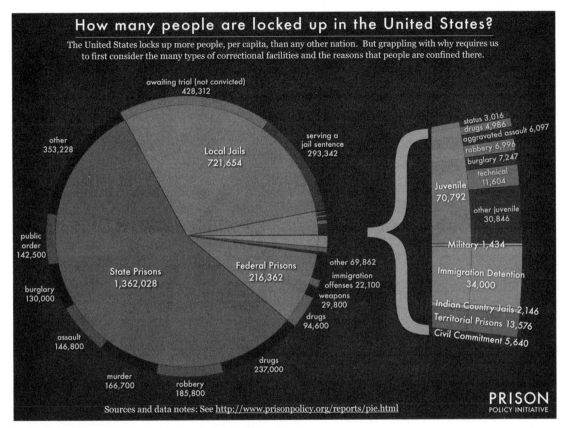

Figure 1.1. The Whole Pie. *Courtesy of the Prison Policy Initiative*

rity, noting that the U.S. government responded to this economic crisis by abandoning social welfare in favor of corporate welfare. Cutbacks targeted public housing, Aid to Families with Dependent Children (now Temporary Assistance to Needy Families, or TANF), food stamps (now Supplementary Nutritional Assistance Program, SNAP), and other social programs. More resources went into security, including the expansion of prisons and jails. This shift was complemented by a campaign on the part of political leaders to draw attention to crime and promote a tough "law and order" approach as the solution.[26]

The drive for greater corporate profits led many U.S. companies to move manufacturing jobs offshore—to countries with much lower wage rates and fewer regulations on production. This capital flight increased domestic unemployment levels, particularly in large cities with sizable African American populations, such as Detroit, Cleveland, and Chicago. High levels of unemployment frequently left criminal activity as one of the few ways to secure an income. That's why Gilmore and others have concluded that globalization caused changes that precipitated mass incarceration.

Several analysts have emphasized that once mass incarceration took off, prison expansion continued to gain support because it represented a new source of profits and a livelihood for many people. This strand of the economic argument stresses how a range of business interests profit from carceral growth. In their collection *Prison Profiteers: Who Makes Money from Mass Incarceration*, Tara Herivel and Paul Wright describe how each step of prison and jail expansion represents a new flow of revenue—first for the financiers who provide loans for these massive construction projects; then for the architects, engineers, and construction firms involved in the building phase; and then later, once the facility is operational, for the companies who supply goods and services to the prison population.[27] Everything from food to toilet paper to prisoner phone calls is an entrepreneurial opportunity. As the prison system expanded, more and more people, from prison guards to bureaucrats in departments of corrections, relied on incarceration for their jobs. By 2012 nearly a million people were employed in corrections. Largely because of its profit possibilities and economic benefits for certain people, many critics refer to the prison system as the prison-industrial complex, a system that benefits small groups of people at the expense of the majority. Scholar and activist Angela Y. Davis has argued that this system while generating economic activity actually drains rather than produces wealth.

The penal system as a whole does not produce wealth. It devours the social wealth that could be used to subsidize housing for the homeless, to ameliorate public

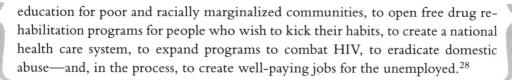

education for poor and racially marginalized communities, to open free drug rehabilitation programs for people who wish to kick their habits, to create a national health care system, to expand programs to combat HIV, to eradicate domestic abuse—and, in the process, to create well-paying jobs for the unemployed.[28]

POLITICAL REASONS

In *The New Jim Crow*, Michelle Alexander argues that a political agenda motivated changes in the criminal legal system after 1980. She contends that the gains won by the civil rights movement in the 1960s and '70s unleashed fear and insecurity among large sectors of the white population. She maintains many whites believed their jobs and educational opportunities were imperiled because of affirmative action.

Alexander describes how conservatives, led by President Richard Nixon and later by President Ronald Reagan, played on this fear to win whites to the ranks of the Republican Party. She shows how politicians used the discourse of "colorblindness" to mask their strategy of exploiting racism among the electorate. Because of the success of the civil rights movement, Alexander contends, no political leader could mobilize support during the 1970s and '80s with an *explicitly* racist agenda. Instead, she documents how conservatives used crime as a symbolic way of referring to African Americans. Without ever mentioning race, a common understanding developed among whites that the word *criminal* meant a young Black male.

Alexander cites statements by Nixon's closest advisers, Bob Haldeman and John Ehrlichman. According to Haldeman, Nixon concluded that "you have to face the fact that the whole problem is the blacks. The key is to devise a system that recognizes this while not appearing to." Ehrlichman declared quite explicitly "that subliminal appeal to the anti-black voter was always present in Nixon's statements and speeches."[29] In Alexander's view, this undercurrent of racism among whites was essential to making mass incarceration feasible.

PHILOSOPHICAL REASONS

In their book *The Punishment Imperative: The Rise and Failure of Mass Incarceration in America*, Todd Clear and Natasha Frost argue that a key shift in criminal justice philosophy occurred after 1980. In previous decades, the dominant ethos in criminal legal circles was the goal of rehabilitation.[30] Prisons, jails, and juvenile justice facilities were viewed as institutions that provided people with a "second chance," often through extensive education and job training programs or substance abuse treatment. With the rise of mass incarceration, however, attitudes began to change. Gradually the proponents of mass incarceration and the general public began to call for the system to punish or incapacitate people rather than rehabilitate them. The sense was that prisoners were "criminals" who, because they had broken the law, didn't deserve further investment or a second chance. The solution was to isolate them from society. Clear and Frost called this the punishment imperative—a popular urge to respond to a perceived threat of crime in a punitive manner.

This punishment imperative didn't mean only criminal prosecution but also included political disenfranchisement. For example, many states introduced prison gerrymandering, a process through which, for election purposes, people in prison are counted as residents of the district where they are incarcerated, not as residents of the district where they lived prior to arrest. The result is more political power to the predominantly white rural areas where most prisons are located and less power in the hands of the urban communities of color where most people in prison come from.

This shift in philosophy came with a change in beliefs about the root cause of crime. In the 1970s, most sociologists and criminologists linked crime to social problems. They believed that it grew out of poverty, inequality, and lack of opportunity. Furthermore, they argued that crime and punishment reflected the racial and class fault lines in U.S. society. The mainstream political rhetoric of the 1980s encouraged a heightened sense of individual responsibility for crime. From this perspective, people turned to crime not because of lack of opportunity or obstacles such as racial or class discrimination, but because they made "bad choices." Under this punishment paradigm, halting crime came down to teaching "criminals" to accept responsibility for their actions, take their punishment, and then turn their lives around.

Angela Y. Davis attributes this move toward increased punishment to shifting ideas about poverty and race. She connects this to the philosophy of retributive justice, whereby the criminal legal system exists only to exact retribution—to punish—rather than to offer second chances or the possibility of forgiveness. Davis contends that this punitive philosophy has contributed to the criminalization of acts that were previously either ignored or handled with nonlegal interventions. In a well-known essay on this topic she argued:

> Imprisonment has become the response of first resort to far too many of the social problems that burden people who are ensconced in poverty. These problems often are veiled by being conveniently grouped together under the category "crime" and by the automatic attribution of criminal behavior to people of color. Homelessness, unemployment, drug addiction, mental illness, and illiteracy are only a few of the problems that disappear from public view when the human beings contending with them are relegated to cages.
>
> Prisons thus perform a feat of magic. Rather, the people who continually vote for new prison bonds and tacitly assent to a proliferating network of prisons and jails have been tricked into believing in the magic of imprisonment. But prisons do not disappear problems—they disappear human beings. The practice of disappearing vast numbers of people from poor, immigrant, and racially marginalized communities has become big business.[31]

This chapter has provided some of the basic background to mass incarceration by offering a general profile of the system, a description of who is behind bars, and some historical explanations why this enormous shift in U.S. society took place. Yet the prison system could not have expanded without considerable amounts of popular support. Gaining support for mass incarceration was a complex, prolonged, and intentional process, one that is often ignored in analyses of the criminal justice system.

Courtesy of Mary Sutton

2

BUILDING POPULAR SUPPORT
FOR GROWING THE PRISON SYSTEM

A key social change underlying the advance of mass incarceration has been an increasing respect for the absolute authority of the law and those involved in law enforcement. This attitude has not always prevailed. The social movements of the 1960s and early '70s raised many questions about the fundamental fairness of the U.S. criminal justice system. Martin Luther King Jr. repeatedly challenged the notion of blind respect for the law. In his famous "Letter from a Birmingham Jail," King asserted that "there are two types of laws: just and unjust. I would be the first to advocate obeying just laws. One has not only a legal but a moral responsibility to obey just laws. Conversely, one has a moral responsibility to disobey unjust laws."[1] Such ideas inspired many people of the day to defy racial segregation and eventually gain passage of more egalitarian legislation, including the Civil Rights Act of 1964 and the Voting Rights Act of 1965.

A similar questioning of the law emerged in regard to the Vietnam War. A large number of those in the United States who opposed the war believed it was unjust. Thousands of young men acted on these beliefs by defying the mandatory draft and refusing military service. Many broke the law by fleeing to Canada to avoid being drafted. Even public figures, such as heavyweight boxing champion Muhammad Ali, defied the law and refused to join the military. Ali became one of some nine thousand people convicted of draft-related offenses during this period. A large number of them ended up serving prison sentences.[2]

One of the most famous antiwar activists, Daniel Ellsberg, was a consultant who worked for the Pentagon in the 1960s. He leaked the *Pentagon Papers* to the press. This secret Defense Department study consisted of thousands of military and security documents pertaining to the Vietnam War. In explaining his decision to take this action, he said, "There was no question in my mind that my government was involved in an unjust war that was going to continue and get larger. Thousands of young men were dying each year."[3] Ellsberg was charged with twelve felonies for leaking the documents, but the counts were ultimately dismissed due to government misconduct.

While activists critiqued the legitimacy of the law, many lawyers and criminologists were questioning the efficacy of prison and harsh punishment. Even with an incarceration rate less than a quarter of what it would be by the new millennium, many legal scholars and policy makers pushed for further cutbacks. A National Advisory Commission on Criminal Justice Standards and Goals in 1973 recommended that "no new institutions for adults should be built and existing institutions for juveniles should be closed."[4]

SHAPING PUBLIC OPINION

Public opinion polls also reflected a liberal perspective often critical of the criminal justice system. For example, popular opposition to the death penalty reached its peak in 1965 and remained above 50 percent from 1957 to 1972.[5] (By the mid-1990s, it would fall to 20 percent.) People also doubted the integrity of the police. In a national survey conducted by the City University of New York, only 37 percent of people in 1977 said they rated the ethics of police officers as very high or high (the figure would soar to 78 percent by 2001).[6]

Similarly, significant swaths of official and popular opinion rejected the law-and-order approach to crime, citing social and econom°°,ic factors as the causes of crime rather than individual character issues or a lenient criminal justice system. The 1967 commission led by U.S.

Social Movements Resist Unjust Laws

The social movements of the 1960s and '70s constantly called the legitimacy of the law into question. Particular actions by these movements raised questions about just and unjust laws and the responsibilities of individuals and government. The most prominent actions included: Native Americans' occupation of Alcatraz Island in California from 1969 to 1971 to demand the restoration of Native American land ownership and national sovereignty. Latino activist Reies Tijerina in 1967 led an occupation of a courthouse in New Mexico demanding restoration of land that previously belonged to Mexico. The legitimacy of law came under further attack from those who campaigned for legalization of abortion, homosexuality, and recreational drug use. A number of people who defied the law faced legal repercussions and, in some cases, lengthy prison sentences. Among the most high profile of these "political prisoners" were:

- African American activist Angela Davis;
- Black Panther leader Huey P. Newton;
- Religious war resisters Fathers Daniel and Patrick Berrigan;
- The Chicago Eight, leaders of various social movements charged with sparking a riot at the 1968 Democratic Convention;
- Women who killed men who had sexually attacked them, including Joanne Little and Inez Garcia;
- California prisoner and author George Jackson, killed by prison authorities in 1971;
- Other groups of activists charged collectively with crimes who became known by their group names: the San Quentin Six, the Wilmington (North Carolina) Ten, the New York Twenty-One, the Seattle Seven, Los Siete de la Raza, and Puerto Rican Prisoners of War.

attorney general Nicholas Katzenbach concluded, "The most significant action that can be taken against crime is action designed to eliminate slums and ghettos, to improve education, to provide jobs, to make sure that every American is given the opportunities and freedoms that will enable him to assume his responsibilities."[7]

Incarcerated men and women began to mobilize within prisons in the 1960s and '70s, questioning the legitimacy of the laws that held them in prison. They petitioned for better conditions and more opportunities for education and training, but their aspirations also incorporated the notions of basic rights and human dignity that were integral to the civil rights and antiwar movements. In California in 1970, prisoners went so far as to organize the short-lived United Prisoners Union (UPU). The UPU reflected a new vision of the humanity of "the convicted class."[8] These views were encapsulated in its Bill of Rights, issued in 1970.

> We, the people of the Convicted Class, locked in a cycle of poverty, failure, discrimination and servitude; DO HEREBY DECLARE, before the World, our situation to be unjust and inhuman. Basic human rights are systematically withheld from our class.
>
>   We have been historically stereotyped as less than human, while in reality we possess the same needs, frailties, ambitions and dignity indigenous to all humans. Our class has been unconstitutionally denied equal treatment under the law. . . . We hereby assert before the tribunal of mankind that our class ought not to be subject to one whit more restraint, nor one ounce more deprivation than is essential to implementing the constructive purposes of the criminal law.[9]

THE BACKLASH ON THE RISE

Even as late as 1981, a national poll found that most Americans believed that unemployment was the main cause of crime.[10] As the strength of the social movements of the 1960s and '70s ebbed and mass incarceration became a reality, reformers lost ground to champions of unquestioning support for "law and order."

Although critiques of the law-and-order approach gained considerable traction throughout the 1960s and '70s, powerful political forces kept a "tough on crime" agenda alive. J. Edgar Hoover, director of the Federal Bureau of Investigation from 1935 to 1972, played a key role in maintaining a tough-on-crime perspective in government, devoting considerable effort to characterizing the activities of the social movements of the day as "criminal." He used the bureau's resources to surveil and undermine any movement that he deemed "radical" or "Communist." Hoover paid special attention to Black political leaders, especially Martin Luther King Jr., and tried to establish links between the civil rights movement and international Communism. Under Hoover's direction, the FBI initiated the secret Counter Intelligence Program (COINTELPRO). The inner workings of COINTELPRO, made public in 1971, revealed a consistent effort by the FBI to disrupt domestic political organizations through the use of infiltrators. One of Hoover's priorities, especially after King's assassination in 1968, was to prevent any possibility of the emergence of what he called a "Black messiah"—another African American leader of the caliber of King or Malcolm X.

> ### President Nixon on Crime
>
> *We must declare and win the war against the criminal elements which increasingly threaten our cities, our homes and our lives.*
>
> —State of the Union Address, 1970

NIXON'S WAR ON CRIME

Hoover's views found great resonance during Richard Nixon's presidential years (1969–74). Nixon became a key advocate of law and order. He publicly declared a war on "criminal elements" while actively contesting the notion of just and unjust laws. On the policy front, Nixon promoted the goal of a higher conviction rate as central to the reduction of crime levels.[11] He also greatly increased funding for law enforcement. Between 1969, when Nixon entered the White House, and the spring of 1973, the federal government's law enforcement budget tripled, and federal aid to state and local law enforcement grew from $60 million to almost $800 million.[12]

One of the principal conduits for these funds was the Law Enforcement Assistance Administration (LEAA), established the year before Nixon took office. For the 1972 fiscal year, LEAA received eleven times the funds it had in 1969. LEAA funding provided financial support for closed-circuit video surveillance equipment, computerization of records, and police training.[13] Nixon also signed the Drug Enforcement Agency (DEA) into existence in his final year in office. The DEA soon became an important player in the War on Drugs.

While Nixon kept the law-and-order strategy alive, he never gained strong support for his "war on criminal elements." His approach failed to reduce crime rates, which continued to escalate during his presidency and by 1970 had more than doubled for the decade. During his final three years in office, violent crimes rose significantly, reaching a previously unprecedented level each year.[14]

More important, other issues diverted attention from Nixon's war on crime. First, his order for a secret U.S. military invasion of Cambodia in 1970 precipitated a national student strike. National Guard members and police officers killed four students at a protest at Kent State in Ohio and five students at Jackson State in Mississippi. These deaths prompted widespread outrage. Subsequent revelations of Nixon's involvement in the illegal break-ins at the Democratic National Headquarters in the Watergate office complex eventually forced him to resign in 1974, far from victorious in his war on crime. His own actions undermined his attempts to criticize social justice activists like King who chose to disobey unjust laws.

THE CARTER YEARS

The Carter presidency (1977–81) took criminal justice in a different direction. During his election campaign, Carter came out in favor of decriminalizing marijuana. Once in power, he reduced funding to the LEAA and cut back on surveillance of political activists. Although Carter did attempt to engineer some changes in criminal justice, he lasted only one term as president.

By the time Carter left office, the economy was plunging. The inflation rate had hit 13 percent and unemployment was at about 10 percent. Law-and-order supporters blamed the economic crisis on the social movements of the 1960s and early '70s, laying the rhetorical groundwork for a revival of a tougher approach to lawbreaking.

REAGAN RESTARTS THE WAR ON CRIME

Ronald Reagan's approach to crime followed the tradition of Nixon and J. Edgar Hoover. Reagan became a strong voice for law and order, linking the harsh punishment of "offenders" to a broader political agenda of conservative values laced with the rhetoric of patriotism. Once in office, he immediately adopted a warlike approach to crime, launching a renewed War on Drugs and expanding funding for law enforcement.

Reagan's administration was the key period in the shift to more punitive legislation and prison expansion. When he took office in 1980, there were just over half a million people in American prisons and jails. By the time of his departure in 1988, that population had more than doubled.[15] The passage of the 1984 Federal Sentencing Guidelines laid the groundwork for expanded prosecutions and lengthy sentences, ensuring the continued growth of prisons and punishment. While Reagan was a controversial president often at odds with Democrats over social issues, by the time he left office in 1988 he had built bipartisan support for being "tough on crime." During Reagan's final year, the House voted on an Anti-Drug Abuse Act, which expanded the use of the death penalty in drug cases and added a five-year mandatory minimum prison sentence for possession of cocaine base. The vote tally for this bill was 346 in favor and only 11 against.[16] Virtually everyone from both parties had bought into the agenda of "tough on crime."

THE PRISON BINGE CONTINUES

Reagan kicked off what law lecturer Martin Horn called the "prison binge," but Democrat Bill Clinton took it to a higher level. His Omnibus Crime Bill of 1994 allocated $9.7 billion to prison construction and also opened the door to more participation by private corrections corporations. As a result, during the Clinton years the nation's prison population increased by more than a half million. By the time he left office, federal, state, and local corrections expenditures had reached a total of $57 billion a year, more than eight times the level of 1980.[17] Moreover, the Omnibus Crime Bill and a second piece of legislation, the Personal Responsibility and Work Opportunity Reconciliation Act of 1996, cut the rights and opportunities for people with felony convictions, even eliminating federal college scholarships for people in prison.[18] The Personal Responsibility Act also criminalized many survival strategies for people on federal assistance. According to Clinton, the act marked the "end of welfare as we know it" by limiting welfare recipients to a maximum of five years of benefits and compelling those receiving assistance to work.[19] In fact, Clinton and other Democrats played such an important role in advancing mass incarceration that Naomi Murakawa, in her book *The First Civil Right: How Liberals Built Prison in America*, and other authors have argued that liberals carried primary responsibility for policies that facilitated prison building from the 1980s onward.[20]

THE (BLACK) FACE OF CRIME IN THE MEDIA

The mainstream media promoted the agenda of law and order in various ways during this period. In general, they created the mythical images of lawbreakers that dominated public discussion of crime during the Reagan years.

The proliferation of images embodying the threat of crime helped create public support for mass incarceration. In the media of the 1960s and '70s, political militants became emblematic, fear-inspiring "criminals." Images of African Americans dominated these representations in newspapers and on television—Black Panthers, political prisoners such as George Jackson and Angela Davis, and participants in urban rebellions in Watts, Detroit, and Newark. Media portrayals of other activists also linked struggles for justice and social progress to crime. The media framed actions by the militant Native Americans who occupied Alcatraz Island in 1969, by uniformed Latino youth groups such as the Young Lords and the Brown Berets, by protesters burning draft cards, flags, or bras, and by hippies, linked to drug use and sexual promiscuity, as criminal threats to the mainstream American way of life.

As the War on Crime proceeded, many media images began to criminalize whole classes of ordinary people in certain communities, specifically young Black males. Researcher Melissa Hickman Barlow summarized this phenomenon: "Evening news broadcasts, television crime dramas, and the 'real' crime stories of programs like *Cops* and *L.A.P.D.* bombard the American public with images of 'young black male' offenders under authoritative police control. The message is that the police are the thin blue line protecting law-abiding citizens from dark and dangerous street criminals."[21]

The media also took part in building certain politically motivated criminal personae, legendary or fictional characters who reinforced the linkages between Blackness and crime. Two of the most important were the Welfare Queen and Willie Horton.

Ronald Reagan first raised the image of the "welfare queen" in his presidential campaign in 1976. Though he didn't use that specific term, he named a woman, Linda Taylor, allegedly a resident of the South Side of Chicago, who he claimed had "eighty names, thirty addresses, twelve Social Security cards and is collecting veteran's benefits on four non-existing deceased husbands. And she is collecting Social Security on her cards. She's got Medicaid, getting food stamps, and she is collecting welfare under each of her names. Her tax-free cash income is over $150,000."[22]

Sociologist Patricia Hill Collins contended that the Welfare Queen notion implied that a Black woman typically had "low morals and uncontrolled sexuality" and passed on her "bad values" to her offspring.[23] Writer Julilly Kohler-Hausmann maintained that these

The Welfare Queen

Historian Duchess Harris provided a poignant description of the Welfare Queen image: "The Welfare Queen is the defining social stereotype of the Black woman, a lazy, promiscuous single Black mother living off the dole of society. She poses a threat to the Protestant work ethic that drives America and the American dream of social advancement and acceptability."[24] Creating the image of the Welfare Queen as a criminal misuser of taxpayer dollars and perpetuator of sexual immorality helped build the case for reallocating money from social services to law and order.

images "framed welfare recipients . . . as deceptive criminals."[25] Loïc Wacquant added that mass incarceration and the criminalization of welfare recipients were the two gender "sides of the same historical coin," with men of color locked up and women of color left to survive with less and less government support.[26]

The most powerful media symbol of the criminal Black male in the 1980s was Willie Horton. As a young man serving a life sentence, Horton received several weekend furloughs from prison in Massachusetts in 1988. One weekend he embarked on a crime spree that included the rape and robbery of a white woman. Michael Dukakis, then governor of Massachusetts, had supported the program that led to Horton's release. Dukakis subsequently became the 1988 Democratic presidential candidate. His opponent, George H.W. Bush, capitalized on the Horton story to play on racialized fears of white voters. Images of Horton appeared throughout the media, and while his race was not verbally noted, the pictures told the story.

A CBS News/New York Times poll showed that Willie Horton ads had more impact than any other commercials aired during the 1988 presidential campaign. The percentage of poll respondents who felt that Bush was "tough enough" on crime rose from 23 percent in July 1988 to 61 percent in late October (after the ads), while the proportion saying Dukakis was "not tough enough" on crime rose from 36 to 49 percent during the same period.[29] The ads helped Bush overcome a 17-point Dukakis lead in opinion polls and win the election.[30]

Race, Media, and Political Agendas

The media, itself an arm of mega-corporate power, feeds the fear industry, so that people are primed like pumps to support wars on rumor, innuendo, legends.

—Mumia Abu-Jamal, political prisoner[27]

The media perpetuate ideas linking race with criminality. . . . The prevalent typification of Blacks as criminals seems to justify law enforcement tactics that exploit race in criminal investigations.

—Kelly Welch, professor of criminology[28]

The 1990s saw a huge leap in crime coverage in local and national news. From 1990 to 1998, the number of crime stories on the three major network news programs rose from 542 per year to 1,392—in a period when crime rates were falling.[31] A similar trend prevailed in local news.

Important additions to TV programming during the era of mass incarceration also reinforced negative images of prisons and prisoners. The program *Oz* depicted an unprecedented level of prison violence. Cultural critic Elayne Rapping summarized the impact of *Oz* as gratifying "a public eager to see monstrous and alien 'criminals' apprehended and taken away in police cars, *Oz* takes the next step by assuring us that . . . these incorrigible demons are being properly disposed of."[32]

Moreover, portrayals of incarcerated men as violent and predatory homosexuals also became common in the era of mass incarceration. Jokes and skits about men using soap and

Black Faces and "Mismemory"

Blacks are the repository for the American fear of crime. Ask anyone, of any race, to picture a criminal, and the image will have a black face. The link between blackness and criminality is routinized by terms such as "black-on-black crime" and "black crime."

Moreover, research by a [Penn State] media-studies expert reveals that memory of crime stories with the suspects' pictures reflects racial stereotypes, and African Americans are especially likely to be mistakenly identified as perpetrators of violent crimes. When readers were asked to identify criminal suspects pictured in stories about violent crime, they were more prone to misidentify African Americans than white suspects. The same readers, to a far lesser degree, tended to link white offenders more with nonviolent crime. . . . In essence, the Penn State findings support the notion that stereotypes of black men as violent criminals are reflected in what people recall from news reports. This kind of mismemory has many implications ranging from issues related to law enforcement to issues related to everyday activities such as greater fear or distrust of others."

—Dennis Rome, professor of criminal justice[33]

other lubricants to force anal sex on other prisoners became a commonplace theme. This combination of homophobia and the stereotyping of men in prison perhaps reached its nadir with the appearance of the board game Don't Drop the Soap in 2007. The game is set in a prison and penalizes players who drop the soap while showering.[34]

THE PROMISE OF ECONOMIC DEVELOPMENT

While mass incarceration played on many negative images of criminals, prison expansion also made promises about bringing economic development to certain parts of the country. The rash of prison building in the 1980s and 1990s had a definite geographical pattern. In states such as California, Illinois, Michigan, and New York, prisons were sited in rural areas, far away from the communities from which most of the incarcerated came. According to re-searcher Tracy Huling, twenty-five prisons per year were built in rural areas during this time. She noted that in many cases entire rural regions became dotted with new prisons. Texas alone built forty-nine prisons in rural areas in the 1990s, most of them in the West Texas Plains. Small "prison towns," such as Susanville, California (subject of the 2007 public tele-vision documentary Prison Town, USA), Florence, Colorado, and Coleman, Florida, became sites for multiple prisons. In the case of Coleman, the population of more than four thousand people incarcerated in the four local penal institutions far outstripped the count of 703 people living in the entire town.

Part of the promise of prisons was that they would bring jobs and business opportunities. In that expectation, local authorities even offered incentives to prison builders: free water, free land, roads, and reduced tax rates. While prisons did create employment, in many places the jobs did not go to local residents. Local businesses also often lost out on contracts to out-side competition. Huling's research on fourteen prisons built in rural counties in New York between 1982 and 1999 revealed that counties where a prison was built fared no better than counties without a prison in terms of employment rates or per capita income. Other studies in Colorado, Texas, and California have yielded similar results.

Despite the mixed economic results, some companies and individuals did benefit and continue to support mass incarceration, along with the politicians who promoted prison construction as a way of bringing prosperity to their communities. Even if all the economic promises didn't become a reality, such politicians enhanced their profile as "tough on crime," which during the era of mass incarceration became an essential component of electability.

Furthermore, the siting of so many prisons in rural small towns had implications for race relations. The local populations and the prison workforce are overwhelmingly white. By contrast, large cohorts of the prison population are urban men and women of color. Researchers Tracy Huling and Kelsey Kauffmann found a number of instances of overt racist activities inside these institutions. Their research revealed that in at least six states, guards have appeared at work in mock Ku Klux Klan uniforms. Black guards in some thirteen states have filed lawsuits alleging racist harassment or violence from white co-workers. Lawsuits in the state of Washington claimed that white guards referred to Martin Luther King Jr. Day as "Happy Nigger Day" and that some white guards greeted one another with "Heil Hitler" and the Nazi salute.[35] Ruth Wilson Gilmore reports in *Golden Gulag* on some efforts at overcoming such sentiments by bringing together urban residents of color with poor residents from rural towns identified as potential prison sites and trying to develop an economic development strategy alternative to prison building. In general, though, political campaigns, legislation, and the media combined to create a base of support for mass incarceration and punishment. Without this, lawmakers would have been unable to pass the required legislation and budget allocations to make mass incarceration a reality.

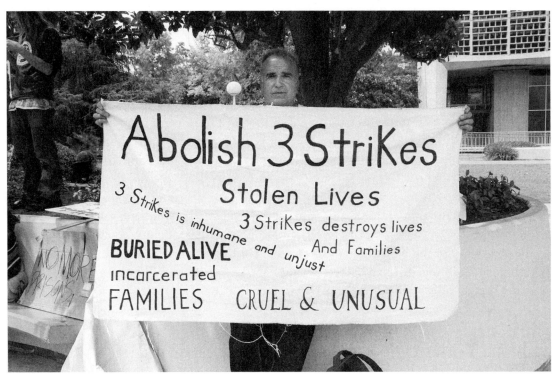

Courtesy of Mary Sutton

3

"LOCK 'EM UP AND THROW AWAY THE KEY": THE RISE OF MASS INCARCERATION

Mass incarceration was aided and abetted by harsher sentencing measures: mandatory minimums, truth in sentencing, three strikes, more frequent life sentences, increased use of the death penalty, sentencing youth as adults, and "sentences within the sentence"—the proliferation of ultrarepressive isolation units where solitary confinement is the rule. Many people have described the attitude informing these sentencing practices as "lock 'em up and throw away the key."

The rebellion at Attica Prison in western New York in 1971 was one of the key historical triggers for harsh sentencing. On September 9 of that year, hundreds of men in the D block of the prison seized control of the building, taking thirty-nine guards hostage. Some of their demands were practical, such as improved diet, better medical treatment, and expanded recreation programs. At the heart of their rebellion, however, was the more general issue of human dignity. L.D. Barkley, one of the prisoner leaders, articulated this demand: "We are Men! We are not beasts and do not intend to be beaten or driven as such. The entire prison populace has set forth to change forever the ruthless brutalization and disregard for the lives of the prisoners here and throughout the United States. What has happened here is but the sound before the fury of those who are oppressed."[1]

Despite pleas from the men inside, prison authorities, and a wide range of citizens, Governor

Rockefeller refused to go to the prison to negotiate a peace. Instead, on September 13, he sent in state troopers and other armed law enforcement officers. In the end, L.D. Barkley and twenty-eight other prisoners were killed, along with ten guards. For social justice actvists of the day, the "Attica brothers" who died became instant heroes. "Attica is all of us" became a prominent slogan in their circles.

On the other side of the political fence, Governor Rockefeller blamed the uprising on a permissive criminal justice system, linking rebelliousness and criminality to increasing illegal drug use. Over the ensuing two years, the governor drove a set of measures through the New York state legislature that became known as the Rockefeller Drug Laws. These laws kicked off a national swing toward the "lock 'em up and throw away the key" approach. Instead of rehabilitation, incarceration came to have the aim of punishment, deterrence, and incapacitation.

THE RISE OF MANDATORY MINIMUMS

The Rockefeller Drug Laws broke new ground by instituting harsh, inflexible penalties known as mandatory minimums. The New York legislation set the sentence for selling two ounces (57 grams) or more of heroin, morphine, raw or prepared opium, cocaine, or cannabis or possessing four ounces (113 grams) or more of the same substances at a minimum of fifteen years to life. A judge had no choice but to impose these sentences. The adoption of this legislation gave New York State the toughest laws of its kind in the entire United States.[2] Other states soon followed suit. For instance, Michigan enacted a "650-Lifer Law," which called for life imprisonment without the possibility of parole for the sale, manufacture, or possession of 650 grams (1.43 pounds) or more of cocaine or any opiate.[3]

Throughout the 1980s, states continued to pass mandatory-minimum legislation. This process accelerated after the launch of the renewed War on Drugs by President Reagan in 1982 and the spread of the use of crack cocaine in the mid-1980s. By 1994, all fifty states had enacted some kind of mandatory minimum sentencing. Perhaps the most important of these measures were the Federal Sentencing Guidelines, passed by Congress in 1984. These guidelines applied throughout the federal system. They ultimately stipulated mandatory minimums for drug offenses and spelled out specific required sentences for nearly every crime on the federal books. These sentencing guidelines provided a clear-cut indication that the tide had turned to punishment.

THE IMPACT OF MANDATORY MINIMUMS ON CRIMINAL JUSTICE

Mandatory minimums have played a key role in increasing the prison population in the United States. Under these minimums, more people are sentenced to prison, and they generally stay there much longer than under previous sentencing laws. Moreover, these laws have led to major changes in the way criminal justice functions.

> *Our reliance on mandatory minimums has been a great mistake. I am not convinced it has reduced crime, but I am convinced it has imprisoned people, particularly non-violent offenders, for far longer than is just or beneficial. It is time for us to let judges go back to acting as judges and making decisions based on the individual facts before them. A one-size-fits-all approach to sentencing does not make us safer.*
>
> —Senator Patrick Leahy, chairman of the Senate Judiciary Committee, March 20, 2013[4]

First, mandatory minimums took away much of the power of judges to consider mitigating factors when imposing sentence. A person's previous criminal record, family responsibilities, service to the community, history of employment, or any other achievements became irrelevant to a judge under mandatory minimum laws. A judge simply consulted the guidelines or the statute and imposed the prescribed time.

Mandatory minimums have shifted power from judges to prosecutors. Despite the media images of a gavel-wielding judge being the final authority, under mandatory minimums the charges a prosecutor files are more likely to determine the sentence than any actions taken by a judge.

More than 90 percent of criminal cases in the United States never go to trial. They are resolved by plea bargaining—taking a deal. Let's say police arrest John Smith, a small-time drug dealer in New York, for selling three ounces of heroin. Mr. Smith has no criminal record. Despite his lack of priors, the mandatory minimum is fifteen to life. In most such cases, the prosecutors will use their discretion to move toward a lower sentence by constructing a plea bargain. They may reduce the charges to simple possession or charge Smith for selling one ounce instead of three. Then the prosecutor can offer him a reduced sentence—say, five years in prison instead of fifteen. Mr. Smith then has the option of accepting the plea bargain or taking his case to trial. If he's found guilty in a trial, the judge has to give him at least the mandatory minimum of fifteen years to life. Frequently the prosecutor will make the deal contingent on Mr. Smith cooperating with investigators by telling them who sold him the heroin, who he sells heroin to, and who else he knows who might be involved in the drug trade. If Mr. Smith is reticent to accept the plea bargain, the prosecutor may delay the processing of the case, leaving Mr. Smith languishing in a very uncomfortable county jail until he agrees to plead guilty.

To further complicate such situations, not all those who cooperate with prosecutors tell the truth. They may falsify information in order to protect kingpins for fear of retribution. They may embellish what they know by adding names of totally innocent people just to impress the prosecutor in the hopes of getting a better deal.

Mandatory minimums put great pressure on defendants to accept plea bargains so as to avoid the risk of a trial. In some cases, even people who are totally innocent of any charge plead guilty because of the risk of a draconian minimum if they are wrongly found guilty.

Perhaps worst of all, mandatory minimum sentencing laws have encouraged the use of more confidential informants—"snitches." Faced with a long sentence, many people peripherally involved in drug cases or other criminal activity often opt for becoming a state's witness against a co-defendant as part of a deal to avoid the mandatory sentence. The use of informants often sows mistrust within communities as neighbors end up testifying against one another.

The punitive philosophy behind mandatory minimums, coupled with the urge to curb the discretion of "liberal" judges, has led to a number of other changes in sentencing laws throughout the country. The two most important of these are "truth in sentencing" laws and "three strikes" or "habitual criminal" legislation.

TRUTH IN SENTENCING

The phrase *truth in sentencing* arose in reaction to the fact that in the 1960s and '70s a person could often serve far less time than stated in the sentence due to "time off for good behavior." Most jurisdictions used indeterminate, parole-based sentencing. For example, a person sentenced in a federal court to serve nine years in prison would be eligible for parole after completing one third of that time. After serving three years, the individual would go before a parole board, which would consider a number of factors, such as the person's disciplinary record in prison, her or his prospects for finding employment or housing upon release, and her or his participation in required programs such as education or drug treatment while in prison. After making its evaluation, the board could either release the person or extend the sentence. The purpose of this approach was to provide incentives for people to participate in their rehabilitation and avoid disciplinary problems during their incarceration.

Truth in sentencing removed those incentives and shifted to a punishment model. Under typical truth-in-sentencing laws, certain people would have to serve 85 percent of the time on their sentence before they could be released. Someone sentenced to ten years would have to serve eight and a half. Their time could be extended to the full ten years

Prisons as Breeding Grounds for Racial Hatred

Many prisons have become hotbeds of racist ideology and violence. In many facilities, white supremacist groups, such as the Aryan Brotherhood or the Nazi Low Riders, have proliferated. In California, state men's prison authorities have reinforced this racism by following strict racial segregation in assigning people to two-person cells and even by instituting racial group punishment. For instance, if two white men have a fight, the white population may be subjected to a lockdown, while the remainder of the men continue with regular activities. Prisoner Garrett Johnson filed a lawsuit against such segregation and won a favorable decision from the U.S. Supreme Court in 2005, but prison authorities have never fully desegregated cell assignments or ended race-based lockdowns.

if they had disciplinary problems in prison, but there was no option of time off for good behavior. In 1984 Washington became the first state to adopt truth in sentencing. By 1998 twenty-seven states and the District of Columbia had truth-in-sentencing statutes in place that required people with violent offenses to serve at least 85 percent of their sentences before being considered for release.[5] The federal system and notoriously severe states, such as Virginia, applied truth in sentencing to everyone convicted of a felony, not just those with violent offenses.

The implementation of truth-in-sentencing laws received an enormous stimulus from funding made available through the Violent Crime Control and Law Enforcement Act of 1994. This act made incentive grants available to states to increase prison capacity to house those incarcerated under truth in sentencing.[6] From 1996 to 1999, federal grants for this purpose amounted to $1.8 billion. A large portion of this funding went to prison construction, leading to the addition of more than forty thousand new prison beds throughout the country.[7]

THREE-STRIKES LAWS

Three-strikes laws applied the principle of mandatory minimums to people with extensive criminal histories, particularly those with repeated convictions for violent crimes. More than two dozen states have enacted them in some form. Three-strikes laws emerged during the era of mass incarceration, although a number of states did have previous "habitual offender" legislation that allowed extra penalties for people with repeat offenses. The three-strikes approach increased those penalties and made them mandatory. Twelve states impose a mandatory sentence of life without parole for those convicted of three violent crimes.

Perhaps the most stringent of these statutes was California's initiative, passed by a popular referendum named Three Strikes and You're Out in 1994. The ballot measure was approved by 72 percent and made a sentence of twenty-five years to life mandatory for anyone convicted of a felony who had two prior convictions for violent offenses. A twenty-five-to-life sentence made a person eligible for release only after serving twenty-five years. An additional feature of the California law was a "second strike" provision, mandating double the normal sentence for someone convicted of a second crime of violence.

The implementation of this law has been particularly controversial. According to a report by the Justice Policy Institute, in the first decade California sentenced more than 4,000 people under three strikes while some 35,000 received doubled sentences as a result of a second strike.[8] While three-strikes sentences usually apply to convictions for violent crimes, in a number of cases people have been "struck out" for relatively minor offenses. For instance, Santos Reyes of El Monte was given twenty-five years to life for lying on the written portion of a driver's license test. Curtis Wilkerson of Los Angeles got "struck out" for stealing a pair of socks worth $2.50. Perhaps the most famous California three-strikes case was that of Jerry Dewayne Williams, the "pizza thief." Williams was sentenced to twenty-five years to life in 1995 for stealing a piece of pizza from some children at Redondo Beach. He served five years before a judge reviewed his case and set him free.

FAMILIES AGAINST MANDATORY MINIMUMS

Families Against Mandatory Minimums (FAMM), a national advocacy group led primarily by those with loved ones serving time due to harsh sentencing laws, has been active in pressing for changes to existing legislation. Through the group's work the stories of hundreds of people given extremely long sentences because of mandatory minimums have been told.[9]

CLARENCE AARON

In 1992 Clarence Aaron was a twenty-three-year-old African American college student in Mobile, Alabama, with no previous criminal record. Then he made a big mistake. He introduced two groups of people he knew were in the drug game. He received $1,500 for making this connection. He never bought or sold drugs. When the others were arrested, they fabricated testimony against Aaron. In order to avoid long sentences, they cast him as a kingpin. A federal court sentenced Aaron to three life terms. He served just over two decades before

President Obama commuted his sentence in December 2013 after a public campaign for his release.

WELDON ANGELOS

Weldon Angelos is serving a mandatory fifty-five years in prison for selling a few pounds of marijuana to an undercover police agent while possessing a firearm. Before his arrest, he had a successful music career and founded a Utah-based rap label, Extravagant Records. He wrote and produced songs for many artists, including Snoop Dogg. Twenty-nine former judges and prosecutors filed a friend-of-the-court brief beseeching Angelos's sentencing judge to declare the sentence unconstitutional.

SHARANDA JONES

In 1999, Sharanda Jones, who had worked as a hair stylist and restaurant manager, was convicted of selling crack cocaine. She was a small-scale, part-time drug seller with no previous criminal record. She was also the sole provider for her eight-year-old daughter. Under the Federal Sentencing Guidelines for selling crack cocaine, she was given life without parole.

As a teenager, her daughter reflected on her mother's sentence: "I was eight years old at the time and my world as I knew it was shattered. . . . Being without my mother for over thirteen years of my life has been extremely difficult. But the thought that she is set to spend the rest of her life in prison as a first-time nonviolent offender is absolutely devastating. . . . My mother does not deserve to come out of prison in a casket."

JUDGES SPEAK OUT

A number of judges have expressed their concerns with mandatory minimums. In 1997 a twenty-seven-year-old African American woman named Stephanie George was given life in a Florida court for holding her boyfriend's cocaine stash. At sentencing, Judge Roger Vinson said, "I wish I had another alternative. . . . Your role has basically been as a girlfriend . . . , so certainly in my judgment it does not warrant a life sentence." But Vinson had no choice.[10]

In 1999 Massachusetts judge Judd Carhart had this to say about sentencing Michaelene Sexton, then forty-eight, to ten years for selling coke: "Ten years is an awful long time. When I look at this case compared to crimes of violence, I wonder."[11]

In 2003 Supreme Court Justice Anthony Kennedy publicly attacked the federal mandatory minimums: "Our resources are misspent, our punishments too severe, our sentences too long. I can accept neither the necessity nor the wisdom of federal mandatory minimum sentences. In too many cases, mandatory minimum sentences are unwise or unjust."[12]

LIFE AND LIFE WITHOUT

Mandatory minimums and three-strikes laws have greatly expanded the use of life sentences. A 2013 report by the Sentencing Project found that more than 159,000 people were serving life sentences in federal and state prisons.[13] In five states—Alabama, California, Massachusetts, Nevada, and New York—at least one in six prisoners was doing life.[14]

Moreover, while the majority of lifers will be eligible for parole at some point, more than 49,000 were serving what is known as LWOP (pronounced EL-wop), life without the possibility of parole. Federal courts, as well as those in Illinois, Iowa, Louisiana, Maine, Pennsylvania, and South Dakota, offer no chance for parole to anyone with a life sentence.[15] A 2012 study by the ACLU, which focused on the federal system and nine states, found more than 3,200 people doing LWOP for drug convictions that involved no violence.[16]

JUVENILES

In the 1990s, in response to an upsurge in violent crime largely related to the influx of crack

Terms People in Prison Use for a Life Sentence

Doing all day

Through with money

All washed up

Got wheels (life will keep going around and around in the same place)

Struck out (for a life sentence through a three-strikes law)

cocaine, states passed legislation to facilitate trying and sentencing juveniles as adults. Under the slogan "adult crime, adult time," these measures gave judges the power to transfer certain juvenile cases to an adult authority. Typically states set a minimum age for a juvenile to be eligible to be tried as an adult. In Kansas, that age was set at ten for certain crimes. Most other states fixed the age at fourteen. Some states, such as New Jersey, allow transfer to adult courts only for certain violent crimes or serious property crimes. Arizona, on the other hand, allows a transfer for any felony. In a number of states, people can be sentenced to life imprisonment for crimes committed as a juvenile.[17]

SENTENCES WITHIN SENTENCES: SUPERMAXES AND CONTROL UNITS

As the criminal justice system grew more punitive, the use of isolation and solitary confinement increased. The most widely known institutions based on isolation are the prisons known as supermaxes. These facilities are allegedly intended to house the most notorious and dangerous people among the prison population. Perhaps the most famous supermax is the federal government's Administrative Maximum Facility, known as ADX, in Florence, Colorado. The Florence ADX houses 490 men who are kept in their cells twenty-three hours a day, allowed out only for an hour a day of solitary recreation. For at least the first year of their sentences, they are not permitted to interact with anyone else in the prison. The facility is designed so people's only view of the outside is through skylights and windows in the ceiling. A former warden, interviewed by *60 Minutes*, described the Florence ADX as "a cleaner version of Hell."[18]

Many state prisons have set up units with conditions much like those of the supermaxes. They are called special housing units, security housing units (SHUs), control units, or behavior modification units. From 2011 to 2013, men housed in one of these units at Pelican Bay State Prison in California staged three separate hunger strikes protesting their lengthy terms in isolation. Many of them had spent decades in the unit, confined to cells at least twenty-two hours a day. Authorities claimed that they had committed serious disciplinary violations or had gang affiliations. Yet the strikers and their supporters alleged that many times such

American Supermax
Joseph Dole

A guard informed me upon arrival that
there are benefits to this isolation.
He promoted the fact that we are now
all safe from gang retaliation.

I had to ask "But what of the
retaliation of the prison administration?"
He smiled cryptically as he enjoyed
this in ecstatic contemplation.

None of what I was experiencing was
making me feel safe. But then, by "grace,"
I see a new definition. I'm safe from
my family's loving embrace.

I'm safe from having education take
ignorance's place.
I'm safe from recreation keeping my
heart's healthy pace.

How I wish I could articulate this quasi-
existence that I've grown to hate.
Or get an answer to why so many strangers
sadistically enjoy my monotonous fate.

They say societal enlightenment takes time, but what if it takes
longer than your life, and you're forced to wait?[19]

(Joseph Dole is serving a life sentence in Illinois. He spent several years in Tamms supermax. Tamms was closed in 2013.)

charges were trumped up, based solely on something as insignificant as a tattoo that purportedly depicted a gang insignia or a supposedly subversive book in someone's possession. At the outset of their third strike in 2013, some 30,000 people inside California state prisons joined in the strike. The action continued for two months, with 128 people remaining without food until organizers called the strike off on day sixty. While the strikes gained national attention, including an editorial in the *New York Times*, only minor changes took place in the control unit. A few dozen people were released into the general prison population, but hundreds

What Is a Political Prisoner?

Many countries jail people explicitly for political activities or beliefs. While there are many definitions of political prisoner, there is general agreement that people who are incarcerated because of political beliefs or politically motivated activities against the government or because of their racial, ethnic, gender, or religious identity are political prisoners. Officially no one in the United States is classified as a political prisoner. Yet many people held in U.S. prisons claim political prisoner status. The best-known are those arrested after 9/11 and held in the Guantánamo Bay prison as "enemy combatants." The United States also continues to incarcerate a host of people who were convicted for politically motivated activities in the 1960s and '70s.

The most well-known long-serving political prisoners in the United States are Leonard Peltier and Mumia Abu-Jamal. Peltier, a leader of the American Indian Movement, was convicted in 1977 of the 1975 killing of two FBI agents on the Pine Ridge Reservation in North Dakota. Amnesty International placed his case in the "unfair trials" category in its 2010 report.

Abu-Jamal was a journalist and a member of the Black Panther Party in Philadelphia. He was convicted of the murder of a New Jersey state police officer in 1981 and sentenced to death in 1982. His sentence was commuted to life in 2012. In 2001 the *New York Times* called him perhaps the world's best-known death row inmate.

Other high-profile people incarcerated in the United States and often listed as political prisoners include:

more remained in it. Lawyers acting on behalf of the strikers, as well as the strikers themselves, filed a number of lawsuits to continue to press the issue.

THE DEATH PENALTY

A final expression of the harshness of the U.S. criminal justice system is the more frequent imposition of the death penalty. The United States reinstated the death penalty in 1976 after a

- The Angola Three, three men held in isolation in the Angola, Louisiana, prison. All were members of the Black Panther Party and were accused of killing a prison guard in 1972. One of the men, Robert King, was released after twenty-nine years in solitary in 2001. A second man, Herman Wallace, was released in 2013 with terminal liver cancer. He died three days after his release. The third, Alfred Woodfox, remains in prison.

- Members of the Black Liberation Army, an offshoot of the Black Panther Party. Their still-incarcerated members include: Sundiata Acoli (imprisoned in 1973), Herman Bell (1973), Jalil Muntaqim (Anthony Bottom, 1971), and Robert Seth Hayes (1973).

- Oscar Lopez Rivera, a member of a Puerto Rican independence organization, the Armed Forces of National Liberation (FALN), in prison since 1981.

In more recent times, people engaged in antiwar and environmental justice actions have received long sentences for a variety of offenses. These include:

- Chelsea (formerly Bradley) Manning, a U.S. Army soldier convicted in 2013 of leaking documents concerning army activities in Iraq and sentenced to thirty-five years in prison.

- Marius (formerly Marie) Mason, an environmental activist convicted of arson and property damage in 2009 and sentenced to twenty-two years in prison.

four-year suspension. Executions peaked at ninety-nine in 1999 and declined steadily to thirty-nine in 2013. More than twenty people have been executed for crimes committed while they were juveniles.[20] With regard to the death penalty, the United States is a global outlier. More than 140 countries have abolished capital punishment, including all members of the European Union.

PRISON OVERCROWDING

Even with the enormous rate of expansion of prison and jail construction in the past three decades, federal facilities and many state systems remain above capacity. In 2012 Alabama had the most overcrowded system, at 195.7 percent of capacity. The federal system has hovered around 130 percent of capacity since the mid-2000s. By 2011 California prisons were so overcrowded that a federal judge ordered their population reduced by 46,000 because the overcrowding made effective health care delivery impossible. Other states at more than 140 percent capacity in 2012 included Alaska, Delaware, Illinois, Nebraska, and North Dakota.[21]

The interim response by many correctional authorities has been to pack two or three people into cells designed for one person or to house people in gyms, dayrooms, and warehouses that were not designed as living spaces. Overcrowding has led to a number of problems: increased potential for violence, a decline in the quality of medical care, a reduction in recreation, and health hazards, particularly in regard to infectious diseases.

Moreover, much of the overcrowding is due to the aging profile of the incarcerated population.[22] The extremely long sentences handed down over the past three decades have led to a situation where by 2015 one in ten prisoners was more than fifty-five years old, double the rate in 2008. Wheelchairs, walkers, and oxygen tanks are increasingly becoming part of the prison landscape, all at increasing costs to taxpayers.

SENTENCING BY RACE

Harsh sentencing has heightened racial inequalities in the criminal legal system. Perhaps the most famous instance of racialized sentencing was the federal penalty for possession of crack

The Innocence Project

The zeal to incarcerate has spilled over into prosecuting and sentencing many people who are completely innocent. In recent years, advances in forensics, especially the use of DNA evidence, has provided the basis for overturning many convictions of people who have been in prison for decades. The Innocence Project, founded by Barry. Scheck and Peter J. Neufeld, has investigated hundreds of cases. Their work has led to the exoneration of more than three hundred people, including eighteen who served time on death row. Robert Bain, a Florida man who served thirty-five years, is the longest-serving individual freed by the work of the Innocence Project so far.[23] Beyond the Innocence Project, lawyers and other individuals have also pursued investigations of possible wrongful convictions. In 2014 alone 125 people were freed from prison because they were incarcerated for crimes they did not commit. Many had pled guilty because of poor legal advice or because they were threatened with longer prison terms if they took their case to a trial and were found guilty.[24]

cocaine compared to that of powder cocaine. In the mid-1980s, a federal law targeted at the spread of crack cocaine use set the penalties for an ounce of crack roughly equivalent to those for a hundred ounces of powder. Because the majority of those convicted on crack cocaine charges were African American, this prompted protests concerning racial inequity. In 2010 Congress passed the Fair Sentencing Act, which reduced the relative penalties. Even under the new law, however, penalties still remain grossly unequal: possession of twenty-eight grams of crack cocaine yields a five-year mandatory minimum sentence for a first offense, while it takes five hundred grams of powder cocaine to prompt the same sentence. Despite these inequities, the law offered twelve thousand people serving time for crack possession under the hundred-to-one rule a chance to apply for sentence reduction and earn their releases.[25]

While crack cocaine is the most obvious example of racial disparity in sentencing, harsh sentences *have* intensified the racial disparities in the criminal justice system. As early as 1991, a federal commission concluded that use of a mandatory minimum "appears to be related to the race of the defendant."[26] The commission found that for white defendants either judges more frequently found a way around the mandatory minimum or prosecutors more often reduced the charges to avoid an offense where a mandatory minimum applied.

A 2005 study by Tushar Kansal for the Sentencing Project reviewed dozens of studies on racial disparity in sentencing conducted between 1980 and 2000. While the results varied in different jurisdictions, overall Kansal concluded that:

- Young Black and Latino males are subject to particularly harsh sentencing compared to other offender populations, especially if they are unemployed;
- Black and Latino defendants typically receive longer sentences than whites for taking a case to trial instead of accepting a plea bargain;
- People of color also are less likely to receive substantial sentence reductions for cooperating with government prosecutors, i.e., serving as an informer, or snitch;
- Black defendants convicted of harming white victims suffer harsher penalties than Blacks who commit crimes against other Blacks or white defendants who harm whites;
- and Black and Latino defendants tend to be sentenced more severely than comparably situated white defendants for less serious crimes, especially drug and property crimes.[27]

Since that time, other studies have shown disparities in the application of specific harsh sentencing measures.

- In California, African Americans are only 7 percent of the general population but make up 28 percent of the prison population and 45 percent of those serving life for three strikes.[28]
- Nationally, the application of life sentences reveals serious inequities. African Americans make up 47 percent of those serving life and 77 percent of those serving life for a crime committed as a juvenile.[29] African Americans constitute 65 percent of those

given life without parole for nonviolent crimes. In Louisiana, African Americans are 91 percent of those sentenced to life without parole for nonviolent offenses.[30]

- A number of studies have revealed racial bias in applying the death penalty. A report by Amnesty International on the first two decades of resumption of capital punishment in the United States showed that roughly a third of those executed were African Americans. The study also showed that capital punishment has been imposed most often when the perpetrator is Black and the victim is white.[31]

- Testifying on mandatory minimums before Congress in 2010, Marc Mauer, the director of the Sentencing Project, made it clear that such sentences "serve to exacerbate racial disparities within the criminal justice system. A combination of circumstances virtually ensures that this will be an inevitable outcome of such penalties."[32]

In sum, harsher sentencing policies not only have greatly increased the number of people in prison, but also have been applied most harshly to people of color. They have allowed racially discriminatory punishment on a massive scale without overt reference to race—as Michelle Alexander put it, a "colorblind" system. A key factor in this process has been the War on Drugs.

PART TWO

THE MANY FACES OF
"TOUGH ON CRIME"

The War on Drugs has targeted African American youth and drained money from public defenders and other social services that help prevent people from being locked up. *Courtesy of Brian Dolinar*

4

THE WAR ON DRUGS

Prosecution of drug cases has stood at the heart of both the expansion of the prison population and the philosophical shift to a more punitive system since the late 1970s. While the sentencing laws formed a crucial part of the implementation of mass incarceration, the chief vehicle to put those laws into effect was the War on Drugs.

The use of drugs has been an issue of legal and political contention for more than a century in the United States. Not surprisingly, the criminalization of drugs has often been associated with racism and anti-foreigner sentiments. The first anti-opium legislation in the United States came about in the 1870s as a reaction to the influx of Chinese laborers who worked on the railroads. Hostility directed at the Chinese spilled over into a desire to punish the use of their frequent drug of choice, opium. Similar processes occurred with anti-cocaine legislation aimed at African Americans in the early 1900s and with the criminalization of marijuana from the 1910s to the 1930s, which was aimed at Mexican immigrants. The media of the day also demonized drugs and drug users. Perhaps the best example was the famous 1936 film *Reefer Madness* (originally titled *Tell Your Children*), which stoked public fears of crime and violence associated with the use of marijuana.

The social movements and youth rebellions of the 1960s and '70s represent the most direct historical links to the current Drug Wars. Many people in these movements experimented with marijuana, LSD, cocaine, and other drugs. The popular music of the day, by artists

The Racist Origins of the War on Drugs

Dr. Hamilton Wright became the first opium commissioner of the United States in 1908. The March 12, 1911, *New York Times* quoted Dr. Wright's comments on drug use: "Cocaine is often the direct incentive to the crime of rape by the Negroes of the South and other sections of the country." Wright also stated that "one of the most unfortunate phases of smoking opium in this country is the large number of women who have become involved and were living as common-law wives or cohabitating with Chinese in the Chinatowns of our various cities."[2]

such as the Grateful Dead, Jimi Hendrix, the Doors, Sly and the Family Stone, and the Beatles, reflected an antiestablishment outlook that accepted recreational use of drugs other than alcohol, nicotine, and caffeine.

These cultural influences had a major impact on people's social lives. In a 1969 Gallup poll, only 4 percent of American adults said they had tried marijuana, but by 1977 the figure had risen to about 24 percent.[1] The broader usage of marijuana and other banned drugs led to a political tug-of-war at the state and federal levels.

On the one hand, a number of liberal reformers advocated decriminalization. At the same time, conservative forces, led by President Nixon, called for a condemnation of all unapproved drug use and first introduced the term "war on drugs" into American politics. In 1971 Nixon issued a message to Congress on drug abuse prevention and control, in which he declared drug abuse (by which he meant all use of any drug banned by the government) to be "public enemy number one."[3] Despite the militaristic rhetoric, the majority of funding under Nixon went toward treatment rather than law enforcement. To this end, Nixon set up the Special Action Office for Drug Abuse Prevention (SAODAP) "to mount a national attack on a national problem."[4]

Nixon's antidrug campaign faltered after his resignation in 1974, however, and liberal reformers gained some ground. Between 1973 and 1977, ten states passed marijuana decriminalization measures. In his message to Congress in August 1977, President Jimmy Carter said, "I support legislation amending Federal law to eliminate all Federal criminal penalties for the possession of up to one ounce of marijuana."[5] The reform spirit was short-lived, though, and Carter lost the 1980 election to Ronald Reagan.

RONALD REAGAN ESCALATES THE WAR

President Ronald Reagan escalated the war. Framing drug use as an attack on American tradition, he pushed a concerted campaign to construct consumption and sales of illegal drugs as a critical political issue. His efforts succeeded. According to a Gallup poll in the early 1980s, only 2 percent of people in the United States identified drugs as the major problem facing society. By the late 1980s, however, that figure had risen to more than 60 percent, during a period when actual drug use was in decline.[6]

What Is Decriminalization?

Decriminalization of drugs means reducing criminal penalties for drug-related offenses. A range of measures fall under the heading of decriminalization—including giving citations, similar to traffic tickets, for those possessing small amounts of marijuana. The most radical decriminalization is full legalization of all drugs, almost certainly with regulations like those that currently apply to alcohol and to nonprescription or prescription medicines.

The Reagan administration's offensive was multifaceted. The leader of the media blitz on the drug issue was First Lady Nancy Reagan, with her famous slogan "Just say no." Beginning in 1982, she took her show on the road, making more than 250 appearances promoting abstention from the use of drugs and alcohol. Her efforts brought a range of entertainers on board. Popular TV programs, including *Diff'rent Strokes*, devoted entire shows to "Just say no."[7] Singer Michael Jackson appeared on an episode of *The Flintstone Kids* as Michael "Jackstone," singing a song about drugs to the tune of his hit "Beat It."[8] The FBI took up the theme as well. The bureau's shield, with the phrase "Winners Don't Use Drugs," was emblazoned on every arcade game sold in the United States from 1989 to 2000.

This colorful media blitz was complemented by more hard-hitting efforts from law enforcement officials such as Los Angeles police chief Daryl Gates, who once argued that "we're in a war," so "casual drug users should be taken out and shot."[9] In 1984 Gates founded the Drug Abuse Resistance Education (DARE) program to warn young people about drug addiction. The DARE program organized visits to schools by police officers bearing the "Just say no" message. In some classrooms, DARE Boxes were installed in which children could submit names of people they suspected were using or selling drugs. By 1999, DARE programs had been delivered to schoolchildren in every state and more than forty-four countries.[10]

DARE even had its own theme song and a reinterpretation of the Three R's: "Recognize, Resist, and Report."[11] The campaign to create popular support for the War on Drugs pushed politicians to take a "tough on crime" stance or risk losing votes. The War on Drugs became one of the few truly bipartisan issues.

Demon Crack Cocaine

In the early 1970s, underground chemists developed a solid (as opposed to powdered) form of cocaine that could survive the long storage and smuggling routes of prohibition without degrading. This form was called crack, and in the mid-1980s an epidemic of its usage swept the United States, largely in inner-city African American communities. Tens of thousands of people became dependent on this "rock" form of cocaine. The use of crack contributed to both increased profits of drug lords and a rise in violent crime. In 1996 a California reporter named Gary Webb broke a story that tied members of the CIA to the origins of crack cocaine and alleged that a specific drug dealer named Freeway Ricky Ross (not the rapper by the same name) was a major conduit for CIA-sourced crack that flooded many African American communities.

Webb's revelations and investigations by others provoked charges from many African Americans that the crack boom was a genocidal plot to destroy their communities. In the words of Glen Ford of *Black Agenda Report*, "Clearly, the crack cocaine laws are models of efficiency in the mass destruction of Black lives under color of law. Any civilized court would treat such blatantly race-based mass punishment as a crime against humanity—possibly an element in a broader charge of genocide."[12]

MILITARIZING THE POLICE

The Reagan administration built on the infrastructure established during the Nixon days to fund extreme forms of policing: drug squads that ran entrapment schemes and networks of spies, Special Weapons and Tactics (SWAT) units for commando raids, and various other military structures in law enforcement. These groups expanded through a vast outpouring of federal dollars into all aspects of drug law enforcement, from surveillance technology to enhanced weaponry.

Legislation expanding policing powers was critical to building the War on Drugs. In 1981, an amendment to the 103-year-old Posse Comitatus Act (which had forbidden using the military against American civilians) removed barriers that had prevented the National Guard from involvement in domestic policing. The amendment opened the door for the National Guard to allocate troops to join in local drug arrests.

From the mid-1980s to the late 1990s, SWAT squads proliferated. By 1997, according to researcher Peter Kraska, 90 percent of cities with populations of 50,000 or more had at least one SWAT team, twice as many as in the mid-1980s. The number of towns with populations between 25,000 and 50,000 with a SWAT team increased 157 percent between 1985 and 1996. Their level of operations skyrocketed from three thousand annual SWAT deployments in the early 1980s to thirty thousand by 1996.[13]

Militarization of SWAT squads was greatly accelerated by measures such as the 1033 Program, which allowed surplus Department of Defense equipment and weapons to be distributed free of charge to other government agencies. After 1989, when Congress passed legislation to make this redistribution possible, local law enforcement agencies aggressively grew their arsenals. Journalist Radley Balko reported that the Pentagon distributed 3,800 M-16s and 2,185 M-14s to civilian police agencies from 1995 to 1997 alone. Domestic police agencies also acquired bayonets, tanks, helicopters, and even airplanes. This military hardware fundamentally changed the way police carried out arrests. Police drug squads began to operate as if they were engaged in wartime military operations and Blacks were the enemy.[14]

DRUG SQUADS IN ACTION

Hundreds of drug raids have prompted public protest and, in some cases, legal action. Here is the story of a typical one, a San Francisco Police Department raid in 1998.

Just before dawn on October 30, 1998, ninety law enforcement officers stormed the Martin Luther King Jr.–Marcus Garvey Square Cooperative Apartments, blowing doors off with special "shock-lock" shotgun rounds and clearing people out of rooms by throwing flash-bang grenades.

Five days later, many of the residents, all African American, appeared at a police commission meeting and "described how officers slapped them, stepped on their necks and put guns to their heads while other officers ransacked their homes." They alleged that weeping and terrified children, some as young as six, were handcuffed and separated from their parents. Some urinated in their pajamas. The residents claimed the raid was a violation of their civil rights. Scores of people with no charges against them and no criminal records were put in disposable plastic flex-cuffs. Civil servants and grandmothers were held at gunpoint. One woman was hospitalized after a fit of seizures; other people were so distraught they couldn't return to work for days.

The officer who planned the operation, SFPD narcotics lieutenant Kitt Crenshaw, said the action went off, "more or less, without a hitch." He said he felt "bad for the innocent women and children that were there, but in a way they do bear some responsibility for harboring drug dealers."[15]

ASSET FORFEITURE

A number of federal and state laws passed in the 1980s and '90s gave drug squads a direct financial incentive essentially to rob their targets legally. Asset-forfeiture laws enable police to retain most of the assets they seize in drug raids as long as they were generated by criminal activity. Such assets include cash, bank accounts, cars, airplanes, and even houses. Moreover, as asset forfeiture has grown more lucrative, assets belonging to family members or friends of those charged have been seized and not returned. One 2010 study in Texas reported that police were consistently confiscating any large sums of cash they found during routine traf-

The 1033 Program and Ferguson

In 2014 the police shooting of Michael Brown prompted national outrage and large-scale demonstrations in Ferguson, Missouri. Police response included the use of massive military vehicles acquired from the Pentagon's 1033 Program. Subsequent research revealed that more than four hundred law enforcement agencies had received such vehicles, sparking widespread condemnation of militarized police. When informed that his county had acquired a 25,000-pound military vehicle, Champaign, Illinois, resident Stuart Levy said, "We should think about these things in terms of not whether they're cheap to acquire, but whether they're good for our community."[16]

Protesters also targeted excessive use of force on the population in general, citing a number of killings of young Black men—the strangling of Eric Garner in New York, the shooting of John Crawford in a Walmart in Ohio, the fatal armed attack on Ezell Ford in Los Angeles, and the gunning down of twelve-year-old Tamir Rice, who was playing with a pellet gun in a Cleveland park. A survey by ProPublica found that from 2010 to 2012 police fatally shot 1,217 people and that Blacks were more than twenty times more likely to be shot than whites. International research showed that police in the United States employ an extraordinary level of violence. In England and Wales, which have a combined population of about 56 million, many police don't even carry sidearms while on foot patrol. From 2009 to 2012, police in all of England and Wales opened fire only eighteen times, killing nine people, about one-twenty-fifth of the level of fatal police shootings in the United States.[17]

fic stops, in many instances without any indication at all that the money came from criminal activity.[18] Throughout the country, police have seized real estate, personal property, and cash totaling more than $15 billion, which they legally pocketed to upgrade their operations and equipment. In 2000 alone drug-case-related seizures netted more than $669 million nationally.[19] As former California deputy attorney general Gary Schons observed, "Much like a drug addict becomes addicted to drugs, law enforcement agencies have become dependent on asset forfeitures. They have to have it."[20]

Testimony from a Victim of the War on Drugs

Little did I know, but that decision to become involved in gangs and the drug trade put me on a collision course not only with other gang members and law enforcement, but with the Federal Government's War on Drugs. Overnight I had unknowingly transformed from a "kid" to "public enemy number one" in the eyes and perception of the public and government. In order for the government to wage a "war" on drugs, it had to identify the enemy, or create "public enemies" the public can vilify and fear in order to justify its war and multibillion-dollar budgets. The enemies were identified. The government had declared war on a substantial segment of its citizenry—in particular, youth of color, i.e., the "gangbangers."

—Robert Saleem Holbrook, an African American man serving life without parole in Pennsylvania for a conviction imposed when he was sixteen[21]

FEDERAL SENTENCING GUIDELINES

The final key to effective implementation of the War on Drugs was the passage of the Federal Sentencing Guidelines, discussed in chapter two.

The guidelines were particularly rigid on drug charges, providing a detailed list of point allocations for every illegal drug and a specific sentence for the amount possessed or sold. This formula sent millions of people away for decades. While on the surface the guidelines contained a seemingly impartial mathematical formula for sentencing, in practice the guidelines were racially biased.

THE CLINTON YEARS

While President Clinton had a more liberal approach than Reagan on most social issues, during his years in office aggressive policing and prison expansion escalated. Under this administration, the incarcerated population rose from 1.3 million to more than 2 million. To ensure that Democrats appeared "tough on crime" to voters, the Clinton administration added new twists of its own to the War on Drugs and mass incarceration. Clinton's attorney general, Janet Reno, set the tone for the administration in a 1993 speech to a meeting of defense and intelligence specialists who had been involved in the recently ended Cold War with the Soviet Union. "Let me welcome you to the kind of war our police fight every day . . . and let me challenge you to turn your skills that served us so well in the Cold War to helping us with the war we're now fighting daily in the streets of our towns and cities across the nation."[22]

As noted in chapter 2, Clinton created legal barriers for people with felony drug convictions even after they had served their sentences. His 1996 Personal Responsibility and Work Opportunity Reconciliation Act facilitated lifetime bans on Temporary Assistance to Needy Families (TANF, or "welfare") and Supplementary Nutrition Assistance Program (SNAP, or food stamps) for those with felony drug convictions, including marijuana possession. He also developed a "one strike and you're out" policy for public housing, allowing local housing authorities to exclude anyone with a drug offense. The housing policy effectively blocked the reunification of families of those returning from prison, forcing parents, siblings, or partners to choose between their homes and their loved ones.

THE WAR ON DRUGS AFTER 9/11

After the destruction of the Twin Towers on September 11, 2001, authorities began to link the War on Drugs to the need to protect the United States from terrorism. Connecting drug usage to terrorism injected new energy and resources into arresting and incarcerating drug traders at home and abroad. The Office of National Drug Control Policy (ONDCP) produced ads that implied that those who consumed illegal drugs were supporting terrorists. Several of these ads appeared during the 2002 Super Bowl, including one called "AK-47," which featured rental cars packed with automatic weapons, a safe house, and a man buying box cutters, the tools used by the 9/11 plotters. The tag line was "Where do terrorists get their money? If you buy drugs, some of it might come from you." Ads with this theme of recreational drug users' complicity in terrorism appeared in more than three hundred newspapers throughout the country, adding a new dimension to the War on Drugs.[23]

Many police forces used 9/11 as a reason to beef up their SWAT teams and drug squads. A sheriff in Syracuse, New York, summarized the situation: "We're in a new era, a new time . . . the bad guys are a little different than they used to be, so we're just trying to keep up with the needs for today and hope we never have to use it." Towns as small as Jasper, Florida (population: two thousand), grew their police arsenals in the name of fighting terror, prompting a story in a state newspaper about Jasper with the headline "THREE STOPLIGHTS, SEVEN M-16S."[24]

THE GLOBALIZED WAR ON DRUGS

The American War on Drugs went global in 1961 with the Single Convention on Narcotic Drugs, a treaty that essentially extended U.S. drug laws to most of the rest of the world. In 2000 President Clinton built on this precedent by signing a pact with Colombian president Andres Pastrana that provided hundreds of billions in aid to Colombia to fight the drug cartels that were supplying cocaine to the U.S. market. Unfortunately, the Colombian government used large parts of these funds to fight political opponents, not to cut off the drug trade.

Mexico has been another important international front in the War on Drugs. The Merida Initiative, signed by President Bush in 2008 and renewed by President Obama, has kept billions in aid money flowing to Mexico supposedly in efforts to stop the drug trade. The money has done little to stem the flow of drugs. With the annual income of Mexican cartels in 2007 estimated by the U.S. Government Accountability Office at upwards of $20 billion, the drug trade continued to reap profits for many people. One drug lord, Joaquín "El Chapo" ("Shorty") Guzmán Loera, even made the *Forbes* billionaire list in 2009.[25]

Moreover, since the beginning of the Merida Initiative, violence by drug cartels and the police has escalated. In 2011 sixteen thousand people died in Mexico as a result of drug violence. Journalist Anabel Hernández has estimated that altogether some eighty thousand people died between 2006 and 2011 as a result of drug-war-related killings.[26]

Critics, such as Witness for Peace, have argued that the money spent on these international efforts to stop the flow of drugs would have had more impact if it went toward supporting antipoverty programs in the United States along with drug treatment and rehabilitation for U.S. drug consumers.[27]

THE RESULTS OF THE WAR ON DRUGS

The War on Drugs provided the main impetus for mass incarceration from the early 1980s to the end of the twentieth century. From 1980 to 2005, drug arrests tripled, leading to enormous increases in the prison population. From 1985 to 2000, drug offenses accounted for half the rise in state prison populations and two-thirds within federal institutions. By 2000, about 500,000 people were behind bars for drug-related offenses, compared to 41,000 in 1980.[28] The bulk of these arrests targeted users, not kingpins, even in recent years. Throughout the 2000s, more than 80 percent of all drug arrests were for possession, half of which were for marijuana.

Moreover, virtually all aspects of the War on Drugs were and are heavily racialized. Violent raids on suspected drug operations were disproportionately targeted at working-class African American and Latino communities that were already impoverished by high rates of unemployment and declining systems of education and social services.

According to a national survey by the American Civil Liberties Union (ACLU), Blacks and whites use marijuana at about the same rate, but Blacks are four to five times more likely to be arrested for marijuana possession. The ACLU study found that in every single state Blacks had higher arrest rates than whites for marijuana possession.[29] Despite the high publicity given to methamphetamine, particularly via the TV series *Breaking Bad*, arrests for synthetic drugs in this century have consistently remained below 5 percent of all drug arrests.[30] At the same time, according to Marc Mauer of the Sentencing Project, increased use of mandatory minimum sentences for meth offenses has led to a higher percentage of whites in the prison population nationally.[31]

Although by the early 2000s many college campuses had become hotbeds of drug usage and the drug trade, policing remained focused on poor communities of color. A 2009 study for Human Rights Watch concluded that Blacks were far more likely than whites to be prosecuted for drugs. While people of color increasingly were incarcerated for drug offenses, statistics repeatedly showed that whites were at least as likely to buy, sell, or use prohibited drugs.[32]

Perspectives on the War on Drugs

You have to understand that the War on Drugs has never been about drugs. . . . We're watching poor, uneducated people being fed into a machine like meat to make sausage.

—Charles Bowden, Pulitzer Prize–winning reporter and author of *Murder City: Ciudad Juarez and the Global Economy's New Killing Fields*[33]

Of the 2,600 people I've sent to prison, I've seen three or four kingpins. We're incarcerating poor, uneducated people who are drug addicts.

—federal judge Mark Bennett[34]

Why serve an arrest warrant to some crack dealer with a .38? With full armor, the right shit, and training you can kick ass and have fun.

—"Mike," U.S. military officer who trained SWAT squads in the 1990s[35]

It's kind of a funny war when the "enemy" is entitled to due process of law and a fair trial. By the way, I am in favor of due process. But that kind of slows things down.

—William Bennett, secretary of education under President Reagan and head of the Office of National Drug Control Policy under George H.W. Bush[36]

For all our science and sophistication, for all of our justified pride in intellectual accomplishment, we must never forget the jungle is always there waiting to take us over. Only our deep moral values and our strong institutions can hold back that jungle and restrain the darker impulses of human nature.

—President Ronald Reagan, September 28, 1981[37]

Moreover, a person's race and class position had a heavy bearing on his or her fate when she or he did face a drug charge. Studies focusing on all stages of the criminal justice system, from racial profiling in traffic stops to charging and sentencing, showed that whites typically received preferential treatment, while low-income people of color were disproportionately penalized.[38] This prejudice has been borne out in the racial composition of those in state prisons. By 2011, the Bureau of Justice Statistics showed that 45 percent of those serving prison time for drug offenses were African Americans, far in excess of their 13 percent presence in the country's population.[39]

> *The ruling class shifts dope to you and me*
> *And don't get arrested, this is lunacy*
> *or is it pimp low magic in unity?*
> *Is it a war on drugs, or just my community?*
>
> —The Coup, "Drug Warz"

The War on Drugs was the driver of mass incarceration. It contributed the ideological spark and the money required to put millions of people behind bars and leave hundreds of communities devastated. In the late 1990s, however, the mass incarceration movement added a second area of focus: the criminalization and arrest of immigrants.

In 2010 immigrants' rights activists staged nationwide actions against harsh immigration laws, such as Arizona's SB 1070. *Courtesy of Mary Sutton*

5

THE WAR ON IMMIGRANTS

The War on Drugs catalyzed mass incarceration in the 1980s, and while it continues, since the mid-1990s a second phase of mass incarceration has emerged—the detention and deportation of immigrants. This has involved focusing legislation, policing, security practices, and the prison industry on the targeting of undocumented people.

IMMIGRANTS IN U.S. HISTORY

The United States often claims to be "a nation of immigrants." Mainstream history books tell us stories about the early settlers near Plymouth Rock and the waves of Europeans in the nineteenth century, yet another type of immigration has deep roots in U.S. history as well: involuntary immigration. This refers to the enslavement of Africans and the Middle Passage that brought them to the United States, the expropriation of land that often forced Native Americans to relocate outside their own territory, and the Treaty of Guadalupe-Hidalgo after the Mexican-American War of 1846–48, which instantly made thousands of Mexicans residents of a different country. Nevertheless, although the United States prides itself as a "melting pot" where people from all over the world share one national identity and culture, anti-immigrant sentiment and repressive policies have been a recurring feature in U.S. history.

Among the earliest anti-immigrant laws in the United States were the Alien and Sedition Acts of 1798. They limited the political rights of certain immigrants, especially those from France and Ireland. The philosophy that inspired these acts and the later upsurges of anti-immigrant sentiment was known as nativism. In the mid-1800s, nativists tried to restrict the immigration of Roman Catholics to the United States, arguing that their loyalty to the pope would undercut their allegiance to the United States.

Several nativist political organizations emerged to target Catholics, including a secret society called the Order of the Star Spangled Banner. This led to the formation of the American Party, which enjoyed a brief round of success in the mid-1850s, electing eight governors and more than a hundred congressmen.[1]

ANTI-CHINESE BIGOTRY

Later in the 1800s, nativists focused on Asian immigration. At this time, thousands of Chinese immigrants were arriving to work on building America's railroads. Many had fled the Opium Wars in their homeland but found hostility rather than peaceful refuge in the United States. Large numbers even met violent deaths. In 1856, California's *Shasta Republican* reported, "Hundreds of Chinamen have been slaughtered in cold blood in the last five years by the desperados that infest our state. The murder of the Chinaman was almost a daily occurrence; yet in all this time we have heard of but two or three cases where the guilty parties were brought to justice."

Atrocities against Chinese became so common that the phrase "a Chinaman's chance" was coined, meaning no chance at all. In fact, an 1850 law prohibited the Chinese—along with Native Americans and African Americans—from testifying in court against a white person. Similar to African Americans in the South, Chinese children were prohibited from attending public schools with white children.[2]

In 1882 Congress passed the Chinese Exclusion Act, intended to stop nearly all immigration from China. This was the first law ever passed in the United States that excluded immigrants from a specific ethnic group. Not until 1943, when the Chinese Exclusion Act was superseded, were Chinese from all backgrounds allowed to immigrate to the United States, though a strict quota limiting their numbers remained in place until 1965.

TWENTIETH-CENTURY NATIVIST BACKLASHES

The 1920s saw the rise of the Ku Klux Klan (KKK). At its peak, the Klan had as many as 4 million members. Best known for its attacks on African Americans, the KKK also recruited on the basis of anti-Semitism as well as an anti-Catholic prejudice that focused on Irish and Italian immigrants. This anti-immigrant sentiment ultimately inspired the passage of the Immigration Act of 1924, which extended the Chinese Exclusion Act to all Asian immigration and instituted national origin quotas favoring northern Europe over southern and eastern Europe. The act stood until 1965, when the Immigration and Nationality Act finally abolished the national origin quota system that had sharply limited the number of immigrants of color.[3]

Another important tide of anti-immigrant sentiment arose during World War I (1914–18), when nativists feared that immigrants from Germany, which was then at war with the United States, might be spies. The Russian Revolution of 1917 prompted a similar backlash. Because the revolution was led by an explicitly communist party, many people in the United States feared that immigrants with communist, socialist, or anarchist sympathies might organize a similar upheaval in the United States. A 1919 bombing that damaged U.S. attorney general A. Mitchell Palmer's house triggered a "Red Scare," and a repressive campaign known as the Palmer Raids ensued. The raids netted about three thousand arrests and more than five hundred deportations, including deportation of some U.S. citizens. The Palmer Raids halted after opposition arose among the public and in Congress.[4]

During World War II, suspicions were directed at immigrants and citizens of Japanese descent after the attack on Pearl Harbor in 1941. President Franklin Roosevelt approved internment camps throughout the country, which housed more than a hundred thousand people of Japanese descent for the duration of the war. Many of them were U.S. citizens.

LATINO IMMIGRANTS

During the latter part of the twentieth century, the most intensive immigration debate focused on Latinos, primarily those from Mexico. In 1942 the federal government initiated the bracero program in the wake of labor shortages due to World War II. This program provided work permits for a specified number of people from Mexico, largely for railroad and seasonal farm work. While this provided work permits for thousands of immigrants, deportations of the undocumented also persisted. In the 1950s, the government launched a massive deportation program targeting Mexicans who were in the United States without permits. This measure, known as Operation Wetback, resulted in the deportation of more than a hundred thousand people, mostly to Mexico.[5]

Three decades later, President Reagan began two major shifts in the treatment of undocumented immigrants. First, in 1981, his administration initiated immigrant detention programs, causing the creation of a new network of largely privately owned facilities to detain people awaiting the results of a deportation or asylum hearing. Second, Reagan pushed for the 1986 Immigration Reform and Control Act, which gave amnesty to 3 million undocumented immigrants while providing funds for tighter border security. The act also established penalties for employers who knowingly hired undocumented workers. These two actions laid the groundwork for future immigration debates and harsher policy measures.

Anti-immigration politics began another resurgence in the 1990s, typified by efforts to block immigrants from government aid and services. Much of this backlash was a reaction to changes going on within Mexico that precipitated increased immigration to the United States. In particular, Mexico's implementation of the North American Free Trade Agreement (NAFTA) in 1994 eased the ban on foreigners owning large tracts of land in Mexico. This enabled large-scale U.S. agribusinesses to buy huge tracts of Mexican farmland, dispossessing about 1.5 million people, many of whom had lived on the land for generations. Large numbers of these landless people went north to seek work.

The key federal legislative responses were the 1996 Personal Responsibility and Work Opportunity Reconciliation Act (PRWORA), mentioned in previous chapters. This made citizenship a requirement for certain federal benefits and allowed states to discriminate against noncitizens in administration of Temporary Assistance to Needy Families (TANF) and other federal aid programs. All of this made life much harder for immigrants.

During this decade, anti-immigration sentiments also began to find their way more fully into criminal justice policy. While being in the country without legal immigration documents remained a mere civil violation subject to deportation, a range of laws enhanced the channels through which the undocumented could face criminal prosecution.

The Anti-Terrorism and Effective Death Penalty Act (AEDPA), enacted in April 1996, and the Illegal Immigration Reform and Immigrant Responsibility Act (IIRIA) passed in August of the same year provided the legal framework. These laws expanded the list of offenses that made detention compulsory for noncitizens. With AEDPA and IIRIA, immigrants whose records included minor drug charges or decades-old convictions suddenly became subject to arrest. These laws also restricted immigrants' options to contest their deportation through the courts, particularly for those who were applying for refugee status and those who had been living in the United States for many years. Largely as a result of this legislation, deportation figures began to escalate after 1996. The number of people deported from the United States because of a criminal record rose astronomically—from 37,724 in 1996 to 90,426 in 2005.[6]

How Does Deportation Work?

When you get deported, you don't simply get picked up by the police and get dropped off at the border. After you have an encounter with police, several things can happen. If you're very lucky, the police will simply let you go. In most instances, however, you will be taken to jail. From there you may be released or picked up by Immigration and Customs Enforcement (ICE) and taken to an immigration detention center. If you end up in a detention center, you wait for a deportation hearing. It may take months or even years before this hearing takes place. During that time, you may be released or held in the detention center. You may also be moved to an immigration detention center in another part of the country while you wait. Some people may also be subject to criminal charges before they have a deportation hearing. If you have no previous conviction for illegal entry, you may be sentenced to a federal prison for up to six months. If you have previous illegal-entry convictions, you may spend several years in prison even if you are guilty of no other crime. Once you complete that term, you will be returned to an immigration detention center to have your deportation hearing.

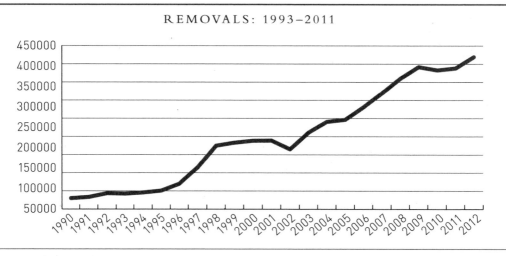

Figure 5.1. Source: Department of Homeland Security, *2012 Yearbook of Immigration*, Table 39.

Overall removals also rose and, in 1997, for the first time in history, exceeded 100,000, soaring to nearly 250,000 by 2005.

THE FUNNEL EFFECT

Part of the United States' enhanced border security effort in the 1990s intended to redirect immigrants from busy Texas and California crossing points with navigable terrain to the deadly desert of Arizona. According to a report compiled by the Binational Migration Institute, this policy created the "funnel effect," which left immigrants with no alternative but desert crossing points. In a 1994 strategic planning document, the Border Patrol made this goal explicit: "The prediction is with traditional entry and smuggling routes disrupted, illegal traffic will be deterred, or forced over more hostile terrain." This funneling over "more hostile terrain" drastically increased the number of deaths of border crossers. From 1990 through 1999, authorities recovered an average of fourteen bodies per year of failed border crossers. After the funneling decision, from 2000 to 2005 the average rose to an annual toll of 160. Since then, despite a reduced total flow of immigrants from Mexico and Central America, deaths have remained at a high level.

AFTER 9/11

The attacks of September 11, 2001, opened the floodgates of further anti-immigrant sentiment, causing a remarkable shift of law enforcement resources into immigration-related issues. Four important changes took place.

1. THE ROUNDUP

Immediately after 9/11, roundups of immigrants captured more than 1,200 people, mostly Muslims from the Middle East, South Asia, and North Africa. A Human Rights Watch report on the process alleged that many people were detained solely on the basis of religion or national origin and that some were physically or verbally abused.[7]

2. THE PATRIOT ACT

In November 2001, Congress passed the Patriot Act (actual title: The Uniting and Strengthening America by Providing Appropriate Tools Required to Intercept and Obstruct Terrorism Act of 2001). The law placed a number of additional constraints on immigrants, as well as mandating an enormous expenditure to tighten border control.

More important, the Patriot Act precipitated a restructuring of the enforcement of immigration law. The act dissolved the old Immigration and Naturalization Services (INS) and established Immigration and Customs Enforcement (ICE) under the newly formed Department of Homeland Security. The mission of ICE was to help ensure national security and fight terrorism, as opposed to INS's primary charge of managing the flow of immigrants. ICE immediately became the largest law enforcement body within Homeland Security, with funding that exceeded the combined budgets of the FBI, the U.S. Marshals, and the Drug Enforcement Administration.

3. THE BORDER FENCE

Fears of terrorism linked to immigrants helped prompt massive expenditure on border security. The most prominent example of this was the construction of a fence along the nearly two-thousand-mile-long Mexican border, mandated by the Secure Fence Act of 2006. A Government Accountability Office report stated that Customs and Border Protection spent $2.4 billion to build 670 miles of the fence between 2006 and 2009.[8] The extension of the border fence also intensified the funnel effect—from 2001 to 2014, more than 2,100 people died trying to cross the border.[9]

The building of the fence was complemented by a massive influx of Border Patrol officers to the area. By 2012 the number of Border Patrol staff surpassed 21,000, more than triple the number in 1997 and double that of 2004.[10] The extension of the fence has provoked considerable controversy. Even Michael Chertoff, a former secretary of homeland security, has questioned its viability: "I think the fence has come to assume a certain kind of symbolic

Who Gets Deported?

Although the majority of those deported are from Mexico, in 2013 the other countries in the top five destinations for people deported were Guatemala, Honduras, El Salvador, and the Dominican Republic. Many of those removed are workers. In 2008 ICE agents conducted a major raid on a meatpacking plant in Postville, Iowa, a town with a population of less than three thousand. Within days nearly three hundred workers, mostly from Guatemala, had been deported.[11]

Some of the deportations are surprising. According to the group Banished Veterans, several thousand men and women who have fought for the U.S. forces in Vietnam and Iraq have been deported after an encounter with police upon their return to civilian life.[12] In some cases, deportation even follows good fortune for immigrants. For instance, an undocumented Arizona woman was deported after she won $1,200 in a state lottery. When she went to collect her winnings, the clerk in store suspected her ID was fake and reported her to authorities. She was deported soon thereafter.[13]

significance which should not obscure the fact that it is a much more complicated problem than putting up a fence which someone can climb over with a ladder or tunnel under with a shovel."[14]

4. TARGETED ANTI-IMMIGRANT PROGRAMS

To enhance the power of ICE, the federal government put two crucial policy measures in place after 9/11—Operation Streamline and Secure Communities.

Operation Streamline, begun in 2005, mandated the criminal prosecution and detention of all people found without documentation, a zero-tolerance policy. Previously, those picked up by police or ICE but not accused of any crime other than illegal entry were placed in deportation proceedings without being criminally prosecuted. Under Operation Streamline, individuals typically first have gone through a court hearing and been sentenced to up to six months in detention, then have been put into deportation proceedings. Because there was such a huge number of prosecutions, sometimes up to eighty people would enter a mass guilty plea and be sentenced at the same time, totally bypassing due process. Operation Streamline led to skyrocketing costs for immigration enforcement. In 2005 the federal government spent $591 million on incarcerating immigrants. After Operation Streamline, the figure rose to $1.02 billion in 2011.[15]

Secure Communities was launched under the Department of Homeland Security and required local authorities to check the identification of anyone taken into custody with ICE records. By the end of 2012 at least 3,074 jurisdictions from all fifty states were participating in Secure Communities. For the period 2011–13 about 81,000 people per year were deported through this program.[16] President Obama terminated Secure Communities in 2014, replacing it with a similar program called the Priority Enforcement Program.

Since 9/11, this shift in immigration policy and law enforcement has placed ICE at the cutting edge of the expansion of police power and the capacity to incarcerate. As an editor for the *South Asian Magazine for Action and Reflection* has written, "Over the last two decades a paradigm shift has taken place. Immigration law, once a set of civil administrative rules to regulate population flow—has become part of the enforcement apparatus of a government

An Undocumented Success Story

As of 2013, there were an estimated 11 million undocumented immigrants living in the United States. In essence, the undocumented are everywhere. One of the most high profile among them is Jose Antonio Vargas, a journalist, filmmaker, and immigration activist. Born in the Philippines and raised in the United States from the age of twelve, he was part of the *Washington Post* team that won a Pulitzer Prize in 2008 for coverage of the Virginia Tech shootings. In 2011 he revealed in an article in the *New York Times Magazine* that he was undocumented and had lived in fear of deportation all of his adult life.[18] Since then he has become an ardent immigrants' rights activist. About his immigration status, he says, "I am an American. I just don't have the right papers."[19]

that functions increasingly as a police state. The politics of fear have changed the whole nature of the immigration system."[17]

OUTCOMES OF HARSHER IMMIGRATION POLICY

People can be deported from the United States in two ways: forced removal or return. Forced removal typically involves an arrest and detention, then an order of removal if no immigration defense is available. Forced removals are entered as an offense into a person's criminal record, making them liable for felony charges if they enter the United States illegally again. In a return, usually a person is simply dropped at the border without the criminal record entry that a removal entails. Only immigrants from Mexico and Canada can be returned, because that process requires a common border with the United States.

Since 2005, the government has decreased returns and drastically increased forced removals. From 1970–96, forced removals were never more than 5 percent of deportations. In 2003–6 they were 19 percent. By 2012, the figure had increased to 65 percent. The number of forced removals increased from 51,000 in 1995 to a peak of 409,000 in 2012.[20] The majority of those subjected to forced removal were deported to Mexico.

The increase in forced removals has been coupled with increased prosecutions for reentry. Under the letter of the law, people with a prior removal order can be sentenced to up to two years in prison before being repatriated. Those with a previous felony conviction who enter the United States illegally can receive up to ten years, twenty if it was an "aggravated" felony. These sentences were rarely applied in the twentieth century. Since 2005 federal criminal prosecutions for illegal entry, largely as a result of Operation Streamline, have nearly doubled, however, from just over ten thousand to more than nineteen thousand in 2011. In 2012 according to data from the U.S. Sentencing Commission, 92 percent of those charged with reentry were categorized as Hispanic. The average sentence for reentry was nineteen months.[21]

The Changing Demographics of the Prison Population

Year	Total Prisoners—Black	Total Prisoners—Hispanic	Total Prisoners—White
2000	572,900	206,900	436,500
2005	547,200	279,000	459,700
2011	555,300	331,500	465,100

Figure 5.2. Source: E. Ann Carson and William J. Sabol, *Prisoners in 2011* (Washington, DC: Bureau of Justice Statistics, Department of Justice, 2012).

The Growth in Immigration Detention Centers

Year	Number of Detention Sites (includes detention centers and space rented out in jails and prisons)	Average Daily Population
1981	18	54
1991	176	6,423
1996	242	8,951
2001	404	20,192
2011	204	32,095

Figure 5.3. Note: The number of facilities declined from 2001 to 2011 due to centralization and the construction of larger new detention centers. Source: Immigration and Customs Enforcement, "ICE Total Removals"; and Gretchen Gavett, "The U.S. Immigration Detention Boom," *Frontline*, Public Broadcasting System, www.pbs.org/wgbh/pages/frontline/race-multicultural/lost-in-detention/map-the-u-s-immigration-detention-boom.

These changes in immigration policy and enforcement practices occurred during a decade where immigrants from Mexico and Central America were arriving in the United States in rapidly increasing numbers. In fact, the population of U.S. Hispanics rose by roughly 15 million from 2000 to 2010.[22] These factors contributed to a major shift in the demographics of the U.S. prison population. During the period 2000–2011, the number of people classified as Hispanics in state and federal prisons increased by more than 50 percent, from 206,900 to 331,500. During that same period, the Black prison population declined by about 25,000. The figures for whites rose by about 7 percent. The per capita rate for Blacks, however, still remained more than one and a half times the rate for Hispanics.[23]

A BONANZA FOR PRISON CORPORATIONS

To accommodate the newly imprisoned immigrants, the federal government has expanded its detention facilities. Often it has rented space in local jails and state prisons, but it has also built new detention centers, funded from a federal budget for detention and deportation that doubled between 2005 and 2010. These detention centers have given a new lease on life to the private prison industry, whose fortunes were flagging in 2000. While private companies hold only about 8 percent of the incarcerated population nationwide, they own or manage more than 40 percent of the immigration detention beds.[24] A leading executive for one of the private prison firms, Steve Cornell, had this to say about 9/11 and company bottom lines: "It is clear that since September 11 there's a heightened focus on detention, more people are gonna get caught. So I would say that's positive . . . the Federal Business is the best business for us and September 11 is increasing that business."[25]

Figure 5.3 shows that the daily population of immigration detention centers, which primarily hold people awaiting adjudication of deportation or asylum cases, had risen to more than 32,000 by 2011, with the two largest private prison firms, Corrections Corporation of America (CCA) and the GEO Group, controlling about a third of the beds.

To help sustain the profitability of the detention business, in 2006 Congress imposed a mandatory quota for immigration detainees, requiring that ICE not let the number of detainees fall below a given figure. By 2013, that quota had risen to 34,000. Another special feature of immigration incarceration has been the building of separate facilities for immigrants serving prison sentences. These prisons, called criminal alien requirement (CAR) institutions, are owned primarily by the private operators CCA and the GEO Group. CAR prisons housed some 25,000 in 2013.[26]

THE FINANCIAL CRISIS AND ANTI-IMMIGRANT LAWS

The financial crisis of 2008 precipitated feelings of economic insecurity among many U.S. workers. As always during economic depressions, many people feared that immigrants would take jobs from U.S. citizens. As a result, a number of states pushed for stricter controls on immigration. The result was legislation to compel law enforcement to determine a person's immigration status during any lawful contact, especially if there is "reasonable suspicion" that the person might not have legitimate immigration papers. In 2010 Arizona passed the first of these laws, SB 1070, or the "show me your papers" law. Georgia, Alabama, and South Carolina subsequently enacted similar laws. Opponents have argued that these laws promote racial profiling of Latinos and people of Middle Eastern descent. Some provisions were blocked by federal courts, including a clause in the Alabama bill that would have required schoolchildren to provide information about their parents' immigration status.

Anti-Immigrant Voices

Illegal immigration is bankrupting states along the border, but this is about more than economics—we're placing our national security at risk. . . . Terrorists are also walking in unopposed; our southwestern border is littered with Arabic papers and Islamic prayer rugs.

—Jim Gilchrist, leader of the Anti-Immigrant Minuteman Project[27]

It should be legal to kill illegals. Just shoot 'em on sight. That's my immigration policy recommendation. You break into my country, you die.

—Carl, a Vietnam War veteran[28]

THE IMMIGRANT RIGHTS MOVEMENT

While the movement for immigrants' rights has been active on many fronts, likely the most important mobilization was the 2006 protest in response to proposed national legislation, known as HR 4437. This bill would have made it a felony to enter or remain in the United States without official permission or to help anyone else do so. The protests against HR 4437 lasted more than two months, beginning in Chicago on March 10 with a march of about a hundred thousand. More than a million people took part in these actions, including marches of four hundred thousand each in Chicago and Los Angeles. The bill ultimately failed to pass the Senate.

Marchers not only were protesting the proposed legislation but were also calling for com-

Voices of DREAMers

Being undocumented doesn't define who you are. By coming out we take back our right of speech that for years others have been trying to control and oppress. . . . Nobody, not even the Senate, can stop us. We're here and we're not leaving. Be proud and be loud!

—Angy, New York State Youth Leadership Council[29]

Now, no one can stop us . . . not only are we undocumented and unafraid, but we are also unapologetic. We are and we deserve to be a part of this country, and we won't let anyone tell us differently.

—Mohammad, DreamActivist.org[30]

Right now I can't get any form of government i.d. that will prove my age . . . there are all these constant reminders . . . every store and bank, every transaction . . . every travel poster, every place of work is a little Post-it that says . . . not yours.

—Stephanie Solis, undocumented UCLA graduate[31]

prehensive immigration reform, which would include a path to citizenship or permanent residence for those who had lived in the United States a long time, as well as amnesty from deportation for a large portion of the 7 million undocumented people working in the United States at the time.

Another key component of this immigrant rights movement has been the many undocumented youth who identify themselves as "DREAMers"—supporters of legislation called the DREAM (Development, Relief, and Education for Alien Minors) Act. This proposed legislation would give those who came to the United States as young children a path to legal residency and freedom from the fear of being deported. As of 2014, fifteen states had enacted a version of the act covering state institutions, but the national version had yet to pass. Throughout the country since 2010, thousands of undocumented DREAMers have "come out" (made their immigration status public) as they campaigned for the federal DREAM Act to become a reality and for comprehensive immigration reform.

Erika Andiola

Erika Andiola was an undocumented student in Arizona when state law changed and greatly reduced financial aid for those without papers. She began to campaign for the rights of DREAMers, and then ICE took her mother and brother into detention. Erika responded by immediately going on YouTube with a video telling her story. Her clip got twenty thousand hits, and she began an extended campaign to reverse her family members' deportation. After a few months, she succeeded in gaining a one-year extension of her mother and brother's permits to stay in the United States.

After winning victory for her family, Andiola became part of a national campaign entitled Not One More (Deportation). Members of the campaign have highlighted their disappointment with President Obama, whom they labeled the "deporter in chief," since more than 2 million people had been deported during his administration, more than under any other president. They called on him to halt all deportations and provide deferred action for adults as well as students.[32]

DREAMers have been active on a number of fronts. For example, they played leading roles in successful resistance to the construction of privately owned immigration detention centers in Joliet and Crete, Illinois, in 2012 and 2013.

In 2012, in response to the vigilante killing in Florida of Trayvon Martin, an African American teenager, a coalition led by youth of color formed an organization called the Dream Defenders. They linked their demands about the DREAM Act to the bigger issue of the American Dream. They organized both for immigration reform and against mass incarceration.

THE FUTURE OF IMMIGRATION AND MASS INCARCERATION

Since 9/11, deportations and criminal charges for illegal entry have continued to increase. Despite massive campaigns, no decisive legislative action has substantially changed the situation. In 2011 Congress failed to pass the DREAM Act. The following year, in response to popular pressure, President Obama initiated a deferred-action program, which offered a two-year renewable delay in deportation of students who came to the United States at an age of less than sixteen and had no criminal record. In 2014 he issued an executive order to provide temporary exemption from deportation for about half of the undocumented immigrants, prioritizing relief for those who had been in the country for a number of years and had children resident in the United States. He also issued an order to deport only those with criminal records.

While these actions brought temporary relief to some, key issues remained unresolved. In particular, millions of undocumented adults remained vulnerable. Conservatives prioritized securing the border and blocking people without papers from entering the country while continuing the deportations. Liberals proposed to strike a balance between securing the borders and finding a way to offer pathways to citizenship and legal resident status for some of the undocumented. Immigrant rights organizations mostly aimed at ending the deportations and securing permanent status for all undocumented people in the country. As one Dream

Defender phrased it, "A new generation of youth, leaders, and organizers for social change must be identified, engaged, trained, and sent back to their communities to build. . . . We are building concrete power and committed to defending the dreams of our community and our generation."[33]

Graduating class of Free L.A. High School, youth who have come through the criminal justice system and continued their studies to completion. *Courtesy of Mary Sutton*

6

THE DEATH OF REHABILITATION

Ninety-five percent of those in prison will one day return to the community. In 2013 this meant about six hundred thousand a year were leaving prison to reenter life on the outside. Yet for the majority of these people, departure from prison will be temporary. According to 2012 figures, more than two-thirds of those who left prison in 2005 were rearrested within three years. More than three-quarters were rearrested within five years.[1]

Mass incarceration not only has captured more people for the prisons and jails but also has created a revolving door that ensures they will return. Because programs in prison and postrelease regimes have abandoned rehabilitation, the era of mass incarceration has become an era of mass recidivism.

REHABILITATION AND ITS DEMISE

Rehabilitation has a long history. The first prison to attempt rehabilitation was the Walnut Street Jail built by the Quakers in Philadelphia in 1790. The Quakers believed that rehabilitation would occur through silent, solitary reflection, so everyone in the jail remained in solitary confinement. The idea was one of seeking penitence (sincere and humble regret for one's misdeeds). From this notion of penitence comes the modern word *penitentiary*, a place where a person seeks penitence.

Throughout most of the twentieth century, prisons in the United States operated on the fundamental principle that a person could be rehabilitated by incarceration. Underlying this notion was the idea that, while incarcerated, prisoners should have access to opportunities that would help them to change their orientation from criminal activity to a more mainstream lifestyle that included a wage-paying job, paying taxes, and taking part in family and community life. To this end, most prisons, particularly those outside the Southern states, set up education and job training programs. Moreover, positive performance in such programs could mean early release. This approach was referred to as indeterminate sentencing, wherein the amount of time served depended on a person's actions while incarcerated.

As noted in chapters 2 and 3, in the late 1970s criminal justice policy makers and scholars began to question the viability of this rehabilitative model. One of the most famous critics of rehabilitation was a criminologist named Robert Martinson. In 1974 he wrote a paper entitled "What Works?"[2] In this paper, Martinson presented evidence that none of the programs offered either in prison or upon release were affecting people's behavior. Basing his conclusions on a review of the cases of 231 individuals who had been through rehabilitation programs, he questioned the value of attempting to do anything at all to help people in prison change their lives. Martinson found that "the present array of correctional treatments has no appreciable effect—positive or negative—on rates of recidivism of convicted offenders."[3]

The idea that nothing works entered the debate concerning rehabilitation at a crucial moment. Throughout the 1970s, crime rates were rising, prompting calls from conservatives for harsher treatment of criminals. In a parallel development, many liberals were posing an argument against indeterminate sentencing. A key component of this argument was that indeterminate sentencing promoted racial bias, because the assessment of who should be released and who should be kept in prison rested with parole boards, which were suspected of treating Black and Latino prisoners less favorably than whites.

Ultimately this debate resulted in the passage of the harsher determinate sentencing regimes, such as mandatory minimums and truth in sentencing. Determinate sentencing became the norm in almost every state, removing all incentives for people to reform.

The demise of rehabilitation had an enormous effect on life in prison and the difficulties people experienced upon reentering their communities afterward. With the removal of rehabilitation as a goal, prisons and jails began to strip away programs that used to help prisoners to improve their education, gain access to job training, or enhance their social skills. More and more, they began simply "warehousing" people, offering minimal activities and leaving prisoners to spend much of their time idle in cells or yards. The decline of education is perhaps the most striking aspect of the change. In 1979 41 percent of all state prisoners were enrolled in some form of education program. By 1995 that number had fallen to 22 percent.[4] Furthermore, while the number of state prisoners more than tripled during that period, the number of educational staff slightly decreased.

Perhaps the bellwether in the move away from rehabilitation programs in prisons was the 1994 ban on Pell Grants for incarcerated people. The 1993 congressional debate on Pell Grants for prisoners was intense. Supporters, including Claiborne Pell, the senator who had sponsored the creation of the grants, argued for the rehabilitative impact of a college education: "America's wardens and parole officers know what few in the Senate and House are willing to acknowledge in the crime bill debate: The more education inmates receive while in prison, the less likely it is they will commit crimes on release. Education equals prevention. Diplomas are crime stoppers."

Opponents, such as Kay Bailey Hutchison of Texas, contended, "The American people are frustrated by a Federal Government and a Congress that cannot seem to get priorities straight. They are frustrated and angry by a Federal Government that sets rules that put convicts at the head of the line for college financial aid, crowding out law-abiding citizens."[5]

Before then, these grants had given prisoners access to full college scholarships covering tuition and books. At the time, there were more than 350 college education programs in prisons. Once prisoners lost access to Pell Grants, the number plummeted. By 2005 only a dozen were still in operation.[6]

THE CHANGING ROLE OF PAROLE AND PROBATION

In the rehabilitation model, the task of parole and probation officers was to facilitate a successful transition for their clients. They were often trained as social workers. After 1980, under the punishment paradigm, parole and probation took on a function much closer to law enforcement: surveillance and control. Parole officers often carry sidearms and frequently patrol neighborhoods in the company of police, looking to find one of their clients in a compromising situation.[7]

The rules and regulations of parole and probation changed as well. With the advent of the War on Drugs, most parole and probation regimes came to include drug testing, even for those whose crimes did not involve drugs.

Perhaps the most important development in parole was expanded use of "technical violations" as a way to send people back to prison. Technical violations are failures to comply with a rule or regulation, not new criminal activity. Technical violations can include missing a scheduled meeting with a parole officer, failing to tell the parole officer of a change in employment or residence, failing to disclose parole status to an employer or landlord, being in the company of someone with a criminal history, being in a prohibited area, traveling out of your county without permission, and getting a positive drug test. In 1980 only about 17 percent of those entering prison entered as a result of parole violations. By 1999 more than a third were parole violators, and two-thirds of those were returned for technical violations.[8] These 1999 figures remained fairly constant until 2012, when, with minor modifications of parole conditions in some large states, the percentage of admissions due to parole violations fell slightly, to 27 percent.[9]

The proliferation of technical violations contributed to high rates of recidivism. In a study of more than four hundred thousand people released from state prisons in 2005, more than two-thirds were rearrested within three years.[10] This was a 5 percent increase over the rate among people released in 1983 who were the subject of a similar study.[11]

LEGAL OBSTACLES FOR PEOPLE ON PAROLE

As noted earlier, the 1996 Personal Responsibility and Work Opportunity Reconciliation Act paid particular attention to people's criminal records in regard to eligibility for state benefits such as food stamps and public housing. Further challenges to those on parole come from employment certification boards in a number of sectors, which add extra hurdles for people with a criminal

How to End Up Back in Prison

If you are on parole, you could risk being sent back to prison for months or years if you:

1. Have dinner with your brother if he has a felony conviction.
2. Ride an unlicensed bicycle.
3. Visit your mother if she lives in a zone where your parole conditions don't allow you to go.
4. Chop onions in the dining room with a knife that has a blade more than 2.5 inches long (you can use it only in the kitchen).
5. Fail to give your parole officer a monthly financial statement.
6. Respond to a family emergency outside your county without permission.
7. Work for an employer who refuses to allow your parole agent to search your work premises.

record. A study carried out by the city of Chicago in 2002 found that of the ninety-eight employment licensure acts in Illinois, fifty-seven had restrictions for people with felony convictions.[12] A number of these completely banned anyone with a particular felony conviction from certain jobs, including employment counselor, funeral director, hazardous waste equipment operator, and horsemeat dealer. Jobs such as barber, boiler vessel repair, interior design, dead animal disposal, and livestock dealing also had limitations for people with felony convictions.

Since 9/11 many employers have also begun to use criminal background checks as a way to screen employees in the name of public safety. Those who fight for the rights of people with felony convictions have argued against this move. According to a leading advocacy group on the issue, the National Employment Law Project, "studies have shown providing individuals the opportunity for stable employment actually lowers crime recidivism rates and thus increases public safety."[13]

As part of screening for criminal background, many employers ask candidates to check "the box" on job applications if they have ever been convicted of a crime. Activists around the country have argued that this box discriminates against people who admit to having a criminal record, often leading to their disqualification from the selection process. As a result of these concerns, campaigns against the box have resulted in a number of cities, counties, and states passing "Ban the Box" measures. These outlaw the use of the question about criminal background on job applications and usually permit the employer to ask about criminal background only once a job offer is on the table. Minnesota, Illinois, and Massachusetts have banned the box for all job applications in the public and private sector, with the exception of municipal employment in large cities.

In addition to employment restrictions, many states ban people with felony convictions from voting. In at least twelve states, a person with a felony conviction may be blocked from voting even after having completed parole or probation. In Virginia and Kentucky, people with a felony conviction must apply for clemency from the governor to get their voting rights restored. Whereas in most European countries individuals can cast a ballot while incarcerated, only two states, Maine and Vermont, allow people in prison to vote. Estimates from the Sentencing Project indicate that in 2010 some 5.85 million people with felony convictions were not allowed to vote. Given the racial bias of mass incarceration, this meant that one in thirteen African American men were banned from voting. In three states, Florida, Kentucky, and Virginia, more than 20 percent of Black adults were disenfranchised.[14] In many states, disenfranchisement includes exclusion from jury duty eligibility as well.

FINANCIAL OBSTACLES FOR PEOPLE ON PAROLE

Encounters with the criminal justice system increasingly come with financial charges. The largest of these charges usually come in the form of fines known as restitution. The 1984 Victims of Crime Act and the 1996 Mandatory Restitution Act added such fines to most federal cases, and every state now has a crime victims' restitution fund of some kind. The Federal Office of Crime Victims is the main distributor of these funds. As of 2013 the fund had a

Coming Home
The Voices of "Returning Citizens"

My son wasn't a baby anymore and he hadn't seen me in 10 years. Now he was 12. He wouldn't let me hug him. He wouldn't even shake my hand. I'm trying to understand this. I cry every night.

I want to prove to myself and those who stuck by me that I can make it right. I'm so scared of letting anyone down after the burden I've been.

The first few days are the hardest, just getting your senses used to not being in an institution can be overwhelming. The smells of urban life, the sounds, eyes adjusting to home lighting. Feet hardly know how to walk on wood floors and carpeting (vs. concrete). Being able to close a door and not be watched, the softness of cushions and blankets.

Last I checked, life doesn't come with instructions. You just got to take it how it comes sometimes. I wish I knew how to make it through a trip to the grocery store without becoming overwhelmed and traumatized by the experience of too many choices. Ice cream was a 30-minute decision-making event for me. I have not yet adjusted to thinking for myself completely.

I worry about violating parole every time I step outside, by resembling someone or just by talking to the wrong person. Every time I see the police go by, even though I'm not breaking any law, makes my heart skip a beat because they love to harass Blacks and Latinos; it's a game to them. I only did five years and I still jump at the sound of keys or two-way radio.

It is frustrating to lay awake and think, "Well, if I go back to prison at least my life will be assigned to me: job, clothes, bed and food will all be handed to me and I don't have to worry." Don't get me wrong. I have no intention (for now) of committing a crime; however, I wonder what I will do if push comes to shove and I'm truly out of cash and have no way to eat or support myself at all.

(continues)

(continued)

We're not seen as community members when we get out, and we face discrimination in employment, housing, etc. People don't necessarily see the value of former prisoners or understand that we have a right to be part of the community and have something to contribute. We need to get that sense of self and value as part of community.[15]

balance of about $9 billion and distributed more than $700 million annually to crime victims throughout the states.[16]

These funds aim to compensate victims of crime for their loss. For example, if someone has a car stolen and wrecked, the restitution fund might provide money for the person to buy a new car. In cases of assault, the compensation fund might pay the victim's medical expenses or fees for counseling.

In many states as well as in federal cases, however, even victimless crimes such as drug possession include "restitution" fines, often of thousands of dollars. This money becomes a permanent debt for the prisoner, and mandatory repayment may begin even during incarceration. Many prisons deduct a percentage of all money a prisoner receives as payment toward restitution. For example, in California if a mother sends her incarcerated son $100 to buy toiletries and food from the commissary, 55 percent of that money will be deducted and put into the Victims' Compensation Fund. The woman's son would get only $45. Similarly, if a prisoner receives wages for work done in the prison, 55 percent will go toward restitution.

In addition, people in prison now often have to pay for prison medical services. Items such as eyeglasses, canes, walkers, and wheelchairs are all billed to a person's account. Medical and psychiatric services now frequently require a co-pay from people inside.

While most states provide "gate money"—a little cash on release—it's not enough to help people get on their feet. The amounts range from $200 in California down to $10 in Illinois, and several states give no gate money at all.

Moreover, when people do hit the streets, they may incur costs for their parole or probation. These may include a monthly fee to be under supervision as well as separate charges for drug testing; compulsory classes, such as anger management courses; or mandatory treatment programs.

SUPER-SUPERVISION

Technology has enabled new types of carceral control. Electronic monitors, typically in the form of ankle bracelets, are used widely. Laws for monitors vary from state to state. In some states people can serve an entire sentence on a monitor. In others, monitors can be used only for parole or probation. Electronic monitors increasingly use GPS technology, which enables an authority to track the location of a client in real time. In addition, some monitors can be programmed with exclusion zones. These monitors will sound an alarm if one enters an area where one is not supposed to go. Exclusion zones are most frequently used for people with sex-offense or gang histories. In the case of those with sex-offense convictions, parks and schools are typically exclusion zones. Those with gang affiliations are usually banned from the areas where their gang is alleged to operate.

How Long Should the Stigma Last?

In 2007 Yolanda Quesada had worked at Wells Fargo Bank in Milwaukee for five years. For some reason, the bank decided to do a criminal background check on her. They found that Yolanda had two shoplifting convictions when she was eighteen, some forty years earlier. Although she had a clean record for four decades and an excellent job history at Wells Fargo, the company fired her, claiming that federal law prohibited it from employing anyone with "a criminal record involving dishonesty or breach of trust." For some employers, the stigma of a criminal conviction never goes away.[17]

Human rights advocates have argued that exclusion zones render reentry almost impossible for many people with sex-offense histories. More than thirty states have such laws in place. In many instances, these laws bar people with sex-offense histories from coming within a specific distance—typically a thousand feet—of any place where children might congregate.

In some urban areas, this effectively makes the entire city an exclusion zone, leaving people with no place to live or work. These restrictions can force people on parole to resort to desperate measures to find a place to live.

In Miami, a number of people with histories of incarceration for sex offenses were banned by exclusion zones from living near parks, places of worship, and schools. Minister Richard Witherow, who calls people with sex offense histories "the modern day lepers," assisted them in relocating to a small town, Pahokee, Florida, which had no such restrictions. They called their settlement Miracle Village. As of July 2013, about a hundred people with sex offense histories were living there. The settlement's website calls Miracle Village "a thriving community where retired sugarcane workers and ex-offenders rebuilding their lives live in friendship and God's love."[18]

LOOKING FOR SOLUTIONS

The release of millions of people back into communities after incarceration has prompted many attempts to create programs that allow people to reenter society successfully. These programs have taken a wide range of approaches, from "tough on crime" zero-tolerance programs to those that involve using formerly incarcerated people as peer mentors.

Hawaii's Opportunity Probation with Enforcement (HOPE). In Honolulu, probation authorities attempted to address the problem of high recidivism, especially by drug users, with a quick-response, quick-punishment approach. Before HOPE was started, people on probation who tested positive for drugs were given several warnings before any punishment was implemented. Under HOPE, a person who tests positive for drugs or commits any other technical violation is immediately sent to jail. The first violation results in a couple of days in lockup, with each violation thereafter incurring a longer period in jail. The advocates of this program claim that it has drastically reduced the number of positive drug tests and technical violations and is relatively cheap and easy to administer.

The Allegheny County Jail Collaborative. In Allegheny County, Pennsylvania, criminal justice authorities set up the Jail Collaborative committee, which included the county sheriff, the chief prosecutor, and the head of probation. This group is responsible for setting up and maintaining a program to facilitate reentry with relevant services. At the heart of the program is risk assessment. Each person coming into the jail is administered a risk-assessment test to assess the level of threat the person might pose to the community and to identify the specific services individual might require (e.g., substance abuse treatment or anger management therapy). Those with low risk might be given a diversion program not involving jail time but requiring them to participate in specific programs. Others with higher risk would be provided services during their time in jail, and those services would be continued and intensified upon release. Each person in this program would be assigned a case manager who would assist the individual with planning and link him or her to relevant services in the community, including those offering help with housing and employment. Two points are central in this plan: (1) relevant services, especially for substance abuse and mental health, begin while the person is incarcerated, and (2) postrelease efforts focus on strengthening ties between the individual and his or her family and community.

St. Leonard's Wraparound Services. St. Leonard's Ministries in Chicago focuses on men and women returning from prison, not jail. Central to the approach of St. Leonard's is the notion of peer mentoring—that formerly incarcerated people need to play a major role in supporting people returning from prison during their transition. St. Leonard's provides comprehensive (wraparound) services, which incorporate transitional housing for up to two years. These include job training on-site, computer literacy classes, substance abuse counseling, and the development of a range of life skills. Eighty-five percent of St. Leonard's staff are former prisoners, including the executive director and other major administrators. St. Leonard's claims to have reduced recidivism to 20 percent, well below the Illinois average of about 50 percent.

A New Way of Life in Los Angeles. A New Way of Life also focuses on the participation of formerly incarcerated people but exclusively serves women. Founded by Susan Burton, who spent many years behind bars in California, a New Way of Life provides services and a path to reentry for women coming out of prison while also functioning as an advocacy group for the rights of the formerly incarcerated. Burton also founded a leadership project called Women Organizing for Justice, which trains formerly incarcerated women to advocate for themselves and others, as well as a Reentry Employment Rights Project to challenge employment discrimination against the formerly incarcerated.

THE DEBATE OVER REENTRY

The yardstick that many corrections systems use to measure the effectiveness of rehabilitation or reentry programs is the recidivism rate. This is typically defined as the percent of people leaving prison or jail who return to custody within three years after release. Many criminal justice analysts question the value of this statistic, arguing that it can be easily manipulated and may depend as much on how strict the rules of parole are as on how the persons being supervised behave. Criminal justice scholar Joan Petersilia explains:

> We just decide to revoke people under different things. We all know that game. That's just a shell game. Okay. Let's don't violate technical violations. I can get that down. Okay. Let's just decide we are going to let people fail three or four times and not violate them. I can get your arrest rates down. I can get a lot of things down. But have we really changed behavior? And so that's a much different thing.[19]

Recidivism rates may have value as one measurement among many, but, as Petersilia points out, the key question is whether we can really measure the success of people who are released from prison by their arrest record. This is not, however, the only area of debate over reentry.

Some analysts have argued that, while reentry programs may help a few individuals, they are futile without investment in the poor inner-city African American and Latino neighborhoods from which most prisoners come. Loïc Wacquant and other writers contend that until we address the root causes of violent and property crimes, the idea of reentry is meaningless.

He points out that people are returning to neighborhoods riddled with violence that lack opportunities for employment or job training and where they're subject to the constant presence of heavily armed police and parole and probation officers. Wacquant asks how "former prisoners [could] be 're-integrated' when they were never integrated in the first place and when there exists no viable social structure to accommodate them outside?"[20]

One response to the deeper problems is justice reinvestment. According to advocates Susan B. Tucker and Eric Cadora, "The goal of justice reinvestment is to redirect some portion of the [billions] America now spends on prisons to rebuilding the human resources and infrastructure—the schools, healthcare facilities, parks, and public spaces—of neighborhoods devastated by high levels of incarceration."[21] This justice reinvestment approach toward transforming criminal justice is discussed in more detail in chapter 14.

Activists in Champaign County, Illinois, staged a mass march to the local jail in October 2013 as part of their campaign to stop efforts by county authorities to spend $20 million on new jail facilities. *Courtesy of Brian Dolinar*

7

JAIL—THE LOCAL FACE OF MASS INCARCERATION

The vast majority of counties in the United States, as well as some cities, have their own jails. While most studies of mass incarceration focus on prisons, in the last three decades jails have continued to swallow up more people and consume larger and larger chunks of local budgets. Jails hold a key position in the criminal justice system as the first stop for most people after arrest. The number of people in jails on any given day is less than that in prisons, but because stints in jails are typically quite short, far more people end up in jail every year than in prison. Hence, to understand mass incarceration, we need to understand how jails work, their impact, and how they differ from prisons yet are intimately linked to them.

The majority of people in jails are waiting for their cases to be resolved in the courts, typically in a plea bargain or a trial. A small number of people who are convicted of misdemeanors or low-level felonies may serve their entire sentences in a jail.

Racial disparity is a reality in most jails, with African Americans and/or Latinos disproportionately represented. This racial disparity has increased due to both the War on Drugs and the increased incarceration of immigrants.

Because people tend to spend a short time in them, jails usually have fewer activities and less space than prisons. Unlike most prisons, jails typically aren't designed with extensive education facilities or large outdoor recreation areas. Conditions and regulations for visiting people in jail are also normally more restrictive than in prisons. In many jails, people spend virtually all day in their cells. Most people who have spent any length of time incarcerated prefer prison to jail. Because of the limited facilities, the per-prisoner cost is generally less than in a prison.

THE GROWTH OF JAIL POPULATIONS

In the last three decades, jail populations have grown astronomically. In 1985 the average daily jail population in the United States stood at 256,615. By 1990 the figure had risen by more than 50 percent to 405,320. At the turn of the twenty-first century, the number was 621,149. The count kept rising, peaking in 2007 at 776,523, and then declined slightly over the next few years to just over 731,000 in 2013. Racial disparity has also grown during this period. In 1985 whites comprised 47 percent of the national jail population, while Blacks made up 36 percent. By 1990 the Black proportion had risen to 41 percent, a level that has remained fairly constant since then.[1]

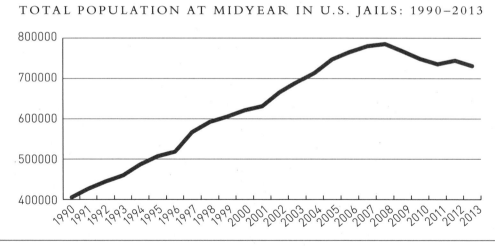

TOTAL POPULATION AT MIDYEAR IN U.S. JAILS: 1990–2013

Figure 7.1

Figure 7.1 counts the population in all jails on a specific day of the year. Because people generally stay in jail for a short time, these figures fail to capture the volume of people who enter and exit jails each year. In 2013 nearly 12 million people spent some time in a jail, roughly one in every twenty adults. While jail populations have grown, the number of jails has remained relatively constant for the last three decades at just over three thousand.[2] To accommodate the larger numbers of prisoners, counties have torn down old jails and built new ones, added on to existing facilities, shipped people to other counties, or just packed people in more tightly.

A number of important changes have contributed to the expansion of the jail population during the last three decades. One of the most important has been the alterations of bail regimes. Bails are typically set much higher than previously, and the use of "own recognizance" (releasing people without bail) has declined. This means more people are waiting in jail until the resolution of their cases. In 1990 money bonds were being set in 53 percent of felony cases. By 2006 that figure had jumped to 70 percent. As the use of money bonds has gone up, pretrial release rates have gone down because fewer people are able to meet the cost of posting bail. In 1990 65 percent of felony defendants were released while awaiting trial, compared to 58 percent in 2006.[3] Research has also revealed racial disparity in bail levels. According to the Pretrial Justice Institute in Gaithersburg, Maryland, African Americans' bail averaged 35 percent higher than that of whites with similar charges. Latino bail was 15 percent higher.[4]

Harsher penalties for driving under the influence of alcohol have also contributed to larger jail populations. Laws against driving while under the influence have stiffened greatly. From 1986 to 1997, the number of people incarcerated for such offenses increased from 21,900 to 58,700, with most of them serving their sentences in jails.[5]

FURTHER EXPLAINING JAIL POPULATIONS' GROWTH

The explanation for expansion of jail populations runs deeper. While the War on Drugs, severe sentencing laws, and harsher immigration policies have contributed to the growth of jail populations, cutbacks in state social service provisions, local ordinances that criminalize the poor, and the increased use of fines and fees in criminal justice have also played a role.

CUTBACKS IN SOCIAL SERVICES

In 2012 the Treatment Advocacy Center, a national advocacy group for mental health care, reported that there were more than 350,000 people with serious mental illness in prisons and jails—nearly ten times the number in state mental health facilities.[6] Over the course of the past three decades, states have systematically cut back on mental health services. This means that when people experience a mental health crisis in a public space, typically referred to as "acting out," police often have nowhere to take them except jail. Thomas Dart, sheriff of Cook County Jail in Chicago, described the process: "It's criminalizing mental illness. . . . We've systematically shut down all the mental health facilities, so the mentally ill have nowhere else to go. We've become the de facto mental health hospital."[7] Moreover, the people most likely to be taken to jail for a mental health crisis are the poor, especially the homeless, who seldom have a private place where they can work out their issues. Not surprisingly, the poor are disproportionately African American, Latino and Latina, and Native American. These people often end up with minor charges, such as disturbing the peace or loitering, but even a short stay in jail can traumatize a person who already has mental health issues. According to researchers, people with mental health issues are more likely to be violently victimized in jail, more likely to end up in solitary confinement, and end up spending more time in jail than the average.[8]

While not as drastic as the cutback in mental health services, many communities have also reduced the scale of drug programs, including detox centers and substance abuse treatment. Moreover, large numbers of people in the criminal justice system suffer from what is referred to as dual diagnosis—both mental health and substance abuse problems. In some cases, substance abuse is the result of self-medication to address a mental health issue. While the rich and famous, such as Lindsay Lohan and Charlie Sheen, may check into expensive rehab programs if they have an encounter with the police because of substance abuse, the poor will be taken to jail and possibly face a series of criminal charges ranging from possession of drugs and/or drug paraphernalia to being drunk and disorderly.

THE CRIMINALIZATION OF POVERTY

Throughout the country, policing of urban spaces has intensified in the past three decades as the nation's treatment of its poor has switched, in the words of researcher Christopher Petrella, "from welfare to cellfare."[9] The criminalization of the poor goes hand in hand with the "zero tolerance" or "broken windows" approach to policing that has become the norm in many cities. The broken-windows idea comes from a 1982 article by sociologists James Q. Wilson and George L. Kelling.[10] Writing at a time of escalating crime rates, the authors suggest that small crimes, such as vandalism, window breaking, or defacing public property, are the first step to more serious criminal activity if the tendency is not nipped in the bud.

In response, many police departments, led by New York City's police chief William Bratton, began a zero-tolerance policy by systematically arresting people for minor violations, such as loitering, graffiti writing, or public drunkenness. In addition, many cities passed ordinances making it illegal to engage in some of the survival activities common to the poor, such as "aggressive" panhandling, selling goods and services on the street (such as windshield washing at stoplights), and sleeping or urinating in public. A survey undertaken by the National Law Center on Homelessness and Poverty and the National Coalition for the Homeless in 2009 found that of 235 cities surveyed:

- 33 percent prohibited "camping" in particular public places in the city, and 17 percent had citywide prohibitions on "camping";
- 30 percent prohibited sitting or lying down in certain public places;
- 47 percent prohibited loitering in particular public areas, and 19 percent prohibited loitering citywide; and
- 47 percent prohibited begging in particular public places, 49 percent prohibited aggressive panhandling, and 23 percent had citywide prohibitions on begging.[11]

Some jurisdictions have even made it illegal to share food in public. For example, Las Vegas passed an anti-food-sharing ordinance to halt a program organized by the group Food Not Bombs to feed the homeless in public spaces. Silicon Valley in California was one of the first

Barbara Ehrenreich on Race and Poverty

By far the most reliable way to be criminalized by poverty is to have the wrong color skin. Indignation runs high when a celebrity professor succumbs to racial profiling, but whole communities are effectively "profiled" for the suspicious combination of being both dark-skinned and poor. Flick a cigarette and you're "littering"; wear the wrong color T-shirt and you're displaying gang allegiance. Just strolling around in a dodgy neighborhood can mark you as a potential suspect. And don't get grumpy about it or you could be "resisting arrest."[13]

places to make living in a car illegal, taking away one of the last living-space options for many homeless people.[12]

Apart from these changes in the law, forceful policing has become more common. For instance, in some cities police carry out sweeps of areas where homeless people are concentrated. These often lead to arrests, personal injury to the homeless, the destruction of their personal property, or confiscation of their medication.

FINES AND FEES

The array of new legal sanctions against urban survival activities has been accompanied by the increasing use of fines and fees as additional punishment. The American Civil Liberties Union has said that this amounts to a restoration of debtors' prisons, a form of punishment the United States outlawed in the 1800s. Many states impose charges simply for entering the criminal justice system. In 2009, for example, the North Carolina state legislature passed a set of fees to be levied on all defendants, regardless of whether they were eventually found guilty. These included a "general court fee" of $95.50 to $102.50 and a "facilities fee" of $30. Louisiana has a $300 fee that goes into a judicial expense fund, while Washington State adds $100 for taking a mandatory DNA sample and a $600 legal financial obligation for each felony conviction. Washington authorities also charge 12 percent annual interest on money owed to the criminal justice system. Arizona levies an 83 percent surcharge on all fines. Hence in Arizona a $500 traffic ticket actually costs $915.[14]

In 2010 the Brennan Center for Justice of New York University Law School carried out a survey in fifteen large-population states.[15] Its researchers found that fourteen had jurisdictions that used "poverty penalties," adding extra charges onto unpaid debt. All had jurisdictions that incarcerated people for failure to pay fines and fees. Eight of the fifteen suspended driver's licenses for nonpayment, while seven revoked voting rights until the debt was paid. Several offered defendants an opportunity to "volunteer" to serve time to settle their criminal justice debts.

In Alabama and Georgia, further financial complications have come via the outsourcing of probation to private firms, such as Sentinel Offender Services and Judicial Correction Services. According to a report by Human Rights Watch, in some instances these firms offer no real probation program other than collecting fines on behalf of the local government.[16] In addition, they top off the fines with monthly fees for their own services and then use the threat of incarceration on people who fail to pay these service charges. This threat is very real. The Brennan Center lists four ways in which failure to pay criminal justice debt can put someone in the modern version of debtors' prison: parole or probation can be revoked, a civil or criminal court action can order the person to jail, probation or parole can be extended, or a person can "choose" jail as an alternative to cash payments in order to pay off fines.

Despite the severe consequences of fines for the poor, many local authorities argue that these fines are necessary in order to finance the operations of the criminal justice system. The Brennan Center report also questioned this claim and found that most states had not even studied the costs of collecting fines as compared to the revenue generated.

Sociologist Alexes Harris, an expert on criminal justice debt, argues that fines and fees can set up a long-term cycle of debt and incarceration, which in some cases can amount to a "life sentence." She maintains that "as a result of interest and surcharges that accumulate on these financial penalties, this portion of a person's sentence becomes permanent legal debt, carried for the remainder of their lives." Harris advocates the abolition of all criminal justice fines and fees apart from restitution. Other people argue that such fines, along with very high bails, violate the Eighth Amendment of the U.S. Constitution. While many people are aware that the amendment bans cruel and unusual punishment, it also outlaws "excessive bail" and "excessive fines."[17]

What Does a Week in Jail Cost?

Aprisoner's stay in jail typically costs local governments about $60 day, or $420 a week, but for an individual a week in jail can be much more costly. A few nights in jail can wreak financial and personal havoc.

If a person doesn't show up for work because of an arrest, how understanding will the employer be? Many people lose their jobs because of an arrest. Without the income, that person may not be able to pay rent or utilities. Without another job, now harder to find because of the arrest, the person may become homeless. Moreover, for some people, especially those with mental illness or physical disability, even a short time in jail may prove extremely traumatic, leaving lasting psychological wounds that are difficult to heal. If a person has parenting or caregiving responsibilities, children or loved ones may be left without support.

At times, a person's family may not know what happened to her or him for hours or days, because lack of access to a phone once in custody can worsen the impact of a short stint in jail. The assumed entitlement to a phone call that we often see in the media is not a reality in many jails. Moreover, even when phones are available, the costs are frequently prohibitive, keeping people cut off from family and community.

FINANCIAL IMPLICATIONS OF JAIL GROWTH

Most jails are owned and operated by counties and funded by local taxes, chiefly taxes on property. The expansion of jail populations has incurred enormous construction costs, and expanded jails mean more staff salaries and larger bills for energy, equipment, maintenance, and supplies. All told, local expenditure on criminal justice grew fivefold from 1982 to 2006, from $21 billion to $109 billion, while that for local corrections alone increased sixfold in even less time, from $3 billion in 1983 to $18 billion in 2002.[18]

Even if a county government has adequate tax revenue to finance a jail construction project, it typically will have to borrow money to pay for the building, then repay the loan plus

---

Media Coverage: If It Bleeds It Leads

As mentioned in chapter 2, TV news coverage has become an important method of building popular support for harsher policing and more lockups. In 1980 a survey of local TV news in a number of areas throughout the United States found that crime accounted for about 20 percent of news stories.[19] A Pew Center survey with a similar focus that covered thousands of local TV outlets from 1998 to 2002 found that 36 percent of all local stories were either crime or accidents, but 61 percent of the lead stories dealt with crime and accidents. By 2005 a subsequent study reported that the lead-story percentage had escalated to 77 percent.[20] A 2009 study of a similar scale done by researchers at Michigan State University found that 32 percent of all local TV news stories focused on crime.[21]

---

interest over the course of fifteen or twenty years. These bond repayments operate much like a home mortgage, with interest consuming a large percentage of repayments. To raise money for such loans, county officials may put a referendum on the ballot to ask voters to authorize such a loan, or they may raise the capital without voter approval through vehicles called lease revenue bonds. In many counties, jail construction is the largest single capital expense in the budget, with banks or other financial institutions making large profits from interest and other charges on the bond. Because this construction involves so much money, proposals to build new jails have become the focal point of many local social justice activists.

CASE STUDIES OF ANTI-JAIL CAMPAIGNS

From Los Angeles, with a mega jail that holds 19,000 people, to Champaign, Illinois, where the jail has a mere 313 beds, activists on the ground have resisted efforts to sink more funds into local lockups.

A Voice from Inside Debtors' Prison

Harold Brooks, a fifty-eight-year-old veteran, was arrested and jailed for ten days in 2008 after falling behind on payments of court fines. At the time, Brooks was receiving Supplemental Security Income (SSI) disability payments because of cancer and heart problems.

"My court fees started in the '70s, and to get rid of them took over 30 years," Brooks said in an interview. "In my life, I'd say I was in prison for court fines more than five times . . . enough that when I get a court date for a court fine and I know that I haven't got the funds to pay it, I get really shaky when it comes to that time."[22]

LOS ANGELES

Los Angeles County Jail is the largest in the United States. Spread across seven different facilities, the jail housed an average of nineteen thousand people per day in 2014. The jail and its future became the focus of extensive debates in local government from 2011 onward. A number of sources exposed horrific conditions in the jail. For example, a report from the federal government noted fifteen suicides in the jail from 2012 to 2014. In December 2013, eighteen Los Angeles County deputies were indicted for abusing people in custody and beating visitors.[23]

The jail was also beset by serious overcrowding. This contributed to the deterioration of conditions, especially in the Men's Central facility, which was built in 1963 and housed about five thousand people per day in 2014.

In 2012 jail system consultant James Austin came up with three sets of recommendations for Los Angeles: (a) implement programs to reduce the jail population, (b) refurbish and repurpose existing facilities and other government properties to reduce overcrowding, and (c) build new facilities for women.[24] The recommendations added extra complexity to a prolonged battle among law enforcement officials; the Board of Supervisors, which must authorize any major capital expenditure; and anti-jail-expansion groups, led by Californians

United for a Responsible Budget (CURB). In 2014 the board approved spending $2 billion on new construction, but the battle over the future of the jail continued.

The debate centered on how to balance expenditure and priorities among three options: (1) improving conditions for those inside the jail by building new and better facilities, (2) releasing many people from jail and into community-based programs, and (3) reducing crime by addressing problems of mental health, substance abuse, and poverty in the community. These competing priorities face many local governments throughout the country.

Voices from the Debate on the Los Angeles County Jail

I have never experienced any facility exhibiting the volume and repetitive patterns of violence, misfeasance and malfeasance [of] the Los Angeles County Jail system.

—Thomas Parker, a former FBI agent who oversaw the FBI investigation into the Los Angeles Sheriff's Department[25]

The Men's Central Jail is so grossly overcrowded, dangerous and dungeon-like that it puts intolerable stress on the jailed as well as the jailers. The county must do whatever it takes to stop subjecting people to the nightmarish conditions in this jail, and stop denying basic mental health treatment to those who need it.

—Margaret Winter, associate director of the ACLU National Prison Project[26]

We're against any and all jail expansion in LA County because we believe incarceration rates are out of control. Dollars should instead be put into the community to take care of people's needs through social services, rehabilitation, housing, job training. These are much more effective ways to invest in the community and create real and long-lasting public safety, as opposed to dumping poor people, mentally ill people, and people of color in jail.

—Mary Sutton, Californians United for a Responsible Budget (CURB)[27]

CHAMPAIGN, ILLINOIS

By 2011 Champaign County, Illinois, with a population of 201,081 in the 2010 census, had two jails.[28] The sheriff came forward with a proposal to close one facility and add on to the other. Those proposing a new jail were planning to float a bond for $15 million to $20 million and repay it with monthly payments from tax money. People in the community, led by a social justice organization called Champaign Urbana Citizens for Peace and Justice, came out in opposition to the jail. They argued that public safety included more than buildings and that the tax money should be reallocated to social service programs for mental health, substance abuse, and reentry. They also emphasized reversing what they called the New Jim Crow in Champaign County; consistently more than half the people in the jail were African American, though Black people constitute only 13 percent of the county's population.

A two-year political struggle ensued. The county paid for a criminal justice needs-assessment consultancy and formed a Community Justice Task Force to propose alternatives to incarceration. At the end of 2013, the county board decided to set aside the jail construction proposal and put $400,000 into reentry, pretrial release, mental health, and additional funding for the public defender. Law enforcement officials nonetheless came back the following year with a proposal to spend millions to add a mental and medical health facility to the county jail.

The battle over how to change the criminal justice system continued, raising a number of key issues.

- How does a community define public safety? Is it just physical security and combating crime, or does it also have to do with social security—employment, health care, education, job training, and housing?
- Who should decide on enormous capital expenditure projects, such as a jail—elected officials or voters in public referendums?
- Should counties be investing in mental health and substance abuse programs located in jails or in the community?
- How can community groups effectively influence decisions on the criminal justice system?

MARICOPA COUNTY

Maricopa County, Arizona, typifies the hard-line vision of jail—punishment only, and the nastier the better.[29] In the early 1990s, faced with a problem of jail overcrowding, Maricopa County sheriff Joe Arpaio rejected a plan to build a $70 million complex. Instead he erected a tent city with military surplus tents. This outdoor living space accommodated some two thousand people. Temperatures inside the tents at the peak of summer reached 145 degrees. Arpaio added extra humiliation to his tent regime by making the prisoners wear old-style striped uniforms and pink underwear. While Tent City solved the overcrowding problem from a financial standpoint, it raised serious human rights concerns. Amnesty International said that it was not an "adequate or humane alternative to housing inmates in suitable . . . jail facilities."[30] Pearl Wilson, whose son died in a fight in Tent City, founded a group called "Mothers Against Arpaio" and called for Tent City to be closed.[31]

NEW ORLEANS

The New Orleans Parish (county) Jail held some 6,500 people in 2005 when Hurricane Katrina struck. The hurricane damaged much of the jail beyond repair. When authorities proposed to rebuild it back to its 6,500 capacity, the community mobilized against the plan. In the end, the community won. The new jail was built to house only 1,438 people. Instead parish officials had to come up with programs to serve people in the community, not inside the jail.[32]

Jails have played a key role in the rise of mass incarceration. Without a great increase in incarceration capacity at the local level, the nation's prison system could never have grown exponentially the way it has. By continually criminalizing the poor and building new cells, local authorities have been key political players in carrying out mass incarceration. Jails attract little attention in the research on mass incarceration, but they are key cogs in the machine and the target of much debate and political struggle over the future direction of the criminal justice system and local government.

Youth have mobilized against the school-to-prison pipeline and the killing of African American youth by police. *Left, courtesy of Mary Sutton; right, courtesy of Frank Johnson*

8

THE SCHOOL-TO-PRISON PIPELINE

The United States incarcerates youth at a much higher rate than other nations—seven times the rate of the United Kingdom and eighteen times the rate of France. Moreover, the education system plays a huge role by preparing a large swath of the nation's youth to live under state control rather than to become successful free adults. Many social justice advocates call this phenomenon the school-to-prison pipeline. The pipeline came fully online in the 1990s, and its delivery of student prisoners increased in intensity in the early 2000s. Three factors contributed to its development.

First, policy analysts began to claim that the nation's education system was in crisis. Among the earliest expressions of this sentiment was a report by the National Commission on Excellence in Education, *A Nation at Risk: The Imperative for Educational Reform*, published in 1983. This report contended that the U.S. education system was falling behind those of many other nations and that tighter regimes of discipline and more rigorous testing were required to improve the performance of American students.

Second, the ethos of the War on Drugs spread the methods and ideology of the criminal justice system into schools. This came in a variety of forms—metal detectors, police on school campuses, zero-tolerance discipline policies, and so on.

Third, in the late 1980s and the 1990s, several high-profile violent crimes committed by young people had a big impact. The Central Park jogger incident was one of the most prominent.

CREATING MORAL PANIC

In the 1980s, the creation of a "moral panic" about drug use and youth violence was key to tightening the screws on juveniles and introducing prison and police practices into schools.[1] The Reagan administration's Drug Abuse Resistance Education (DARE) program, described in chapter 4, brought thousands of police officers into schools throughout the country to talk up the dangers of drugs. The DARE stage was followed in the 1990s by a rash of pundits who promoted the fear of a whole new class of allegedly inherently violent young males labeled superpredators. Although the connection was seldom explicitly made, superpredators always seemed to have dark complexions and African American or Latino features.

In their book *Body Count: Moral Poverty and How to Win America's War Against Crime and Drugs*, John DiIulio Jr., along with former and future White House drug czars William Bennett and John P. Walters, insisted that "America is now home to thickening ranks of juvenile 'super-predators'—radically impulsive, brutally remorseless youngsters, including ever more pre-teenage boys . . . who do not fear the stigma of arrest, the pains of imprisonment, or the pangs of conscience."[2] The authors argued that Americans were "sitting atop a demographic crime bomb." Media promotion of the superpredator theory soon converted pressure into action. This took place on two fronts: among lawmakers and within the schools.

CHANGING THE LAWS OF JUVENILE JUSTICE

A key response to the moral panic was extending adult prosecution to youth under eighteen, as described in chapter 3. National legislation buttressed this approach by clamping down on schools. The Gun Free School Zones Act of 1990 banned possession of a gun near the grounds of any school. The Safe and Gun Free Schools Act of 1994 made expulsion for at least a year a mandatory minimum for any student found in possession of a gun on the premises of a public school.

Moral Panic: From the Central Park Jogger to Columbine

In April 1989 Trisha Meili went jogging one night in New York's Central Park. Along the way, she was attacked, raped, and so brutally beaten that she had no memory of the events afterward. Not long after, five young men, four Blacks and one Latino, were charged with the crime. All were under eighteen. The case drew national attention as four of them signed confessions, then claimed they were intimidated into confessing and pled innocent in court. After two trials, the five were all convicted and sentenced to long terms in youth correctional facilities. They became known as the Central Park Five and the case was called "the case of the Central Park jogger," since Meili was not widely identified in the media at the time. In 2002, after all five had completed their sentences, another man, Matias Reyes, confessed to the crime, and DNA testing confirmed that he was the perpetrator. The convictions of the five were vacated, and they subsequently sued the City of New York. In 2014 authorities announced that all parties had accepted a settlement of $40 million.

A decade later came the Columbine massacre, the first of many highly publicized armed assaults on schools. On April 20, 1999, two students shot dead twelve other students and a teacher at Columbine High School in Colorado. Columbine sparked a range of changes in school discipline regimes, extending the implementation of zero-tolerance policies and catalyzing a federal initiative to impose automatic suspension for possession of a weapon on campus.[3] These measures intensified with the general national move toward tighter security in the wake of 9/11, even at a time when violent crimes in general and those committed by youth in particular were in steep decline.

JUVENILE LIFE WITHOUT PAROLE

The harshest step in tightening juvenile justice was applying the sentence of life without parole to crimes committed by youth under eighteen years of age. The United States is the only country today where kids are sentenced to live the rest of their lives in prison. As of 2013 there were at least 2,500 people serving life sentences without parole in the United States for crimes they committed when they were children.[4] Florida has the highest number of people doing life without parole for crimes committed as juveniles. As of 2009 84 percent of those in Florida serving life without parole for juvenile crimes were African American.[5]

Human Rights Watch reported that more than 50 percent of those doing life for crimes committed as juveniles had no prior criminal convictions. One in six were fifteen or younger at the time of their offense. Many of them had experienced abuse and neglect, their lives marred by instability, poverty, and violent or criminal behavior by the adults in their lives.[6]

After widespread outcry over the issue, in 2012 the Supreme Court ruled in the case of *Miller v. Alabama* that mandatory life without parole was unconstitutional for juveniles. The court's opinion held that, compared to adults, juveniles have a "lack of maturity and an underdeveloped sense of responsibility"; they "are more vulnerable or susceptible to negative influences and outside pressures, including peer pressure"; and their characters are "not as well formed."[7]

POLICING SCHOOLS WITH ZERO TOLERANCE

To solve the supposed crisis in education, many of the principles and disciplinary methods common in the criminal justice system were transferred to the schools. A first step was the application of "zero tolerance." Under zero tolerance, no disciplinary problem would go unpunished. Misbehavior such as arguing with a teacher, coming late to class, or fighting with a schoolmate had previously been handled primarily by interactions among teachers, school administration, parents, and students. Under zero tolerance, such behavior fell under a regime that closely resembled a criminal code.

Future president George W. Bush helped drive the bandwagon. In his first state of the state address as governor of Texas, he declared, "We must adopt one policy for those who terrorize teachers or disrupt classrooms—zero tolerance. School districts must be encouraged, not mandated to start 'Tough Love Academies.' These alternative schools would be staffed by a different type of teacher, perhaps retired Marine drill sergeants, who understand that discipline and love go hand in hand. . . . If we are going to save a generation of young people, our children must know they will face bad consequences for bad behavior."[8]

Zero tolerance led to more frequent use of suspensions, expulsions, fines, and even referrals to the criminal justice system. Though zero tolerance was unheard of in schools in the early 1990s, by the 1996–97 academic year, 94 percent of U.S. public schools had zero-tolerance policies for weapons and firearms, 87 percent had them for alcohol, 88 percent for illegal drugs, and 79 percent for fighting or tobacco. These policies contributed to a meteoric rise in suspensions. By 2010 an estimated 2 million students were being suspended or expelled from high schools every year. This amounted to one in every nine students, an increase of 40 percent from the early 1970s.[9]

Supporters of zero tolerance argued that the use of suspensions had two primary positive effects. First, they contended that the removal of disruptive, unmotivated students contributed to a better learning environment for the other students. Second, they argued that suspensions served as a deterrent, that fear of suspension would motivate better behavior.

Critics took a different point of view. They maintained that frequent use of suspension created a climate of fear in schools that was not conducive to learning. They also stressed that there was a high correlation between students who were suspended and those who failed to complete high school. The contention was that missing classes due to suspension put students in even further academic jeopardy, making staying away from school all the more attractive. Nonetheless, throughout the 1980s and '90s, suspensions steadily increased, reinforced by federal funding for more intensive policing of schools.

SCHOOL RESOURCE OFFICERS

These stringent policies also brought new security technologies into schools, including metal detectors and video surveillance cameras. More important, schools throughout the country employed "school resource officers," or SROs, police assigned to schools. While the stated aim of using these SROs was to reduce conflict and keep the peace, often they became hard-line enforcers of zero-tolerance policies.

After Columbine, the federal government boosted the use of SROs with the allocation of $68 million through the Community Oriented Policing Services (COPS, or Cops in Schools) program. This funding fostered a growth in the number of school police from 9,446 in 1997 to an all-time high of 14,337 in 2003. From 2003 to 2011, Cops in Schools continued its support, contributing a total of $905 million to hire 6,300 school officers and develop other safety measures.[10]

With SROs on campus, a fistfight on the playground or a cigarette in the bathroom no longer meant a visit to the principal's office but likely a trip in handcuffs to the local juvenile court or detention center. In addition, the terminology and routines of prison became commonplace in schools. When violence occurred or drugs were reported on campus, schools were put on lockdown, leaving students unable to enter or leave the building. In some schools, the periodic ritual of a surprise search of students' lockers, bags, backpacks, and purses became routine. In Texas 163 school districts developed their own district level police forces. The Los Angeles Unified School District's five-hundred-person police force came to include a canine unit to sniff for drugs.

Meting out harsh punishments for all disobedience and introducing prison culture into schools increased the number of court referrals from schools. This augmented the trend toward mass incarceration by channeling many kids into the criminal justice system at an early age.

RACE AND ZERO TOLERANCE

A number of studies have concluded that enforcement of zero tolerance, especially by suspensions, expulsions, and criminal charges, has been especially severe in urban schools with a large presence of students of color. According to the Advancement Project, during the period from 2002 to 2007, annual suspensions increased by 250,000.[11] During that same period, suspensions of Black students increased by 8 percent and those of Latinos by 14 percent, while whites' rate went down by 3 percent. By 2012 the Civil Rights Unit of the Department of Education was reporting that:

Where Are the Superpredators?

The predicted wave of crime by juvenile superpredators never came to pass. Murders committed by those of age ten to seventeen fell by roughly two-thirds from 1994 to 2011, according to statistics kept by the Justice Department's Office of Juvenile Justice and Delinquency Prevention.[12] Dilulio admitted that his forecast, based on so-called demography, turned out to be incorrect. "Demography," he says, "is not fate." Although his projections failed to materialize, the laws, policies, and attitudes put in place by the superpredator myth remained. As he put it in a 2014 interview with the *New York Times*'s Retro Report, the trouble with his superpredator forecast was that "once it was out there, there was no reeling it in."[13]

Thousands of young people paid dearly for Dilulio's miscalculations by spending long years in adult prisons. In many instances, youth in adult facilities were held in solitary confinement, allegedly to protect them. This is what Ryan, a juvenile housed in an adult prison, had to say about solitary, also known as segregation: "They take your personality when they put you in segregation. They have everything, mentally, physically, and emotionally. They say it helps us, but it makes everything even worse. I wish that upon nobody. This is what really happens behind closed doors."[14]

Some researchers, such as Elizabeth Cauffman, argue that even youth who commit violent crimes typically change. "Over time, they just stop offending. We call it the 'age-crime curve.' It's shown time and again: Crime peaks at 18 or 19 years of age and begins to decline. Around 26, it really drops off."[15]

- Blacks were three times more likely than whites to be suspended.
- American Indian and Native Alaskan students were also disproportionately suspended and expelled, representing less than 1 percent of the student population but 2 percent of out-of-school suspensions and 3 percent of expulsions.
- While girls received only one-third of suspensions, Black girls had a suspension rate of 12 percent, compared to 2 percent for white girls. American Indian and Native Alaskan girls had a 7 percent rate.

Similar disparities prevailed in referrals to law enforcement. At the national level, Blacks constitute just 16 percent of student enrollments but 27 percent of those referred to law enforcement and 31 percent of those subjected to a school-related arrest.

Students with disabilities also were punished more frequently than average, representing 25 percent of those arrested but only 12 percent of students. Moreover, students with disabilities suffered restraint (handcuffs and straitjackets) and seclusion (isolation in a small room) far more frequently than other students. They endured 58 percent of all applications of seclusion and 75 percent of incidents of physical restraint.[16]

TRUANCY BECOMES A CRIME

Changes in legislation have advanced the school-to-prison pipeline. In many states, absence from school has been criminalized, often leading to fines for parents or punishment for the children. At one point a student in Los Angeles could be fined $250 for being a minute late to class. Three such violations could boost the fine to $985. In 2013, after more than a decade, Los Angeles County eliminated the fine.[17]

In 2012 Texas prosecuted 113,000 truancy cases against youths aged twelve to seventeen. Dallas County alone collected more than $3 million in truancy fines for that year. Texas law requires schools to refer any student who misses ten or more days of school in a single year to state truancy court.[18]

One year Dallas experimented with placing students with truancy violations on electronic monitors, which included ankle bracelets. In addition to wearing the bracelet, students had to call in several times a day to verify their location.[19] Truancy law violators paid heavy prices in other states, as well. In Reading, Pennsylvania, in 2014, Eileen DiNino, a fifty-five-year-old unemployed mother of seven, spent a weekend in jail to try to pay off hundreds of dollars in fines for her children's truancy. Tragically, she died in her cell from what the coroner deemed pulmonary edema.[20] In response state legislators introduced "Eileen's Law," which would let judges substitute parenting training or community service for a jail sentence in truancy cases.[21] The bill passed 198–0 in the state House of Representatives.

THE PRESCHOOL-TO-PRISON PIPELINE

Suspension and other disciplinary measures have even been extended to preschool. During the 2011–12 school year, some five thousand preschoolers were suspended.[22] Once again, research by the Department of Education revealed serious racial disparities in enforcement. Black children represented 18 percent of preschool enrollment, but they constituted 48 percent of preschool children receiving more than one out-of-school suspension.[23]

In 2012 a six-year-old Black girl in Georgia had a temper tantrum, tearing posters off the wall and throwing toys and books and a shelf that supposedly hit the teacher. She ended up being removed from school in handcuffs and being suspended for the rest of the year.

In 2014 African American motivational speaker Tunette Powell reported in the *Washington Post* that her four-year-old son had been suspended from nursery school five times. When she described to white parents what her child had done, they replied their children had done the same things but had not been suspended. She concluded that her son had been victimized by the "preschool to prison pipeline." She decided to join the advisory body of the school and fight for equal treatment for all children.[24]

GENDER AND THE "PIPELINE"

The term *school-to-prison pipeline* has become popular, but there has been some debate over its accuracy. Some scholars have argued that it is too narrow, even suggesting adopting Tupac Shakur's phrase "cradle to the grave" as a more accurate rendering of the breadth of the process.

Other scholars, including Monique W. Morris, argue that the phrase "school to prison pipeline" doesn't adequately describe the experience of African American girls, however. Morris points out that poverty and curtailed education often lead young girls into the difficult terrain of early pregnancy, encounters with the state over welfare services, and substance abuse. In addition, many Black girls who drop out of high school end up as victims in abusive relationships, often with partners who are involved in the underground economy. The

Kids for Cash

One of the most notorious schemes of abusive juvenile justice took place in Luzerne County, Pennsylvania, in the early 2000s. In what became known as the Kids for Cash scandal, judges accepted more than $2 million in bribes for sentencing young people to unnecessary or excessive terms in for-profit detention centers operated by PA Child Care and a sibling company, Western Pennsylvania Child Care. In 2011 former Luzerne County judge Mark Ciavarella was convicted and sentenced to twenty-eight years in prison for his role in the affair. A second judge involved, Michael Conahan, received a sentence of seventeen and a half years. The companies involved paid out $2.5 million to families of the juveniles in a civil suit.[26]

youth advocacy group Rights4Girls uses the term *sexual violence–to–prison pipeline*, maintaining that abuse is a more important factor than school disciplinary policies in propelling young women of color into the criminal justice system.

Still another suggestion comes from sociologist Victor Rios, who created the term *youth control complex* by analogy to the prison-industrial complex to describe the institutions, such as schools and the criminal justice system, that have a critical impact on young people of color.[25]

JUVENILE DETENTION

While many young people are sentenced to adult prisons, a much larger number go to juvenile detention facilities, either local juvenile halls or state juvenile institutions. And juvenile incarceration is costly. According to author Nell Bernstein in her book *Burning Down the House: The End of Juvenile Prison*, the average cost of keeping a youth behind bars is $88,000 a year, more than twice the average cost of imprisoning an adult.[27]

Bernstein traveled across the country studying conditions in juvenile lockups and found a host of troubling abuses, including extensive use of solitary confinement and repeated physical abuse by staff. In one instance, after a fight, young boys in a facility were forced to spend weeks handcuffed and chained to each other while they knelt on a concrete gym floor.

The Argument Against Juvenile Detention

Children, it turns out, will never thrive in storage. We can safely stash away unwanted objects but children are meant to be held close, not banished. . . . Rather than building on young people's existing relationships, rather than helping them forge positive new ones, we've chosen an intervention that flies in the face of all the evidence researchers can offer, everything young people tell us, and all that we know already—as parents, as people—from basic common sense. . . .

We know what works, we know what doesn't, and we know that persisting with what doesn't wastes millions of dollars and destroys thousands of lives. We are clearly not getting what we say we are seeking: improved public safety and better outcomes for children. Instead, we are inflicting untold harm on the thousands of young people who pass through our juvenile prisons each year. . . .

How, knowing what we know, can we do what we do? How can we continue to deprive so many young people of what we understand as essential to their growth, if not their survival, with no evidence of any public benefit?

—Nell Bernstein, author and journalist[28]

Bernstein also found that in the state institutions, which house the "most dangerous" youths, about 40 percent of those incarcerated had committed what she called "very-very low-level offenses," such as truancy, shoplifting, loitering, or disturbing the peace. She estimated that only about a quarter were behind bars for violent crimes.[29]

Further research by the federal government's Office of Juvenile Justice and Delinquency Prevention found particularly troubling conditions affecting the health of girls in detention. Up to 90 percent of these girls had experienced physical, sexual, or emotional abuse, including 41 percent who had signs of vaginal injury consistent with sexual assault. An astonishing 8 percent had positive skin tests for tuberculosis.

Bernstein argues for the elimination of juvenile institutions altogether. She contends that even the most reform-minded programs remove adolescents from what they need most—

contact with family and loved ones. Furthermore, she maintains that confinement of juveniles is the best predictor of their incarceration as adults.[30]

COUNTERING THE SCHOOL-TO-PRISON PIPELINE

People in a number of communities throughout the country have attempted to shut down the school-to-prison pipeline. In fact, juvenile justice is the area where decarceration has made

---

Voices from the Juvenile Justice System

They are pouring more and more money into the incarceration institutions than they are in the educational system. So you're finding your youth coming out of failure factories. These schools are drop-out factories. . . . Some of the schools are becoming like little mini-prisons, preparing the youth for the next thing—juvenile hall, ranches, YAs [youth authorities, or juvenile prisons].

—Parent, California

As a parent of a juvenile that went through the system . . . it affects the whole family. My anxiety and stress level went up, the doctor put me on medication. I was having nightmares that they were killing my child. . . . It affects you mentally and physically having a loved one that's in the system. If you don't know how to navigate the system, you don't know what's going on. So all kinds of things are going through your head.

—Parent, Texas

My son has made mistakes in his life. But he wasn't sentenced to be tortured. He wasn't sentenced to sit in a cold cell by himself all day with no help. And he wasn't sentenced to be viciously beaten by guards. I want my son to get help. I want him to finish high school and to never go back.

—Parent, California

the most significant advances. Through a range of policy changes, including closing at least five juvenile detention centers after numerous reports of abuse, Texas lowered the population of juveniles in state facilities from about 3,500 in 2006 to just over 1,000 in 2015.[31] In the first decade and a half of the twenty-first century, ten states, including some of those with the highest incarceration rates, such as Louisiana and Mississippi, have lowered the number of juveniles behind bars by more than 60 percent.[32] Colorado and at least ten other states have passed laws that forbid holding juveniles in adult facilities before they are sent to trial.[33] Missouri has moved toward the creation of small-scale, community-based programs in which youths can be geographically close to family and friends. The state has claimed this switch has greatly reduced recidivism.[34]

Other efforts have focused on eliminating zero-tolerance policies for school discipline. In 2013 Broward County, Florida, one of the largest school districts in the country, relaxed

Whether we are trying to do what's best for our own child or fight for systemic reform, we as the families of these young people have been blamed, ignored, and cut out of the juvenile justice system. Biases, unequal treatment, and falsely held beliefs have all served to silence the family voice to the detriment of our children and our communities. The time of our silence is over. If we are to improve the lives of all children, we must begin to work with equal respect and equal power, together!

—Grace Bauer, parent of young son who was abused in Louisiana facilities who works with Justice for Families, a national coalition on juvenile justice

For nearly all of us at the Youth Justice Coalition, our push into the prison system started with our push out of school. I hope that all U.S. citizens will support Justice for Families and build schools, not jails, investing in college prep and not prison prep. Without school, we have no future beyond bare survival in low-wage jobs, death in the streets, or a lifetime in and out of prison.

—Veronica Martinez, member of Los Angeles' Youth Justice Coalition[35]

its policy on nonviolent misdemeanors, even those involving alcohol, marijuana, or drug paraphernalia, opting to handle them at the school level without involving police.[36] In early 2014, the federal Departments of Education and Justice recommended abandoning the zero-tolerance approach.

In Denver, San Francisco, Oakland, and Philadelphia, school administrators have replaced zero tolerance with conflict resolution and peace-building processes, which follow the principles of restorative justice. Under restorative practices, those involved in conflict—both the person accused of breaking a law or causing harm and the victim—participate in a facilitated discussion to try to resolve the issues without punishment or incarceration.

In addition, young people have organized, both inside school and in their communities, to change the system. The Youth Justice Coalition in Los Angeles has developed a continuation high school for young people released from the juvenile justice system. The school, named Free L.A. High, offers not only traditional educational programs but also training in community organizing around criminal justice issues. The school motto is "College prep, not prison prep." Members of the coalition play a leading role in social movements opposing prison and jail building as well as advocating the abolition of school resource officers in schools. Their key campaign demands the reallocation of 1 percent of the county's criminal justice budget toward youth development. They calculate that this 1 percent would come to $100 million, enough to support 25,000 youth jobs, fifty youth centers, and five hundred full-time community workers.[37] All activities are planned in support of the Youth Justice Coalition's mission to "build a youth-, family-, and prisoner-led movement to challenge race, gender, and class inequality in the Los Angeles County and California juvenile *in*justice system."[38]

The widening of the net of juvenile justice to include both school regimes and harsher punishment from the courts is one of the defining features of mass incarceration. Mirroring the growth of mass incarceration for adults, the increasingly harsh punishment in schools and the juvenile courts coincided with a *decrease* in juvenile crime. At the same time, a 2011 study by the Vera Institute concluded, "Zero tolerance does not make schools more orderly or safe—in fact the very opposite may be true."[37] In addition, zero tolerance and the widespread use of suspensions and expulsions has thrown a disproportionate number of poor youth of color off the path of success and into the revolving door of juvenile and adult jails and prisons. While zero tolerance and harsh juvenile sentencing have lost favor in some states, they still remain the dominant approach in others.

PART THREE

THE GENDERED THREADS OF PUNISHMENT

Family and community members have become key players in mobilizing against mass incarceration. *Courtesy of Mary Sutton*

9

THE FOLKS LEFT BEHIND

People who go to prison leave behind pieces of their lives—spouses, lovers, children, parents, other family members, friends, jobs, neighbors, businesses, property, accomplishments, and memories—a set of relationships with others in the communities from which they come. Because roughly 90 percent of prisoners are men, the vast majority of those left behind are women and children. Their experiences are seldom visible in our accounts of criminal justice. The experiences of the "other half" outside the walls and the 10 percent inside women's prisons are the gendered threads of punishment, as invisible to ordinary sight as the threads of our DNA but likewise powerful in their effects.

We often think of imprisonment as an individual experience, but the scale of mass incarceration and its concentration in poor urban communities of color mean that it is a social, collective process rather than one person's journey through the criminal legal system.

HISTORICAL CONTEXT

To better understand the situation of those "left behind" by mass incarceration, we need to trace the historical changes that have taken place over the past half century and have severely impacted family and community life among the urban working class. These changes have played a major role in creating a destabilized, increasingly impoverished terrain in many ur-ban communities of color, creating fertile ground for mass incarceration. The central change has been the great reduction in employment opportunities in our cities, especially for young men. To get a better understanding how this fed into mass incarceration, we'll examine one community—the South Side of Chicago.

For much of the twentieth century, Chicago was very attractive to people of color. Be-tween 1916 and 1970, some five hundred thousand African Americans arrived in Chicago from Southern states, part of the Great Migration. Mexican immigrants also started to land there in the 1930s. During its economic peak at midcentury, the South Side was a dynamic part of an industrial boom town, home to massive stockyards, steel plants, and factories, which employed tens of thousands of people. In 1954 Chicago produced one-quarter of the nation's steel. Local factories also were major producers of machinery, primary and fabricated metals, printing and publishing, chemicals, food processing, and radios and televisions. Most of the jobs in these industries were permanent positions with union wages and benefits and brought some semblance of the American dream to working-class people, including people of color.

Beginning in the late 1960s, however, industrial jobs began to disappear as companies relocated factories to low-wage, antiunion regions overseas or within the United States.[1] During the 1970s, Chicago lost 29 percent of all manufacturing jobs in the city. Predomi-nantly African American neighborhoods in the South and West suffered a 46 percent decline in manufacturing employment.[2] As a result, from 1969 to 1989, Black unemployment rates grew from 7 percent to 20 percent. Overall the United States lost 24 percent of its manu-facturing jobs from 1980 to 2005, with urban communities of color taking the hardest hits. Many cities—such as Cleveland, Ohio; Hartford, Connecticut; Scranton, Pennsylvania; and Rochester, New York—lost more than 40 percent of their manufacturing jobs during those years.[3]

Remaining employment opportunities increasingly became low-wage, low-security jobs in the fast-food, retail, delivery, and personal and household service sectors. Under these conditions, according to research by Harvard sociologist Bruce Western and others, selling

A Perfect Storm for Mass Incarceration

For mass incarceration to take root in Chicago, a number of processes had to take place:

1. Loss of well-paying legal jobs
2. Cutbacks in public housing and welfare programs
3. The War on Drugs, creating a hyperinflated Black underground economy that became the major large-scale economic opportunity for Black youth
4. Expansion of police power highlighted by the War on Drugs
5. The rise of gangs, first as a self-defense for ghetto youth, then as the local kingpins and networks of the drug trade
6. Escalating crime rates in the 1980s and 1990s

This perfect storm created a toxic social and criminal justice environment. Chicago police, already with a long history of unnecessary violence, became notorious for torturing dozens of alleged gang members into confessions. Many of them spent decades in prison before being pardoned and released.

banned drugs became one of the few viable economic choices for unemployed young men in the inner city.[4]

CUTTING HOLES IN THE SOCIAL SAFETY NET

Concurrent with the decline in the industrial economy in cities came the scaling down of the federal and state social welfare system. The early 1980s saw massive cutbacks in federal programs, especially those designed to help the poor. In the Reagan administration's first budget, Congress slashed funding for public housing and housing subsidies by 50 percent. Throughout the decade, huge reductions also hit programs such as the Comprehensive

Employment Training Act (CETA), the Job Corps, the food stamp program, and Head Start. Eligibility requirements for federal assistance were tightened.[5]

By the mid-1980s, many people in impoverished urban communities of color, such as the South Side of Chicago, were caught in the complex crossfire of the aggressive, racialized policing of the War on Drugs; the expansion of drug trade and violent gangs on the street; and the demise of jobs, social services, and welfare support. After the mid-1990s, roundups of immigrants escalated, drawing Latino neighborhoods into the same crossfire and making daily life precarious for all those who were undocumented or had family members and loved ones without papers.

Cutbacks in welfare benefits continued beyond the Reagan years. According to a 2010 report, forty-eight states had lowered real welfare payment levels since 1996. In more than thirty states, the real value of Temporary Assistance for Needy Families (formerly Aid to Families with Dependent Children) had declined by more than 20 percent since 1996.[6] This decline in benefits has been accompanied by tighter restrictions on other sources of income. These cutbacks effectively criminalize people on welfare by forcing them to supplement their income with "illegal" activity to earn enough money to survive. In this context, "illegal" activity does not necessarily mean things defined as crimes but rather any informal work, including babysitting, contract house cleaning, or selling secondhand clothes, all banned by welfare regulations.

This tightening of regulations has gender and racial implications, since in 2010 more than 85 percent of those receiving Temporary Assistance for Needy Families were women and nearly 60 percent of all recipients were African American or Latina/Latino.[7] In the context of all these changes, families also had to deal with the imprisonment of hundreds of thousands of their male loved ones. In the Drug War culture, incarceration became, in the words of sociologist Dorothy Roberts, a "rite of passage imposed upon African American teenagers."[8] Mass incarceration became a collective experience. Researcher David Garland summarized the situation succinctly in the introduction to *Mass Imprisonment: Social Causes and Consequences*: "Every family, every household, every individual in these neighborhoods has direct personal knowledge of the prison—through a spouse, a child, a parent, a neighbor, a friend. Imprisonment ceases to be the fate of a few criminal individuals and becomes a shaping institution for whole sectors of the population."[9]

WOMEN CARRY THE BURDEN

As noted in chapter 1, incarceration imposes many financial and emotional burdens on family members. Typically it is mothers, grandmothers, spouses, and lovers who take up the bulk of these additional tasks in the context of the declining economic opportunities and welfare provisions. In such dire economic situations, incarceration of a loved one may a mean major upheaval in family life,

> The law does not care whether this individual had access to good education or not, or whether he/she lives under impoverished conditions because companies in his/her communities have shut down and moved to a third world country, or whether previously available welfare payments have vanished. The law does not care about the conditions that lead some communities along a trajectory that makes prison inevitable.
>
> —Angela Davis[10]

such as a move to cheaper housing or taking in boarders to earn extra money. Some families may even become homeless due to the loss of a loved one to the prison system. Most households will at least have to cut back spending for education, food, clothing, and entertainment. If the incarcerated person was a caregiver, there may also be a need to mobilize more money or people to look after children or the elderly.

Incarceration also comes with another set of financial burdens: meeting the needs of the prisoner. Many prisons don't provide even the basics of personal hygiene, such as soap, deodorant, and toothpaste. In such cases, family members will often buy such items from an approved company and have them sent into the prison or send money to prisoners' accounts so they can purchase them at inflated prices in the institutional commissary. Other things, such as clothing, shoes, or even personal televisions and radios, may help ease the situation for the loved one doing time but become a new expense in the family budget.

Visits are also an important means of support, especially as a way to maintain ties between

Siblings and Parents Speak

During those years, I learned that the saying is true: When a parent, sibling, or child goes to jail, the whole family serves the sentence with that person. My brother made a terrible mistake, but he did not need to spend the rest of his life in prison to recognize that it would have been a terrible waste of taxpayers' money to shelter, feed, and care for someone in prison who was not a threat to society and should have been working and paying taxes.

—Andrea Strong, whose brother was incarcerated[11]

People don't realize that on our side [as parents] it is not about just the pain that we go through seeing our sons and daughters incarcerated, but also the injustice of the system. Sometimes I feel like I am getting treated like a criminal. . . . Unfortunately with stories like mine, there are thousands . . . for you to understand what a mother goes through, you have to live the experience."

—Luisa Borrego, whose son committed a murder when he was fourteen and was sentenced to fifty years

incarcerated people and their children. Organizing visits often means spending considerable money on transportation expenses, hotels, and food. These costs escalate when people are incarcerated in distant rural areas, far from the cities from which most prisoners come.

When personal visits are not an option, the most convenient way to communicate with a loved one behind bars is via the exorbitantly expensive carceral telephone system. In 2012 a national survey found that some states were charging as much as $14 for a fifteen-minute local phone call. Often more than half of the revenue from these calls was returned to corrections departments as a kickback.[12] Families were paying a surcharge to finance the incarceration of their loved one.

COPING WITH ABSENCE

An adult who is experiencing the trauma of separation may have difficulties adjusting to the situation. Some people in such circumstances may turn to alcohol or other drugs as a way of coping with the stress of separation. Moreover, everyday life in a household and a community entangled with the criminal justice system exposes families to increased vulnerability. Beth Richie has done extensive research on women in African American communities that have been affected by mass incarceration. She concludes that "the already overburdened role of caretaker in low-income families is further complicated by the constant threat women face of possible arrest and detention of a family member. . . . Women are busy attempting to shelter their children from dangerous environments, trying to protect them from aggressive law enforcement practices, and keeping themselves out of the state's child protection apparatus."[13]

Marc Mauer and Meda Chesney-Lind have noted further complications, pointing out that in such cases, "Women's contributions are invisible, undervalued, misinterpreted and, in some instances, even criminalized, as in the case of women charged with conspiracy for not cooperating with law enforcement's investigations of their family members."[14]

CHILDREN OF PRISONERS

Incarceration has a critical impact on the children of people in prison. As of 2014 about 2.7 million children in the United States had a parent who was incarcerated. Research surveyed by a National Academy of Sciences report, *The Growth of Incarceration in the United States*, describes complicated patterns of behavioral change in children after a father's incarceration.[15] Some children become more aggressive, while others become more withdrawn. The report also notes that many parents indicate that children's school performance declines if a parent is incarcerated. The effects on children are compounded by poverty, unemployment, reductions in state assistance, and deteriorating public schools.

Nell Bernstein has written extensively on the rights of children and wrote the text for the

Voices of the Children

I didn't know I had rights. . . . I thought I was worthless, somebody without a family that nobody cared for. I felt that whenever someone cared about me, I owed them my life. If somebody gave me a meal that was more than Top Ramen, I thought they had done me a favor. I didn't want to accept help because I felt I'd owe a debt I couldn't pay—not realizing that care was my right as a child.

—Sayyadina Thomas, whose mother was incarcerated during her childhood

Many people have convinced themselves that we're special families, unique families; that we're a different kind of kid. And we're just like everyone else. We love our parents as deeply as everyone else. They love us as deeply. And loss is as painful for us as it is for anybody else.

—Emani Davis, whose father was in prison

When I was 4 years old, my mother started doing drugs. She used to be in and out of jail, and then she started going to prison when I was 7. That's when we first got taken from her. Her friends took me to Social Services, dropped me off, left me there. I've been in about 18 different group homes since then, and three or four foster homes. I don't care how bad whatever we were going through was, I still wanted to be with my mom. At the foster homes they would try to talk to me and I would say, "yes" and "no." I didn't tell them anything else, because I was so hurt about it.

—Antonio, whose mother was in prison[16]

Bill of Rights for Children of Incarcerated Parents, which maintains that children with parents behind bars "have . . . committed no crime, but the penalty they are required to pay is steep. They forfeit, in too many cases, virtually everything that matters to them: their home, safety, their public status and private self-image, their source of comfort and affection. Their lives and prospects are profoundly affected by the numerous institutions that lay claim to their parents—police, courts, jails and prisons, probation and parole—but they have no rights, explicit or implicit, within any of these jurisdictions."[17]

In addition to the effects noted by Bernstein, many children of incarcerated parents end up in foster care. In fact, the expansion of the ranks of children in foster care has moved hand in hand with mass incarceration. The federal Adoption and Safe Families Act (ASFA) of 1997 set in place a policy whereby a child who spent fifteen out of twenty-two consecutive months in foster care would automatically be put up for adoption. This had serious consequences for any parent serving more than a fifteen-month sentence. A further catalyst for increased adoption came from the passage of laws in at least thirty-four states making incarceration a criterion for termination of parental rights.[18]

As might be expected, all of these negative effects on children have a racial component. Nearly 40 percent of children in foster care are African American while they constitute less than 20 percent of all children.

Rights of Children of Incarcerated Parents

San Francisco Partnership for Incarcerated Parents[19]

1. I have the right to be kept safe and informed at the time of my parent's arrest.
2. I have the right to be heard when decisions are made about me.
3. I have the right to be considered when decisions are made about my parent.
4. I have the right to be well cared for in my parent's absence.
5. I have the right to speak with, see, and touch my parent.
6. I have the right to support as I struggle with my parent's incarceration.
7. I have the right not to be judged, blamed, or labeled because of my parent's incarceration.
8. I have the right to a lifelong relationship with my parent.

Poetry from Mothers
Alison Henderson

The Forgotten Victim
That man you condemn has a child and a wife
A Mum and a Dad who has given him life!
What would you do if this happened to yours?
Deny all your love and close all the doors?

Do you honestly think I'd sink to that level
And just turn my back and deem him a devil?
Yes! He's done wrong and is serving his time
And No! I do not agree with his crime.

"That woman" you point at, yes it is me
I was born with a name, as I'm human you see!
I'm innocent! just in case you've forgot
And love him whether you like it or not!

I've had the abuse, the comments and more
It's nothing I haven't heard all before
I mean no offense when I say this to you:
I'm a victim as well—a forgotten one too.[20]

Daddy's Gone
I tried telling my son with emotional tact
The truth of the matter, you can't hide the fact
His Daddy has gone and has gone for a while
You can't say it with flowers or manage a smile.

So how do you sit down and talk to your son
And answer his questions why Daddy has gone?
All you can do is just tell him your way . . .
And pray to the lord he'll be home soon one day.[21]

PAROLE AND PROBATION

When individuals are released on parole or probation, their families often assume the responsibility for their transition to life on the outside. Parole, or supervised release from prison, often involves strict regimentation and personal monitoring. Family members who house or support a person on parole may themselves be subject to searches and limits on their behavior (such as bans on possession of alcohol or weapons). They also often have to take responsibility for paying parole fees or restitution/fines/fees.

Most important, family members have to shoulder the burden of the emotional support for a person's transition from life in prison. People who have been incarcerated for many years may be unfamiliar with things that everyone else takes for granted, such as cell phones, email, computer technology, or using ATM cards instead of a bank book. Even figuring out how to put gas in a car or read a bus schedule may present a challenge. Without assistance from family members in negotiating the details of daily life, many people on parole are doomed before they even start.

While social service professionals, such as social workers, are trained to provide these crucial services, family members typically must try to provide them as best they can without any training or access to professional networks.

Finally, as noted in chapter 6, conditions of supervision may place restrictions on people that create hardships for family members. For example, most people on parole are not allowed to live with or socialize with anyone else who is on parole or, in some cases, with anyone who has a criminal record. The rules about contact with people on parole are especially difficult to follow in neighborhoods where mass incarceration has taken large numbers of people to prison or in families where more than one person has a criminal record.

OTHER TARGETED COMMUNITIES

The Native American "community" is a complex population that includes large numbers of people who live on reservations as well as in urban areas. Within the reservations a semiautonomous political system exists through which 310 tribal authorities exercise some form of sovereignty over their territory, including operating a criminal justice system. Tribal courts can charge and convict people but may not sentence them to more than three years. As a result, the most serious cases are handed over to federal authorities to prosecute. The rise of mass incarceration has also affected criminal justice in Native American territory, delivering more police, stricter laws, and harsher sentencing. As a result, incarceration rates among Native Americans are much higher than among the general population, especially in states with high concentrations of Native Americans. For example, in Minnesota, a state whose population is 1.3 percent Native American, 9 percent of those in prisons in 2010 were classified "American Indian."[22]

While we often think of communities as geographically defined places, people with a common experience or those who face a common oppression are also often said to comprise a community. In terms of mass incarceration, lesbian, gay, bisexual, transgender, and queer (LGBTQ) people can be said to constitute a community.

LGBTQ youth are especially vulnerable to incarceration, largely due to high rates of homelessness. A 2012 national survey found that 40 percent of homeless youth identified themselves as LGBTQ. Within this community, transgender people are the most frequently caught in the poverty-arrest trap. A 2011 survey found homelessness among transgender people at almost double the national average and poverty rates four times the national average.[23] The same survey also revealed that nearly one in six transgender people has been incarcerated at some time—far higher than the rate for the general population. Among Black transgender people, nearly half (47 percent) have been incarcerated. These high incarceration rates contribute greatly to instability in the LGBTQ community.[24]

LOSS OF FAITH IN THE LAW

While undermining the social fabric of communities, mass incarceration has also contributed to an erosion of faith in the political process. First of all, harsh policing and injustices in the courts have undermined the trust in the entire political system in many places. In the words

VAWA and Domestic Violence

In the 1960s and '70s, domestic violence and in some cases even rape were not processed as criminal offenses. They were typically categorized as personal or private affairs beyond the scope of the law. Mobilization by feminists brought these issues onto the radar of the criminal justice system. One outcome of this mobilization was the passage of the Violence Against Women Act (VAWA) in 1994.

The act provided a comprehensive legal framework for court action concerning a range of offenses: domestic violence, rape, stalking, date rape, spousal rape, and violating a civil protection order. In 2013 amendments to the act extended coverage to gays, lesbians, transgender people, Native Americans, and undocumented people. Several states, including New York, California, and Illinois, subsequently passed their own versions of the Violence Against Women Act. Passage and implementation of the VAWA have prompted very different views about the role of the criminal legal system in handling issues of domestic violence and sexual abuse. Supporters of the act claimed that from 1994 to 2011 it played a major role in increasing the number of reported incidents of domestic violence by 51 percent and decreasing the number of homicides of women by intimate partners by 34 percent.[25]

A number of feminists and social justice activists, however, have argued that relying on an untransformed criminal legal system to address this problem ultimately amounts to perpetuating mass incarceration. Rather than supporting more criminal prosecutions for domestic and sexual violence, some groups, such as INCITE!, a network of women of color, have contended that the act is insufficient, arguing that it is "impossible to seriously address sexual and intimate partner violence within communities of color without addressing . . . larger structures of violence (including militarism, attacks on immigrants' rights and Indigenous treaty rights, the proliferation of prisons, economic neo-colonialism, the medical industry, and more)."[26] Researcher Vikki Law also has questioned the efficacy of the Violence Against Women Act's approach. "The threat of imprisonment . . . sets up a false dichotomy in which the survivor has to choose between personal safety and criminalizing and/or imprisoning a loved one. . . . Challenging patriarchy and male supremacy is a much more effective solution."[27]

of sociologist Dorothy Roberts, "a key component of the . . . dynamic of mass incarceration is the negative view of the justice system it generates."[28] Researchers Todd Clear and Dina Rose explain that in such communities, "the workings of the state are seen as alien forces to be avoided rather than services to be employed."[29] In many communities of color, people believe that calling the police is likely to bring them more problems than whatever issues they are facing. This is especially true for families with a resident who is on parole, probation, or public assistance; is undocumented; or may be involved in illegal activity.

This mistrust complicates society's response to domestic violence. Women, the most frequent victims, often hesitate to call the police for fear that involving law enforcement may result in incarceration of their men or threats to custody of their children, especially given the expansion of foster care and adoption. Beth Richie has researched this issue extensively. She concluded that "women of color from low income neighborhoods, where the impact of mass incarceration is most keenly felt, . . . may be particularly reluctant to call the police, to use mainstream social services, or to report incidents of abuse to agencies because of their marginalized social position, their precarious legal status, or their loyalty to their vulnerable (albeit abusive) partners."[30]

THE UNTOLD STORY

Mass incarceration is a complex process that affects far more people than those locked up inside prisons and jails. In many communities, prison is part of the common experience of all members. Moreover, the impact of mass incarceration is highly gendered. Overwhelmingly, it is the women who shoulder the burden of keeping family and community on track in the absence of hundreds or thousands of men due to imprisonment. Their pain and suffering often go unrecognized and unassuaged yet form a large part of the untold story of mass incarceration. Genderization of punishment doesn't stop there, however; women's prisons are another neglected aspect of the story.

Moreover, these effects of mass incarceration have gone hand in hand with decreasing access to resources from the state. Cutbacks in benefits, education, mental health, and substance abuse treatment as well as the closure of many public housing facilities have intensified the struggle for survival for those left behind. In recent years, in addition to these factors, the prosecution and incarceration of women has skyrocketed, with the population of women's prisons growing rapidly. The increasing incarceration of women from poor communities has meant even more difficulties for children and families who must cope not only with the absence of fathers but also the absence of mothers as well.

From 1977 to 2011, the number of people in women's state and federal prisons increased by 600 percent, faster than the growth rate in men's facilities. *Courtesy of Mary Sutton*

10

WOMEN'S PRISONS

Women's prisons and jails hold only about a tenth of the incarcerated population, but they are an important and rapidly expanding element in the system of mass incarceration. According to historian Nicole Hahn Rafter, the first totally separate women's prison in the United States was built in Indiana in the 1870s.[1] After that, the system expanded gradually in the early twentieth century, with two or three prisons built each decade between 1930 and 1950. Seven units opened in the 1960s, and seventeen opened in the 1970s. In the 1980s construction boomed, with the establishment of thirty-four new women's units or prisons.[2] Mass incarceration was moving into full swing.

Hence, from 1977 to 2011, the number of people in state and federal women's prisons increased by 600 percent, from 15,118 to 111,387.[3] The female jail population also increased, both in numbers and as a proportion of total jail population. In 1986 female jails held 7 percent of the total, some 22,000 prisoners; by 2013 the figures were 14 percent and 102,400.

As of 2010 there were about 205,000 people in all women's facilities, about 7 percent of the nation's entire incarcerated population.[4] The percentage of people under correctional supervision classified as female in 2012 constituted 24 percent of all those on probation and 11 percent of those on parole.[5]

Thinking About *Orange Is the New Black*

Women's prisons rarely appear in the media. Yet the hit TV series *Orange Is the New Black*, based on Piper Kerman's book of the same name, has exposed millions of viewers to a totally new narrative. The series has proven extremely controversial. Loyal fans argue that the characters are intriguing and attempt to present the complexity of the people in a women's prison rather than relying on stereotypes. Others are more critical, contending that *Orange* still offers a sanitized version of prison, especially because the lead character is a college-educated white woman whose experiences don't reflect those of most women in prison.

In her book *Resistance Behind Bars*, law researcher Vikki Law paints a very different picture—of organizing inside women's prisons. Law chronicled a number of mass actions by women prisoners in the 1970s, including a sit-down strike in North Carolina Corrections Center for Women in 1975 to demand better medical care and improved counseling services.[6]

MUCH THE SAME AS MEN'S PRISONS BUT . . .

In many ways, the profile of women who are incarcerated parallels that of their male counterparts. As in men's prisons, the population in women's facilities is disproportionately poor people of color. Blacks and Hispanics together constitute about 46 percent of the female prison population, while whites are a slim majority at 54 percent.[7] The racial disparity among Native American women is especially pronounced. For instance, in 2013 the state of Montana reported that, while Native Americans were only 7 percent of the state's population, they occupied 36 percent of the places in Montana women's prisons.[8]

Since 2000 there have been significant changes in the racial makeup of the women's prison population. From 2000 to 2010, the ranks of Hispanic women in prison swelled by seven thousand, a 70 percent rise. The number of white women in prison increased by more than seventeen thousand in the same time, a proportionally somewhat smaller increase of 50 percent. Researcher James Austin studied this growth of female incarceration in Ohio, where the percentage of whites among those serving time in women's prisons rose from 43 percent in 1998 to 80 percent in 2013. He concluded that the women were coming from "predominantly white, rural counties" and attributed the changes to harsher sentencing in drug cases, particularly those related to methamphetamine. He also noted that in many rural areas there were no alternatives to incarceration, such as substance abuse treatment programs.[9] By contrast, the per capita incarceration of Black females nationally declined more than 30 percent during the first decade of the twenty-first century. Despite this decrease, Black women still maintained by far the highest per capita incarceration rates—nearly three times that of whites and almost double that of Hispanics.

Like people in men's institutions, those incarcerated in women's prisons generally have low levels of education and lack economic security. A 2007 Bureau of Justice Statistics survey revealed that 38 percent of people in women's prisons had no high school diploma or General Educational Development (GED) diploma upon admission. More than a third of mothers in prison reported receiving federal benefits such as food stamps or Temporary Aid to Needy Families before admission, while nearly 50 percent in state prison reported a monthly income of less than $1,000 before their arrest.[10]

. . . WITH SOME KEY DIFFERENCES

In their expansion and their racial disparity, women's prisons parallel men's, but there are also important differences between the two populations.

FEWER VIOLENT OFFENSES, MORE DRUG CHARGES

People in women's prisons are less likely to be charged with a violent offense and far more likely to have a drug-related case. In a 2005 study, more than half of the men's prison population had charges involving violence, compared to about a third of those in women's facilities. Women were, however, about 10 percent more likely to face drug charges.[11]

In recent years, criminal justice authorities have recognized that, while women are rarely kingpins in drug dealing, they often know about the illegal activities of their family members or neighbors but choose not to reveal this information to police. Increasingly, police have resorted to charging such women with conspiracy as part of a drug case. An alternative to that charge is to pressure women into becoming confidential informants by threatening to charge them or take away their children. In such predicaments, there are no good choices. Some women refuse to cooperate with police and suffer the consequences. Others inform to save themselves and their children.

MORE PARENTING RESPONSIBILITIES

Women in prison are more likely to have major parenting responsibilities than their male counterparts. In 2010 fully 61 percent of women in state prisons and 56 percent of those in federal facilities were parents of minor children. Among imprisoned mothers, 64 percent had lived with their children before going to prison; the corresponding figure for fathers was 47 percent.[12]

Not only are incarcerated women more likely than incarcerated men to be the primary caregivers for children, but they are also more likely to be criminally prosecuted for allegedly failing to carry out their duties as a parent, usually by being declared "unfit" as a mother. For example, mothers are the most frequent target for prosecution due to truancy on the part of their children. Some cities have rounded up and arrested parents of children whose days of absence from school have exceeded the legal limit. In another twist to the criminalization of motherhood, in 2011 Kelley Williams-Bolar of Akron, Ohio, ended up with a felony conviction and a ten-day jail sentence for falsely reporting that her daughter lived with her father in order to get the girl into a better school.

Another example of this trend is the more frequent prosecution of pregnant women who test positive for drugs or alcohol. National Advocates for Pregnant Women published a report in 2013, which detailed 413 cases from 1973 to 2005 of prosecution or attempted prosecution of pregnant women for allegedly endangering a fetus through drug taking or other "misbehavior."[13]

Not surprisingly, African American women have been disproportionately prosecuted. A study released by the *Journal of Health, Politics, Policy and Law* found that 52 percent of women prosecuted under these laws were African American.[14] One South Carolina judge proclaimed upon sending an African American woman to prison for five years for testing positive for cocaine during pregnancy: "I'm sick and tired of these girls having these bastard babies on crack cocaine and until they change the law, the law they gave me, it said I could put them in jail."[15]

The laws that bar people with certain drug felonies from accessing Temporary Aid to Needy Families, food stamps, and public housing have major implications for women's ability to survive when they are released from prison, especially if they have parental responsibilities. A twelve-state study reported on by the Sentencing Project in 2013 revealed that 180,000 women had been adversely affected by the lifetime bans on these programs.[16]

PREGNANCY

A 2008 Bureau of Justice Survey found that roughly one in thirty of those incarcerated in women's prisons said they were pregnant at the time of admission.[17] In many institutions, women are shackled while delivering babies in prison, making an already painful experience excruciating. The American Medical Association and the American Congress of Obstetricians and Gynecologists have opposed the practice of shackling pregnant women. The latter says that it interferes with proper medical practice as well as being "demeaning and unnecessary."[18] Nevertheless, as of 2014, only eighteen states had outlawed it. The delivery is often intentionally made worse for the mother and more damaging for the infant by the fact that in most states the baby is taken away from the mother after twenty-four hours.[19]

VIOLENCE AND SEXUAL ABUSE BEFORE PRISON

For many in women's prisons, personal or domestic violence and sexual abuse are closely tied to their incarceration. Though exact figures are difficult to obtain, estimates of the percentage of those in women's prisons who have experienced violence, including rape, sexual assault, child abuse, and domestic violence, before being incarcerated range from 40 to 85 percent.[20] For women who are involved in sex work or the drug trade, sexual violence during their working hours may actually lead to their arrest.

Can a Woman Stand Her Ground?

At the first trial I got a hung jury. Before the second trial, that's when I was given a deal—fifteen years. The judge said if I lost in trial she was going to give me the max because she didn't believe that I was a battered woman. It didn't matter to her that I had iron marks on my chest, irons marks to this day on my arms, bruises and scars all up and down my body. Back then, the battered woman syndrome was just becoming a factor. There was no consideration, no compassion for the fact that people like me were fighting for their lives in their own homes. There was no consideration of the fact that I was just like a prisoner coming out of war.

—Sheri Dwight, who pled guilty to killing her husband after more than a year of abuse[21]

The experience of violence, especially in the household, may prompt behavior that can end up in arrest and criminal charges, particularly for poor women. Many women flee circumstances of violence, leaving them homeless, perhaps forced to reside in shelters, on the street, or other locations where they are vulnerable to aggressive policing and other sources of personal violence. A small number of women, when pushed into desperate situations, resort to counterviolence against their attackers, resulting in charges for violent crimes. While some states have passed "stand your ground" laws, which in theory allow people to defend themselves when their lives are threatened, few criminal justice authorities are willing to apply that principle to women who defend themselves against violence or sexual assault, especially if the assailant is a husband or romantic partner.

SEXUAL ABUSE IN PRISON

This pattern of abuse often continues in women's prisons. Women are far more likely than men to be sexually victimized in prison by the overwhelmingly male staff in women's facilities. From 2009 to 2011, national data on sexual victimization in prison showed that those in women's institutions, despite being only 7 percent of the overall prison population, accounted for 33 percent of reported sexual assaults by staff members.[22]

Sexual assault in prison often takes place during strip searches, which are common in most prisons. These are allegedly done to hunt for contraband, especially drugs that may be hidden in bodily cavities. During a strip search, a person typically must remove all her clothing, face the staff member conducting the search, and open her mouth, plus squat down and cough to make sure nothing is hidden in her vagina or anus. In some instances, staff members subject women who are being searched to physical or verbal abuse. The Michigan chapter of the American Civil Liberties Union has called such searches in women's facilities "sexually abusive."[23]

Perrion Roberts, who served time in Tutwiler Prison in Alabama, describes sexual misconduct by staff: "This is how it would go. The guard would stare, maybe slow-stroll through the showers when certain inmates were in there, maybe call a prisoner over to the desk. 'Say, I've just been looking at you. You know, you're a pretty girl.'

"When I was there a lot of the women trade[d] sex to get privileges with the guards. If they approach you and you turn them down, they make it difficult for you."

Federal inspectors who came to Tutwiler found that an unnamed "Officer B" traded underwear for oral sex, "Sergeant C" forced women to touch his penis, "Officer D" swapped romantic letters and then had sex with a prisoner, and "Officer E" raped a prisoner who later gave birth. The list stretched to Officer T.

Six guards at Tutwiler were successfully prosecuted for employee-on-prisoner crimes, including sexual misconduct and abuse, from 2009 to 2011. Reporters from Alabama newspaper conglomerate Advance Publications identified a total of eighteen cases involving thirty corrections employees that were referred to the Elmore County district attorney's office in a five-year period. But only six employees were found guilty, and most served no time.[24]

THE GENDER BINARY

Prison systems operate on what is called the gender binary—everyone must be either a male or a female. Typically, classification is done on the basis of genitalia. This model assumes that men's prisons are the norm and serve as a model for women's facilities. For example, the

Sexual Abuse of Immigrants: Raquel's Story

The huge increase in imprisonment of immigrants has yielded new opportunities for the sexual abuse of women in custody. Here "Raquel" tells the story of being driven from the detention center to the airport by an ICE officer.

We started driving. I was saying the rosary which is something . . . I always do when I am going on a trip. After a while the driver pulled off the road and stopped. He opened the door and unlocked the cage and gestured for me to get out. He told me to raise my hands and I did. Then he started touching me all over. He pulled up my bra, fondled my breasts, and put his hand down my pants. He was talking in English and touching himself. I asked him why he was doing this to me. . . .

He hurriedly shoved [away] anything that was on the floor of the front area of the van and motioned for me to lay down on my back. I refused. When he saw that I wasn't going to cooperate, he went to the back of the van. He pushed my things off the seat in the cage inside the van and gestured for me to get back in. I complied. He followed me into the van. I told him I would report him

jumpsuits that women have to wear are modeled on clothing from men's institutions. Commissary items may be largely based on male needs and preferences and may not include items such as makeup, tampons, or pads. This also applies to the health care framework, which often excludes gynecological care as well as effective breast and cervical cancer diagnosis and treatment. Moreover, the training for most guards is modeled on men's institutions, failing to take into consideration the gender dynamics in women's prisons, particularly the power relations between male staff and the prison population.

The power dynamics have led some women's prison activists to question whether male guards should be allowed in women's prisons. Until the passage of the Civil Rights Act in 1964 and the Equal Employment Opportunity Act of 1972, men rarely worked as guards in women's prisons. That legislation leveled the playing field between men and women for all if he continued to touch me and he pushed me into the van. I was crying and I thought it was the end of my life. I thought he was going to kill me. I thought I should have stayed in my home country if my life was going to end like this because at least I would have had more time with my children. He got in the cage with me and started unzipping his pants and pulling off my clothes. He exposed himself to me. He was angry that I would not take off my clothes. I kept yelling, saying that if he didn't stop I would tell someone.

He finally stopped, got back in the front of the van, and drove fast to the airport. When we got to the airport he opened the door and the cage. I jumped out and I started running. I ran into the airport and I was still crying. . . . Then they let me go through security and I got on my flight and left. . . .

I didn't want to talk to anyone about what happened to me. I left one problem in my home country and encountered another one here. I felt afraid of everyone on the street, men and women, especially if they came near me or touched me. I was very afraid that the man who hurt me had bad friends and they were going to find me and hurt me. I cried at night and had a hard time falling asleep. Every time I closed my eyes, I saw him. I also felt dirty all the time, because his hands had been on my body, and I took two showers every day.[25]

jobs in prisons, however, and has facilitated a huge increase in the number of male guards in women's institutions.

In recent years, LGBTQ activists in particular have questioned the validity of the gender binary in prisons, but those questions have yet to have any impact on the criminal justice system. As a result, transgender activist Alex Lee maintains, the gender binary leads "to especially horrific abuse of transgender and gender-variant prisoners whose genders and bodies do not conform to these stereotypes."[26]

A national survey published in *Injustice at Every Turn*, a report of the National Transgender Discrimination Survey, found that 16 percent of transgender people in prisons or jails reported being physically assaulted and 15 percent claimed to have been sexually assaulted. Among Black transgender respondents, 34 percent reported sexual abuse while in prison

Prison Rape Elimination Act (PREA)

Passed in 2003, the Prison Rape Elimination Act came about primarily as a result of popular pressure to address sexual violence in *men's* prisons. Research revealed, however, that sexual violence was much more prevalent in women's prisons. The act assumed a zero-tolerance perspective and mandated prosecution and punishment for violators. It created a basis to address sexual misconduct of all forms in prison. Some critics have argued that the act can sometimes be used to prosecute the wrong people, though. For example, its zero tolerance bans all sexual activity in prisons, including consensual sex. LGBTQ prisoners and others argue that it is wrong to punish people for consensual sex or even displays of affection such as hugs or hand holding.

or jail. According to the same report, of respondents who went to jail and/or prison, 37 percent reported that they were harassed by correctional officers or staff. Respondents of color experienced higher rates of such harassment than their white peers, with Latinas and Latinos at 56 percent, Black respondents at 50 percent, and multiracial individuals at 44 percent.[27]

Because of the high frequency of assaults on transgender or homosexual-identified people, many institutions choose to place people with these labels in isolation. While this may reduce incidents of assault and harassment from other prisoners, isolation is another psychological trauma and may leave transgender people less protected from assaults by staff.

Because women and transgender or gender-variant people are often extremely isolated while incarcerated, some have turned to various forms of media as resistance and have crafted links to supporters on the outside to discuss their situation. Yraida Guanipa started several newsletters, including an e-mail-based chat site called Prison Talk, while she was incarcerated in the federal system. Women at a state facility in Oregon started a zine in 2002 that, with support from people on the outside, has run for more than a decade under the name *Tenacious: Art and Writings by Women in*

Prison. Black and Pink, a Massachusetts-based "open family of LGBTQ prisoners and 'free world' allies who support each other," sends a monthly newsletter to more than five thousand LGBTQ people inside prisons across the country. The newsletter contains mainly content written by current and former prisoners.

"GENDER-RESPONSIVE" INSTITUTIONS

Some criminal justice authorities and policy makers have proposed special, "gender-responsive" prisons and jails to house those classified as women, transgender, or gender-variant. This idea has gained increasing traction as the rate of incarceration of women has continued to rise. The National Institute of Corrections has been one of the leading promoters of gender-responsive institutions. It defines *gender-responsive* as "creating an environment . . . that reflects an understanding of the realities of women's lives and addresses the issues of the participants. . . . The emphasis is on self-efficacy."[28]

The vision of a gender-responsive institution would include programs, therapy, and treatment to support imprisoned mothers and address substance abuse and mental illness among women, as well as the wounds from violence and sexual abuse on their pathway to prison.

A number of social justice activists have rejected the idea of gender-responsive institutions, however, arguing that they merely perpetuate mass incarceration rather than creating a genuine alternative. Activist Rose Braz from the group Critical Resistance labeled them "gender-responsive cages." Some organizations, such as Californians United for a Responsible Budget, contend that "real reform demands a true reduction in the numbers of people in prison, beginning with a moratorium on new prison construction. We can then redirect funds saved from prison expansion into the local services that women and transgender people need, including housing, healthcare, education, and employment, independent of the criminal legal system."[29]

★ ★ ★

The experiences of those incarcerated in women's prisons, including transgender and gender-variant people, have long been overlooked in research and activism on the issue of mass incarceration. Yet the issues that land people in women's prisons and jails extend deep into communities and reach far beyond the walls of any correctional facility and remain central to any efforts to reverse mass incarceration.

PART FOUR

PRISON PROFITEERS

Privatization of prisons has been a key target of social justice campaigners throughout the country. *Left, courtesy of Mary Sutton; right, courtesy of Brian Dolinar.*

11

PRIVATE PRISONS

Mass incarceration could never have gained traction if it didn't benefit some powerful people. In chapters 4 and 5, we have seen how law enforcement and immigration authorities have gained in power and resources from mass incarceration. In the next two chapters, we look at others who have also benefited, a group Tera Herivel and Paul Wright have labeled the "prison profiteers."[1] In this chapter, we will focus on the most well-known and most controversial of the prison profiteers, the private prison companies.

THE HISTORICAL BACKGROUND

Historically, prisons and jails have primarily been the responsibility of government, but there are precedents for private prison operators. As early as 1825, authorities in Kentucky leased out all the prisoners in the state penitentiary to business owner Joel Scott, who used them as laborers to produce chairs, shoes, wagons, and rope.

This arrangement remained in place for fifty-five years, and "several lessees made fortunes in the process." Scott himself accumulated more than $40,000 (more than $1 million in 2014 dollars).[2] Perhaps the best-known historical example of prison privatization was the prisoner leasing system of the post–Civil War South, vividly described by Douglas Blackmon in his book *Slavery by Another Name*.[3] Under this regime, state or local authorities leased out hundreds of "convicts" to the custody of farm owners, transforming these farms into post-slavery slave labor camps. Local law enforcement carried out roundups of Blacks and arrested them on petty charges, such as vagrancy and loitering, to generate numbers for the leasing system.

In the early 1900s, outcries against the human rights violations of prisoner leasing helped to finally put private prisons and private prison labor largely out of commission. During the 1920s and '30s, nearly all states passed laws that banned contracting of prison labor by private companies. Mississippi was the last to ban the practice, in 1944.[4] In 1979, however, Congress established the Prison Industry Enhancement Certification Program, which once again opened the door to private sector involvement in employing prison labor and operating penal facilities.[5] The private sector began a quiet return to corrections by operating a few halfway houses. In the early 1980s, private prisons staged a full-fledged comeback.

THE RISE OF PRIVATE PRISONS

The Corrections Corporation of America (CCA) opened the first private facility in the era of mass incarceration by winning a contract to run an immigration detention center in Texas in 1983. The building was actually a converted motel. Co-founder and former head of the Tennessee Republican Party Tom Beasley said the company was founded on the principle that you could sell prisons "just like you were selling cars, or real estate, or hamburgers."[6]

The company followed with the first full-blown private prison, in Hamilton County, Tennessee, in 1984. In 1985, it made a bid to take over the entire state prison system of Tennessee, but the authorities declined the offer.

The GEO Group, originally called Wackenhut Corrections Corporation, emerged during this period as well. Wackenhut was an outgrowth of a company that specialized in security and oil industry construction. Wackenhut Corrections incorporated in 1988, a year after the parent company had opened an immigration detention center in Colorado. Several other, smaller firms that remain in business began operations at this time as well, including the Management and Training Corporation in 1987, LCS Corrections Services in 1990, and

Emerald Corrections in 1996. Another sizable firm, Cornell, opened for business in 1984 but was bought out by the GEO Group in 2010.

Beginning in the late 1980s, the private prison companies slowly grew their market share; then privatization began to take off in the 1990s. From 1990 to 2009, the number of prisoners in private prisons increased by approximately 1600 percent, a far higher rate than in public-sector prisons.[7]

The core state for private prison expansion in the early years was Texas. Starting with the detention centers in the early 1980s, by 1996 Texas had thirty-eight private prisons either operating or under construction. Lobbying for private prisons also bore fruit in other states, such as Oklahoma and New Mexico.

Despite this rapid expansion, private prisons also encountered a number of operational problems. In 1997 CCA built a prison in Youngstown, Ohio, on an abandoned industrial site which the city had sold to the company for a dollar. The deal also came with a 100 percent tax abatement for three years. CCA then moved 1,700 prisoners from Washington, D.C., to Youngstown. Within fourteen months, there were two fatal stabbings, forty-seven assaults, and six escapes, creating waves of outrage. Similar problems occurred at two Wackenhut facilities in New Mexico, where four prisoners and a guard were killed, placing private prisons in further disrepute.

In 1997 CCA, which had offered shares on the New York Stock Exchange, had conflicts over dividend payments to shareholders that resulted in several investors bringing successful lawsuits against the company. By 1999 CCA's share value had fallen from a high of eighty-four dollars to eighteen cents. CCA finished the fiscal year with a loss of $202 million. An auditor's report said, "There is substantial doubt about CCA's ability to continue as a going concern."[8]

The passage of mandatory detention for immigration violations in 1996, followed by the increased focus on immigrants spawned by 9/11, breathed new life back into the privatization project. The expansion of immigration detention centers provided a new market niche for private corrections firms. The creation of Criminal Alien Requirement prisons for immigrants with criminal convictions offered more opportunities for the private companies as well.

PRIVATE PRISONS TODAY

By 2014 private prisons had a presence in at least thirty states. The marketing strategy for them had changed significantly from the days of Tom Beasley and his hamburger analogy. In the twenty-first century, private corrections firms stress the formation of partnerships with governments and other stakeholders. While they have enjoyed success since 2000, private prisons still retain a marginal place in the overall system, managing or owning only 9 percent of all prison beds. Moreover, many of the largest state prison systems, such as those of New York and Illinois, have totally blocked private providers over the last three decades. A number of others, including Michigan, Kansas, Minnesota, Arkansas, and Washington, have given up the private prison idea.[9]

Nonetheless, the ethos of private prisons, along with frequent reports of scandals and abuse in private facilities, have often landed them in the limelight. Two megafirms, Corrections Corporation of America and the GEO Group, dominate the market, holding about 58 percent of the private prison cells in the country. As of 2013, CCA owned or controlled fifty-three correctional and detention facilities and managed thirteen others owned by government, with a total capacity of about 86,000 people. The GEO Group's operations included the management and/or ownership of sixty-six correctional and detention facilities with 72,744 beds. The GEO Group also expanded internationally, opening prisons in Australia and South Africa. CCA's total revenue for 2013 was $1.69 billion, while the GEO Group earned $1.52 billion. All told, the private prison industry earned about $5.47 billion in 2013, slightly more than half the corrections budget of California.[10]

The CEOs of these two corporate prison giants are likely the highest-paid employees in the world of corrections. In 2013 CCA's Damon Hininger brought in $3.2 million, while GEO Group head George Zoley received total compensation of $4.6 million.[11]

THE INVESTORS
Unlike most companies in the corrections business, CCA and the GEO Group are publicly traded firms, selling shares on the New York Stock Exchange. CCA first offered shares for

sale in 1983. It put $18 million worth on the market. The GEO Group (then still called Wackenhut) went public in 1994, selling $19.7 million in shares. Both firms then set up front companies to take advantage of tax breaks as owners of real estate. CCA's Prison Realty Trust sold $446.8 million in shares in 1997, and Wackenhut issued $142.6 million as Correctional Properties Trust in 1998. By organizing the companies as realty trusts, their directors avoided millions in corporate taxes.[12]

According to NASDAQ data, the retirement funds of government employees, including public school teachers, are big investors in private prisons. Public employee retirement funds from numerous states, including New York, California, Texas, Kentucky, Ohio, Arizona, Florida, and Colorado, are large holders of private prison stock.[13]

Likely the largest shareholder in private prisons is Henri Wedell, a member of the CCA board. As of 2010, Wedell allegedly owned more than 650,000 shares in the company, valued at more than $25 million. He explained the U.S. prison situation to Vice.com interviewer Ray Downs:

> America is the freest country in the world. America allows more freedom than any other country in the world, much more than Russia and a whole lot more than Scandinavia, where they really aren't free. So offering all this freedom to society, there'll be a certain number of people, more in this country than elsewhere, who take advantage of that freedom, abuse it, and end up in prison. That happens because we are so free in this country.[14]

THE PRIVATE-PRISON TRACK RECORD

Private prisons have expanded primarily because state and federal systems have not been able to cope with the rapid increase in their prison populations. Involving private prisons provided a way for corrections officials to offload some of the burdens of managing more facilities. But the expansion of private prisons has also come with an enormous shift in ideology. Whereas in the 1960s and '70s the dominant thinking held that the state should control and operate

Private Prisons—a Hot Debate

No aspect of mass incarceration has precipitated more heated debate than private prisons. Proponents tend to stress presumed economic advantages, especially to investors.

Private prisons not only have lower costs than public prisons: by introducing competition they encourage public prisons to also innovate and lower costs.

—Alexander Tabarrok, professor of economics at George Mason University[15]

By acting now . . . putting some money behind the CCA could prove to be a portfolio addition that any investor will be happy to have down the road.

—tipster on RT (Russian Television) Online[16]

Critics take a far different view:

Privatization gimmicks are a distraction from the serious business of addressing our addiction to mass incarceration.

—David Shapiro, former staff attorney at the ACLU National Prison Project[17]

Private prisons don't save dollars and they don't make sense. Only reforms that rely less on incarceration make economic, community safety and civil rights sense . . . De-incarceration, not privatization, will save money, keep Florida safe by preventing future crime and protect the rights of all Floridians.

—Byron E. Price, professor of public administration at Medgar Evers College of the City University of New York[18]

The United Methodist Church declares its opposition to the privatization of prisons and jails and to profit making from the punishment of human beings.

—United Methodist Church[19]

If you've read some of the annual reports from prisons and what they give to their stock-holders, they say, "Lookin' good for us. Looks like we can keep filling our beds. We don't want any changes in the drug laws because that might mean fewer people in prison. We don't want any comprehensive immigration reform because that might take people out of our prisons. We want crime."

—Dianne Post, Chair of Legal Redress, Maricopa County, Arizona, NAACP[20]

social service and security services, in the post-1980 era of conservatism and neoliberalism, the private sector became the preferred provider. The prison company directors rode this ideological wave and pitched their companies as a cheap, more efficient alternative than facilities run by the government. Apart from stressing supposed cost reductions, many advocates, such as Irving Lingo Jr., chief financial officer at Corrections Corporation of America, sold their companies as a source of economic stimulus, explaining, "Our core business touches so many things—security, medicine, education, food service, maintenance, technology—that it presents a unique opportunity for any number of vendors to do business with us."[21]

THE INHERENT CONFLICT OF INTEREST

Private prisons have been the target of considerable criticism and political mobilization. Kanye West even protested against them in his song "New Slaves." Some critics charge that private prisons have an inherent, unresolvable conflict of interest: they maximize profit by locking up the largest possible number of people and keeping them locked up for the longest possible time. This conflict is exacerbated by the fact that both CCA and the GEO Group are publicly traded companies, whose primary accountability is to shareholders, not to taxpayers and certainly not to those incarcerated in their facilities. Some critics question the ethics of private prisons on additional grounds. They contend that in the drive to maximize profits, firms inevitably will cut corners, making conditions worse for both the prisoners and those who work in the prisons. Unions have been particularly vocal on this issue, arguing that private prisons underpay staff, provide them with inadequate training, and offer few benefits.

The Buyout Offer

In 2012 the chief corrections officer of Corrections Corporation of America, Harley Lappin, sent a letter to prison officials in forty-eight states offering to buy selected state prisons. CCA claimed to have set aside $250 million for this purpose, but the company put some conditions on the offer. The sale would have to include a contract for CCA to manage the facility for at least twenty years with a guarantee of payment for at least a 90 percent occupancy rate regardless of how many people were in the prison. Such occupancy guarantees already had been a feature of many private prison contracts. The letter brought a round of condemnation from community and religious groups. A letter signed by the American Civil Liberties Union and twenty-six other organizations and sent to the states warned, "Selling off prisons to CCA would be a tragic mistake for your state. . . . [CCA's] proposal is an invitation to fiscal irresponsibility, prisoner abuse and decreased public safety. It should be promptly declined." No states responded positively to CCA's letter.[23]

The unions maintain that this may lead to high rates of turnover and therefore increased violence within the institutions due to the lack of qualified, experienced staff.

SOILING THE POLITICAL PROCESS

Private prison companies spend considerable time and money on lobbying for harsher sentencing laws and further privatization of prisons as well as on campaign contributions to pro–private prison political candidates. Marketing materials from the companies reflect these priorities, indicating that changes in laws or corrections policy that would reduce prisoner numbers pose threats to the firms. Authors of CCA's 2010 annual report stated, "The demand for our facilities and services could be adversely affected by . . . leniency in conviction or parole standards and sentencing practices."[22]

A 2011 Justice Policy Institute report said that CCA spent $1.55 million to back political candidates in twenty-seven states from 2003 to 2010. The GEO Group contributed $2.4 million. In addition, JPI reported that both firms employed huge teams of lobbyists. CCA hired 179 lobbyists in thirty-two states during the same period, and GEO deployed 63 in sixteen states. CCA's past membership in the American Legislative Executive Council (ALEC), a pro-corporation conservative political advocacy group, also came under scrutiny. One report accused CCA of taking part in ALEC sessions during which drafts for Arizona's harsh immigration law, SB 1070 (discussed in chapter 5), were under discussion. SB 1070 passed in Arizona and became the model for similar laws in several other states.[24]

PRIVATE PRISONS' TRACK RECORD

The most frequently cited justification for privatizing prisons is that they save money. Results have been mixed. The Government Accountability Office (GAO) did a study in 1996 that looked at reports analyzing comparative costs in five states—Texas, California, Tennessee, New Mexico, and Washington. The GAO found mixed results in terms of cost savings by private prisons. A similar literature review by the University of Utah in 2009 was also inconclusive.[26] Arizona investigators found that costs in private institutions were comparable to those in public ones for medium-security facilities but that the state prisons were cheaper for minimum security.[27]

The Quota System: Bilking Taxpayers

Contracts with private prison providers are typically paid on a per-occupant basis. Theoretically, if a prison was empty, the private provider would get nothing. To avoid losing money with low occupancy levels, most contracts have a percent-of-capacity quota for guaranteed minimum payment. A 2014 report on sixty contracts by In the Public Interest, a think tank that focuses on privatization, revealed that 65 percent of agreements contained quotas, sometimes referred to in the report as a "low-crime tax." Occupancy guarantees generally hit at least 80 percent; Arizona, Louisiana, Oklahoma, and Virginia have quotas requiring between 95 percent and 100 percent occupancy. If the quota is 100 percent, then the company would be paid as if the prison were full even if it was totally empty.[25]

Researchers who have tried to compare costs of public and private prisons have noted some difficulties in reaching precise conclusions. Private prisons almost universally house low- and medium-security-level prisoners, who require fewer employees and less security infrastructure. In addition, many contracts stipulate that people with serious medical conditions or those who are elderly cannot be housed in a private facility. Such arrangements serve to make the costs per person much lower for private prisons than for state or federal institutions.

A second difficulty in making comparisons is that sending prisoners to private institutions may not dramatically reduce the fixed costs of a Department of Corrections, such as salaries and loan repayments. For example, if a quarter of the population of a state prison is transferred to a private institution, it is unlikely that the prison's staff or energy costs would be reduced by 25 percent. Hence payments to private prisons may add extra costs without making equivalent reductions in the existing expenses of state-run institutions.

Furthermore, saving money is not always desirable. As unions point out, private prisons may reduce costs by cutting back on wages, pensions, and other benefits. In addition, they may decrease expenditure on essential services for the incarcerated population: food, health care, recreation, education, and even security staff. So to be accurate, a comparison would need to find a way to take into account the quality of services.

QUALITY OF SERVICES

In addition to ambiguous results in terms of financial effectiveness, private prisons have been involved in a number of scandals and cases of abuse. Some of these incidents have drawn considerable public attention and led to legal action or termination of contracts.

- On March 11, 2011, the American Civil Liberties Union filed a class action lawsuit regarding the violent conditions inside CCA's Idaho Correctional Center—a "gladiator school" where violent fights were frequent. A second lawsuit was filed in 2012 by men incarcerated there. In 2014 the state reclaimed control over the prison, not long after CCA admitted to having filed false staffing reports that claimed thousands of hours of labor that were never performed.
- In 2010 the Southern Poverty Law Center and the ACLU National Prison Project filed a lawsuit regarding the Walnut Grove Youth Correctional Facility in Mis-

sissippi. The suit targeted the GEO Group, the facility's administrators, and state officials. The complaint alleged abuse, violence, sexual contact by staff, and other inappropriate practices. Federal Judge Carleton Reeves ordered the juveniles at Walnut Grove to be moved to another facility. Mississippi subsequently canceled its contract with the GEO Group for Walnut Grove.

- In November 2008, the State of Texas indicted the GEO Group in the death of Gregorio de la Rosa Jr., who was allegedly beaten to death by fellow prisoners while guards stood and watched. The case resulted in a $42.4 million dollar civil suit settlement by GEO.

- In 2000 a crew from the TV program *60 Minutes* reported that Louisiana authorities seized control of the GEO Group's Jena Juvenile Center for Boys after numerous reports of guards engaging in what a Department of Justice report labeled "cruel and humiliating punishments." Witnesses said that guards were smoking marijuana and that some had sex with some of the boys. The report concluded, "Jena is a dangerous place to be."[28]

Perhaps no one is as well qualified to evaluate private prisons as those who've lived inside them. Alex Friedman spent several years in a private prison in Tennessee. These are some of his reflections:

> The private prison industry is not solely responsible for its many shortcomings. Public officials, including state and federal corrections officials, deserve blame for failing to effectively monitor the industry and hold it accountable. . . .
>
> To be sure, publicly run facilities have problems, too, including corruption, incompetence, or malfeasance at the local, state, and federal levels. Nor are the publics exempt from violence, abuse of prisoners, and civil rights violations.
>
> The difference lies in the *nature* of the two types of facility. Privatization, with its emphasis on cutting corners to reduce costs, produces *systemic* deficiencies that make problems—ranging from riots and stabbings to escapes and murders—more likely

GEO Group Stadium Scandal

In early 2013, the GEO Group donated $6 million to Florida Atlantic University (FAU), the alma mater of the company's CEO, George Zoley. In return, the university agreed to name their newly built football stadium the GEO Group Stadium. The GEO Group is based in Boca Raton, where FAU is also located.

FAU planned to use the money to pay off some of the $70 million in debt accrued to finance the stadium construction. The deal with the GEO Group created a major controversy on campus and beyond. Students staged a sit-in outside the administration building to protest the naming, dubbing the stadium "Owlcatraz," after the school's mascot. The faculty senate passed a resolution against the use of the GEO Group name. Eventually, the American Civil Liberties Union and the United Methodist Church joined the condemnation of the GEO Group's naming rights, as did the Florida Immigration Coalition, which pointed to the company's extensive investments in immigration detention centers. After less than three months, local and national pressure forced the GEO Group to back out of the stadium deal.

"From the beginning, we did not want the university associated with a company that violates human rights," said Gonzalo Vizcardo, a student organizer at FAU, adding that "the GEO Group wanted to legitimize its business, and normalize the idea of private prisons, and they were utterly defeated."[29]

to occur. High employee turnover and inadequate staff training lead to situations such as the deadly violence at CCA's Youngstown, Ohio, prison and the shameless abuse of juvenile offenders at a Wackenhut [GEO Group] facility in Jena, La.[30]

IMMIGRATION AND PRIVATE PRISONS

As noted in chapter 5, increased immigration detention has been a boon for private prisons. From 1996 to 2011, immigration detention center occupancy nearly quadrupled. The bulk of this increase came from the building or contracting out of new immigration detention centers by the federal government.

In 2012 CCA and the GEO Group took in $738 million in federal contracts for immigration detention and incarceration, about a quarter of the firms' total revenue for the year. One 2009 study estimates the average cost to detain an immigrant at $164 a day or roughly $60,000 a year—about the cost of tuition, room, and board at an Ivy League college.[31]

In the post–9/11 era, many new, privately run immigration detention centers have been brought online. They are dedicated to holding the rising number of those awaiting judgment in deportation or asylum cases. For example, the CCA facility in Lumpkin, Georgia, built in 2004 and renovated in 2007, holds more than 1,700 people. The GEO Group opened both the $32 million Karnes County Civil Detention Center in Karnes, Texas, and the 650-bed extension on the Adelanto, California, facility in 2010. It previously had added the 1,900-bed South Texas Detention Complex in Pearsall in 2005. The smaller Management and Training Corporation spent $65 million to build the Willacy Detention Center in Raymondville, Texas, in 2006.[32]

As noted in chapter 5, the early 2000s also saw the arrival of Criminal Alien Requirement (CAR) prisons, for those being held on criminal charges for illegal entry or other crimes. The most notorious is the Reeves County Detention Complex, completely converted to a 3,700-bed CAR facility through a federal government partnership with GEO in 2007.[33]

The Reeves Detention Complex was the site of two major prison rebellions in reaction to problems in medical care and other issues. The death of thirty-two-year-old Jesús Manuel Galindo prompted one of these actions. Galindo had a history of epilepsy and died of a seizure in his solitary confinement cell. A lawsuit filed on his behalf claimed that he had been placed in solitary because he had complained about poor medical treatment. His death was the fifth at Reeves over a two-year period. Allegedly the prison medical staff offered him only Tylenol. Reeves was rated one of the ten worst prisons in the United States in an article in *Mother Jones* magazine.[34]

ACLU Private Prison Recommendations

Many religious groups and social justice activists oppose the very idea of private prisons. Groups including the American Civil Liberties Union nonetheless have issued recommendations on how to improve the existing ones:

- Stop using occupancy quotas;
- Ensure that private prisons are inspected regularly, with findings publicly posted;
- Strengthen oversight and accountability for existing private prisons;
- Reject contract bids from private companies with records of mismanagement, abuse, or substandard care;
- Ensure transparency of private prison operations;
- Stop expanding the use of private, for-profit contractors;
- Return immigration enforcement to civil immigration authorities, through specified measures.[35]

NEW PROFIT FRONTIERS

CCA and the GEO Group have ventured into new markets beyond owning and operating institutions. CCA has spread into the realm of reentry by opening a Correctional Alternatives Division, which runs programs for those returning to the community from prison.

In 2010 GEO bought BI Incorporated, the largest provider of electronic monitoring services in the United States. The purchase fit in with GEO's immigration work, as BI had a multiyear contract with ICE worth more than $600 million to supervise immigrants awaiting adjudication.[36]

Private prisons have been among the fastest-growing carceral entities in recent years. Capturing the niche market in immigration detention has placed them in a position to reap benefits for many years to come. These firms have provoked resistance from a range of people in religious and social justice circles who question the very ethics of privately run institutions of incarceration. Nonetheless, private prison owners and operators are not alone in reaping financial benefits from mass incarceration as a whole. Many other companies, government departments, and key individuals have prospered at the expense of the millions of people who have been locked up in this era of mass incarceration.

Courtesy of Mary Sutton

12

INCARCERATION INC.

In addition to the private prison corporations, a wide range of companies, organizations, individuals, and even towns profit economically or politically from prisons. They all have "skin in the game"—and have a definite interest in opposing attempts to reduce or end mass incarceration.

These prison profiteers recognize that incarcerating people is an economic as well as a political operation. Keeping a person in prison is costly, whether in New York, where in 2010 it cost on average $60,076 a year to lock up one person, or in West Virginia, where the price tag was $26,498.[1] The question is: where does that money come from and where does it go?

It is pretty simple to see where the money comes *from*. Almost all funding for operating prisons and jails comes from tax revenues. The money to build them, however, usually requires issuing some kind of bond. The repayment of the bond then comes from taxes.

Where the money *goes* is more complicated. Expanding and sustaining mass imprisonment requires at least three costly activities:

1. Building the infrastructure. Whether in the public or private sector, those who will run the prison must pay architects, engineers, and contractors to design and build the cells, security fences, guard towers, visiting rooms, offices, et cetera.
2. Employing staff. Once the prison is built, the major operating costs for prisons and

jails are wages and salaries. These are paid not only to guards but to counselors, case managers, administrators, accountants, maintenance people, cooks, drivers, secretarial staff, doctors, nurses, and a host of other employees. All told, staffing costs generally consume at least half of expenditure on corrections.

3. Supplying goods and services to people in prison. Each prisoner needs food, clothing, water, and medical services. Most prisons also have some kind of recreational equipment, televisions, telephones, and a store where prisoners can buy supplemental food, clothing, and hygiene items.

BUILDING

The expense of building a prison varies, depending on the cost of labor, the style of accommodation, and the technology used for security. According to an IBISWorld report, corrections construction brought in an average of $2.8 billion per year from 2001 to 2012.[2] In 1996, at the height of the prison building boom, California conducted a comparative study of construction costs. The average for the nine medium- and high-security prisons the state built at that time was around $200 million each (about $300 million in 2014 dollars). A similar prison in Arizona would have cost a third less; in Texas, 20 percent less. The California average translated to $92,000 per bed, nearly as much as the national average selling price for a house at that time, $115,000.[3]

Prisons and jails are major construction projects. In many counties or rural areas, building a prison or jail constitutes by far the biggest infrastructure item in an annual budget. For most prison building projects, a major construction company manages operations. A number of large global firms have become national leaders in this field. These companies don't build just prisons but also a host of large-scale construction projects—malls, government buildings, bridges, highways, and luxury hotels. Three construction companies account for about 30 percent of the prison market.

Turner Construction, a New York–based firm, is the largest player in corrections construction. It is a subsidiary of the German company Hochtief. Turner's average annual income for prison and jail construction from 2007 to 2012 was $278 million. The company's average annual revenue for all activities in 2013 was $9 billion, making it the fourth largest of all U.S. construction and engineering firms. Perhaps the most famous project in its portfolio is New York's Lincoln Center for the Performing Arts, but Turner has also completed work for the FBI, the Department of Veterans Affairs, and the Centers for Disease Control as well as building corporate headquarters for Boeing and the RAND Corporation. Turner has about five thousand employees worldwide.

Number two in this industry is Gilbane, which had average annual prison construction revenue for 2007 to 2012 of $153 million. Its 2013 total revenue was just over $4 billion. Gilbane built the Baltimore County Detention Center and specializes in courthouses and county jails. The company is based in Providence, Rhode Island.

Number three in the prison construction sector in 2013 was Hensel Phelps Construction, with annual revenue of around $2.3 billion. From 2007 to 2012, it earned an average annual income of $186 million from corrections construction.

Construction companies are not the only businesses that share in the profits of carceral construction, however. A host of architects and consultants are essential to prison and jail building. Before any construction can take place, most authorities want some kind of feasibility or needs-assessment study to give them an idea of the options available and the costs involved. Such needs assessments can be quite costly—from a few thousand dollars in a small county to the $30 million contract Los Angeles County awarded in 2014 for design sketches and an environmental impact study on a $2 billion jail construction project.[4] Firms such as Justice Concepts, Nacht and Lewis, DLR Group, and CGL are leaders in this type of work.

Prisons could not be built without financing, and even small county jails call for expenditure in the tens of millions. Because of the scale of these investments, corrections officials need to secure loans to pay for construction. They then make an arrangement to pay them off over time. In the past, this was done largely by setting aside money in the annual budget to make the required loan repayments, a pay-as-you-go arrangement. Alternatively, local or state authorities have issued general obligation bonds, which are sold in the market as an investment vehicle. These have to be approved by voters. In the late 1980s, however, voters began to sour on bonds for prisons and jails. Because the authorities remained determined to build these facilities, they frequently turned to lease-revenue bonds, which don't require voter approval. State and local authorities in several states, including California, Texas, New York, Florida, Alaska, and Michigan, made use of these bonds to build correctional facilities.

Arranging the financing for prison and jail construction, especially through lease-revenue bonds, is a high-profit enterprise. For the nine prisons the state of California built in the 1990s, the finance charges came to $3.5 billion, nearly twice the cost of the actual construction.[5] The opportunity to fund these prisons attracted some of the biggest names in finance, including Goldman Sachs, Morgan Stanley, the late Bear Stearns, and Bank of America Securities.

EMPLOYEES OF THE CORRECTIONS INDUSTRY

Nationwide approximately 2.4 million people work in the justice system, about one per prisoner. At the financial apex are the CEOs of the large private corrections companies, with their multimillion-dollar annual compensation packages (see chapter 11). Big winners also include the heads of state departments of corrections, the director of the federal Bureau of Prisons, and other high-level officials. They have reaped opportunities for promotion, salary increases, and political power and influence.

Second-tier administrators and professional staff also have benefited from mass incarceration. Salaries for these administrators vary, however. The director of the Oklahoma Department of Corrections earned $160,000 in 2014.[6] In California in 2014, the chief physician and surgeon for the Department of Corrections and Rehabilitation earned $569,000, and eighteen professional staff had salaries in excess of $300,000.[7]

Down another financial rung rest about eight hundred thousand who work directly in corrections, whether inside prisons or jails or in the lower levels of corrections bureaucracies.[8] The employment figure for corrections has almost tripled since 1979. About 60 percent of these corrections jobs are in state departments. Local jails represent about a third of this sector, and the federal prison system employs about 4 percent of corrections workers.[9]

Apart from high-level administrators and professionals, people who work in corrections fall into four broad categories:

1. Office personnel—people who work in offices at departments of corrections or on-site at prisons. These range from professionals, such as accountants, to administrative assistants, clerks, and nonprofessional workers employed outside the correctional facilities.
2. Civilians or "free staff"—people who work in prisons or jails providing a service and dealing directly with prisoners. These might include nurses, cooks, maintenance personnel, teachers, and transport workers.
3. Those who directly maintain custody of prisoners—wardens, guards, counselors, and case managers.
4. Those who work in postincarceration capacities—parole and probation officers.

Guards, officially called correctional officers, make up about half of all corrections employees. In 2013, according to the Bureau of Labor Statistics, 432,688 people were employed as correctional officers.[10] In 2012 the national average pay for a correctional officer was $39,950.[11] In California, the use of extraordinary amounts of overtime has led to thousands of guards earning more than $100,000 a year in wages since 2006.[12] In New York, New Jersey, Illinois, and Massachusetts, guards did almost as well, earning more than $60,000 on average in 2013. By contrast, in Georgia average pay was $29,180.

Much of the financial fortune of correctional employees depends on the presence of unions. Those who work in states where corrections unions are strong tend to earn more money and have better benefits. Four major national unions organize corrections workers. The American Federation of State, County and Municipal Employees is the largest, with 62,000 correctional officers and 23,000 other correctional employees. The American Federation of Government Employees has 30,000 members, all of whom work at federal prisons and detention centers. Others are represented by the Service Employees International Union and the Teamsters Union. In addition, a number of states have their own local unions for correctional officers.[13] Two of the most notable are the California Correctional Peace

Some Unions Change Gears

In more recent years, several labor unions have begun to link mass incarceration to the broader problems of working people. For example, in 2013 the AFL-CIO passed a resolution opposing mass incarceration. The resolution called for full rights for people with felony convictions once they have completed their prison terms and advocated the elimination of "inappropriately long mandatory sentences for non-violent crimes."[15] Many opponents of mass incarceration argue that the unions should go further, however, and press for decarceration and the retraining of corrections employees into more socially useful fields such as public health, environmental protection, and affordable housing.

Officers Association (CCPOA) and the New York State Correctional Officers and Police Benevolent Association.

The CCPOA has been particularly controversial. This association has consistently donated large sums of money to political candidates who back harsh sentencing legislation. In 2002 it made a $2 million contribution to tough-on-crime governor Gray Davis's campaign.[14]

At times unions have clashed with those fighting to end mass incarceration. An extreme case of conflict between unions and social justice activists occurred in the battle over closure of the Tamms supermax prison in Illinois in 2014. Tamms had become the focus of a human rights campaign because of its policy of keeping prisoners in their cells twenty-three hours per day and denying them any contact with other men in the institution. In some cases, people had been held in solitary confinement for more than a decade. After activists from Tamms Year Ten and other groups had pushed for the closing of the supermax for many years, Governor Pat Quinn decided to shut the prison down and relocate those held there, and the workers, to other institutions. The American Federation of State, County and Municipal Employees (AFSCME), the union that represented the Tamms prison guards, came out in opposition to the closing, however, arguing that it would cost jobs and economically disadvantage the small rural town where the prison was located. Ultimately, the prison was closed, but the union maintained its opposition to the end.

SUPPLIERS OF GOODS AND SERVICES

A host of suppliers have found prisons and jails to be a growing source of profits. One company that has flourished in this new marketplace is Bob Barker Industries. Based in Nashville, Tennessee, Bob Barker produces a wide range of goods for prisoners and prison staff. The firm bills itself as a "worldwide leader in delivering innovative products and services to correctional and rehabilitation customers." The company vision invokes religious inspiration: "Transforming criminal justice while honoring God in all we do."[16]

Barker offers prisons and jails a wide variety of cheaply made goods: jumpsuits, sandals, T-shirts, board games, and black-and-white striped canvas shoes. They also sell steel stools and benches for dayrooms and offer staff a range of uniforms, handcuffs, leg shackles, metal detectors, and isolation cells that can be installed in vans to transport "violent prisoners." A company specialty is marketed as the "convict classic" uniform, a retro outfit that puts prisoners back into black-and-white stripes. The company's total sales are about $100 million a year.[18]

Fun and Games

Game developers have found a lucrative market in simulating prison profiteering. The big seller in this realm is Prison Architect, in which the player takes control of building and running a prison. Released in 2012, the game sold more than three hundred thousand copies in a little over a year, bringing in about $11 million. A less commercially successful game was the Prison Tycoon series launched in 2005. That game includes simulated versions of real prisons, including Angola in Louisiana and the Leavenworth federal penitentiary in Kansas. The goal is to build and operate a prison and make money.[17]

HEALTH CARE

Prison and jail administrators have embraced outsourcing, creating more business opportunities. Health care is one of the major services where outsourcing has taken hold.

Carceral Entrepreneurship

Steven Oberfest was working as a personal trainer when one of his clients' friends was convicted of a nonviolent crime. She was worried about what might happen to her in prison, so she asked Oberfest for some hints on how to defend herself when she was behind bars. He took up the offer and an idea for a business was born.

Oberfest founded Incarceration Optimization Program International in New York City, offering a hundred-hour, $20,000 course that instructs white-collar criminals on the art of survival behind bars.

Oberfest teaches his clients slang terms, how to address guards and other prisoners, and generally what daily routines to expect inside. According to a CNN report, his business was going well.[21]

As of 2012, about twenty states had contracted their prison health care to private companies. Many county jails have done the same. Corizon Correctional Healthcare, the largest prison medical provider, takes in around $1.5 billion in annual revenue with contracts for prisons in twenty-eight states and jails in numerous cities and counties. Some of Corizon's contracts are with major municipalities, such as Atlanta, Philadelphia, and New York City. In addition, the company has its own in-house pharmacy division, PharmaCorr.

Unions and many human rights groups are critical of private companies delivering health care in prisons. As Kerry Korpi of AFSCME maintains, "Private correctional health care companies have a track record of cost cutting that puts both inmates and staff at risk. These companies' goal is profit, not public safety."[19]

A number of lawsuits and protests have been lodged against Corizon. In 2012 it paid out almost $1.8 million to settle claims filed by Vermont prisoners from 2007 to 2011.[20]

PRISON FOOD

Another service where outsourcing is the dominant trend is food provision. The giant in this market is Aramark, which has a presence in more than six hundred correctional facilities throughout North America, serving more than a million meals per day according to its website. It holds or has held food contracts with state prison systems in Florida, Indiana,

Kansas, Kentucky, Michigan, and Ohio, as well as with dozens of county jails. The state contracts tend to be the most lucrative. A two-year contract with Ohio in 2013 paid out $110 million. A similar agreement with Michigan was concluded for $145 million.

Aramark's record reveals a number of controversial incidents. In 2014 Ohio fined it $142,000 for various violations, including not hiring enough workers. An $86,000 fine in Michigan in 2014 targeted shortages of food. In both states, there were also several reports of maggots in the food.[22]

PRISON PHONES

The annual value of the carceral phone business is estimated at $1.2 billion.[23] A small number of telecommunications providers have cornered the bulk of this market. In most instances, they have institutionalized extremely exorbitant phone rates. Family members bear the burden of extra costs.

Typically the contracts include not only normal service fees and profits for the telecommunications company, but also, as noted in chapter 9, a "site commission" ("kickback") to the government or institution. In an era when many customers have unlimited long-distance calls, thirteen states charge more than

The Loaf

Many prisons and jails have resorted to serving "the loaf" (also called nutraloaf and prison loaf). Well suited to both punishment and cost cutting, the loaf is an amalgam of various foods compressed into a meat loaf shape and baked. The loaf may include soybeans, oatmeal, eggs, powdered milk, vegetables, and an assortment of leftovers. It has prompted many lawsuits from prisoners. The American Correctional Association has stated that reducing food quantity or quality may not be used as punishment. Correctional authorities and courts have argued that prisons are not obligated to serve food that is tasty. Their requirements are given only in terms of calories and the most basic nutrition. Aaron Fraser, who spent four years incarcerated, described the loaf thus: "They take a bunch of guck, like whatever they have available, and they put it in some machine. . . . I would have to be on the point of dizziness when I know I have no choice [to eat it]."[24]

$5 for a fifteen-minute in-state phone call from a prison. All told, the kickbacks from all prison phone calls come to more than $460 million annually.[25]

The largest firm in this industry is Global Tel★Link, which has about a 57 percent market share. According to its website, the company serves twenty-nine state departments of corrections and more than eight hundred counties. The parent company of Global Tel★Link, American Securities, bought the firm from financial giants Veritas and Goldman Sachs Direct for $1 billion in 2011.[26] The high rates for prison phone calls have sparked a nationwide campaign for federal regulation of the cost of calls. After considerable lobbying led by prisoners and their families, along with groups such as the Media Action Grassroots Network, Working Narratives, Prison Legal News, and the Prison Policy Initiative, the Federal Communications Commission put a cap on the charges for interstate calls from prisons and jails in 2014.[27]

CONTRACT LABOR

A small number of companies have reaped profits from contracting cheap prison labor. Overall estimates are that about sixty thousand incarcerated men and women work under contract.[28] The bulk of these workers produce goods and services for government departments, however—making clothes or mattresses for prisons, assembling telecommunications equipment for the Department of Defense, or, in the most iconic example, making license plates. About 60 percent of these government contracts are with the Department of Defense. The largest contractor, the Bureau of Prisons Federal Prison Industries, often called Unicor, employed some thirteen thousand such workers in 2013.

All incarcerated workers under contract to a private company must be registered with the Prison Industries Enhancement Certification Program.[29] In 2013 just 4,735 prisoners were under such contract. According to the program's regulations, such workers are supposed to receive the legal minimum wage, though this is not always the case. While a few contract workers are employed by large companies, such as Cisco, most are under contract with small firms.

One typical example of a small firm contract involved Lufkin Industries and Direct Trailer, two Texas firms. Lufkin Industries' trailer division was doing well when suddenly a local competitor, Direct Trailer and Equipment Company, began to produce much cheaper trailers. Eventually Lufkin closed down its trailer business and laid off 150 workers. Only later did Lufkin's owners realize that the entire Direct Trailer and Equipment operation had been moved inside a prison, providing not only a source of cheap labor but also factory premises at a rent of $1 a year. Although federal regulations forbid shutting down an entire company and relocating it inside a prison, Direct Trailer and Equipment managed to pull it off.[30]

Apart from those who work for small companies, the largest number of prisoners under labor contract to private firms work on prison farms in southern prisons.

PRISON FARMS

In many facilities in southern states, incarcerated men produce crops on prison farms. Most of these crops are used in the prison system, but some are sold to the public. On the Mississippi State Penitentiary farm, 5,700 acres were planted in 2012 with the value of production totaling $1.3 million. Oklahoma's Agri-Services produces or processes some 723,000 pounds of beef, 115,000 pounds of pork, 1,445,000 pounds of processed meat, and 568,000 gallons of milk, along with 7,500 tons of hay and 4,500 tons of livestock feed, in a typical year. In 2012, in the wake of a labor shortage due to harsher immigration law enforcement, some Georgia farmers employed prisoners as an emergency measure to harvest the onion crop. Due to the rise of high-tech agriculture, however, some states, including Pennsylvania and Iowa, have closed prison farms, deciding that they are unable to compete in the modern marketplace.[31]

A new sector employing people in prisons is call centers. At least a dozen states house call centers inside prisons, employing some two thousand people. Unicor, the government-subsidized contract-labor corporation of the federal Bureau of Prisons, markets its call centers with the lure of Third World labor conditions right here at home, as in this notice on the company website:

> UNICOR now has the authority to work with private sector firms that are sending their work offshore, or in lieu of sending it offshore. We call it "smart-sourcing."

> Let's face it. Outsourcing offshore can be a hassle. There are language barriers, monetary exchange rate concerns, time zone differences, etc. And to visit your offshore operations may require a transoceanic flight. . . . UNICOR can provide call center support at highly competitive rates, right here in the USA!
>
> Imagine . . . All the benefits of domestic outsourcing at offshore prices. It's the best kept secret in outsourcing![32]

The human rights concerns of contract labor are the most worrisome to many. As David Fathi, director of the American Civil Liberties Union National Prison Project, put it, "There's real opportunity for exploitation here. They can't unionize. We don't want a situation where business has an interest in increasing the prison population." Prison owners and

---

The Debate Over Prison Labor

The use of prison contract labor has been the subject of extensive debate. Here are some voices from this debate.

The wages that they earn within the institution allow them to put money in their personal bank accounts, as well as utilize it toward victim restitution and other court-ordered payments.

—Richard Davison, secretary of the Florida Commission on Offender Review[33]

Normally when you work in the free world, you have people call in sick, they have car problems, they have family problems. We don't have that [in prison].

Leonard Hill, owner of Lockhart Techologies, a Texas company that uses prison labor[34]

suppliers obviously have that interest already, but critics worry that contract labor will generalize it to many other businesses.

Despite claims by some writers that penitentiaries have become a "niche market" for the exploitation of prisoners by the corporate sector, the vast majority of incarcerated men and women have no links at all to private companies, however.[35] If they are employed, they engage in basic labor to keep the institution operating—cleaning, cooking, maintenance, and clerical tasks. In 2013 about seven hundred thousand prisoners had this type of employment. The vast majority receive little pay for such labor, from nothing at all to perhaps twenty-five cents an hour, though some clerical jobs may pay up to a dollar an hour.

While private corrections companies, especially Corrections Corporation of America and the GEO Group, have been the most prominent prison profiteers, many other actors have

---

It's bad enough that our companies have to compete with exploited and forced labor in China. They shouldn't have to compete against prison labor here at home.

—Scott Paul, executive director of the Alliance for American Manufacturing[36]

My employees just cannot believe the fact that a prisoner who should be paying a debt to society is being promoted through the federal government to take a job from an American taxpaying citizen.

—Chris Reynolds, president of Campbellsville Apparel in Kentucky[37]

Prisoners should never be used in competition with free labor or to replace free labor.

—AFL-CIO, the nation's largest trade union federation[38]

We're sending jobs overseas when there are plenty of qualified people in prison. Why not pay people a wage to rehabilitate them?

—Rosemary Batt, professor at the Cornell University School of Industrial and Labor Relations[39]

gained financially and politically by promoting mass incarceration. From architects to toilet paper vendors, from construction firms to producers of orange jumpsuits, private concerns have been lining up to secure and maintain carceral contracts. For three decades, government at all levels has continued to spend more and more money on criminal justice, thereby attracting more companies and individuals wanting their share of an ever enlarging pie.

Finally, around 2009, the bubble began to at least leak, if not burst. Gradually some of the focus turned to alternatives—ways to lock up fewer people and spend less money on a sector that has grown beyond all rational boundaries. After years of campaigning by activists and those directly impacted by imprisonment, some policy makers have begun to question the logic of mass incarceration as well as examine possibilities for change and potential alternatives.

PART FIVE

ENDING MASS INCARCERATION

Actor Danny Glover is one of many high-profile individuals who have stepped up to oppose policies like the excessive use of solitary confinement and to advocate for restorative justice instead of the current punitive system. *Courtesy of Mary Sutton*

13

CHANGING THE MIND-SET

In 2009, for the first time since the late 1970s, the number of people in prisons in the United States declined. From 2009 to 2011, the overall prison population declined by about 3 percent.[1] Though the decline was relatively small, it showed that the critique of the criminal justice system had spread well beyond the small core of activists, scholars, and humanitarians who had been sounding alarm bells about this issue since the 1990s. By 2010 critics included mainstream politicians, conservative libertarians, and some business leaders. In addition, public opinion began to shift away from support for further expenditure on incarceration, especially in drug cases. Many people hope this decline is a turning point in the history of mass incarceration, but newfound opportunities for change have provoked considerable resistance. Major changes in mind-set and philosophy will be required to leave the punishment paradigm behind.

Throughout this book we have seen how the spirit of punishment has informed mass incarceration, even in victimless crimes such as prostitution or drug possession. Some people refer to this approach as retributive justice, meaning that the main purpose of the system is to exact retribution rather than rehabilitate or transform the person who commits the crime. Those who have opposed mass incarceration have offered a range of alternatives to this punitive philosophy, including restorative justice, transformative justice, and prison abolition.

RESTORATIVE JUSTICE

In the current criminal justice system, the fundamental logic proceeds this way: Was a crime committed? If so, who committed the crime, and how should that person be prosecuted and punished? In a system of restorative justice, the logic begins with different questions: Has harm been done? If so, how do we repair the harm?

Restorative justice involves promoting a spirit of forgiveness and reconciliation. Practitioners of restorative methods encourage people who do harm to accept responsibility for their actions, take steps to undo that harm, and then be given a second chance to carry on with their lives. The outcomes of restorative justice are not generally measured in terms of arrests and convictions but rather in the quality of relationships that are built among those involved in harmful actions, their victims, and the broader community. Robert Yazzie, Supreme Court justice emeritus of the Navajo Nation, explains it this way:

> The first order of business the relatives would do in the peacemaking process is to get to the bottom of a problem. . . . In court, I would sue you for battery and the state would say we have to prove all the elements of a crime and use the rules or the law to prove that you are guilty. The Holy People say that's beside the point. What matters here is: why did this act happen in the first place? There's a reason why the harm has occurred. Let's deal with that. Maybe we have a history of problems between the two of us. If we can get to the bottom of a problem, all the other stuff will fall into place. The damage can be acknowledged by you, and I can go away happy from the process, knowing that you say that you're not going to do it again.[2]

Restorative practices have been used for centuries by indigenous peoples in the Americas and elsewhere. In more recent times, communities troubled by conflict and violence have employed restorative processes to attempt to heal the wounds of the past and build a lasting peace. Some criminal justice institutions have also implemented restoration-based policies, such as peer courts, to handle low-level cases. The highest-profile uses of restorative practices have been on the global stage, where several countries, including South Africa, Chile, El Salvador, Rwanda, and Liberia, have set up truth and reconciliation commissions to heal the collective and individual wounds of war, tyranny, racial hatred, and social division.

VICTIM-BASED RESTORATIVE JUSTICE

Restorative justice programs can be divided into two types. The first type focuses largely on the victims of crime. Practitioners in these programs normally intervene in a situation after a criminal conviction has been completed. They accept the need for punishment but stress that punishment alone will not undo the harm. Instead they prioritize providing restitution to crime victims and ensuring that those who are convicted take full responsibility for their actions and their implications.

This form of restorative justice emerged with the advance of mass incarceration and played a major role in adding victims' rights to the agenda of the criminal justice system. All states have initiated some form of victims' compensation fund, and Texas even added a constitutional amendment in 1989 to protect victims' rights. The amendment included the right to be treated with fairness and dignity and the right to be protected from the accused during the criminal justice process, as well as the right to information about the conviction, sentence, imprisonment, and release of the accused. The amendment also added a victim's right to restitution. The state subsequently

> *In order for a true discussion of forgiveness/restorative justice to take place, all of us—not just survivors of crime—must learn to see those who commit crime as human beings. It is easy not to forgive or restore when applying the assumption that the person who has caused harm is less than human, incapable of doing otherwise or of changing for the better. Only by rehumanizing those who commit crime is forgiveness/restorative justice (healing) possible.*
>
> —Troy T. Thomas aka Asar I Amen, Lancaster State Prison, California, 2014[3]

established a victim/offender mediation and dialogue process to enhance communication and reconciliation between people convicted of a crime and crime victims.[4]

This kind of restorative justice process operates by fully participating in the existing institutions of the criminal justice system. Practitioners of this school generally do not question the legitimacy or validity of the current legal framework or the dispensations of the courts. Overall they are a form of advocacy for the victims of crime. Apart from restitution, these programs often focus on providing victim-support services, such as post-trauma counseling. In some cases, advocacy of victims' rights and restoration has been combined with lobbying for harsher sentencing for certain types of crimes. For example, Crime Victims United in California promotes victims' right to restoration but also has actively opposed referenda to eliminate the death penalty and reduce the range of offenses covered by three-strikes laws.

COMMUNITY-BASED RESTORATIVE JUSTICE

By contrast, a large number of restorative justice practitioners operate primarily outside the formal criminal legal system. Many of their programs emerged as a reaction to what they believed were the excesses of the punishment paradigm. They attempted to set up alternative processes and institutions that would empower individuals and communities to resolve conflicts through their own initiatives before criminal prosecution took place.

To get a better idea of how such programs operate, let's begin with a simple example of restorative justice. A young man we'll call John works at a restaurant. While seemingly alone in the break room, John sees the purse of one of his co-workers, Sally. He reaches into her wallet and steals twenty dollars. Sally has set aside this twenty dollars to buy new school shoes for her young son. When she returns to the break room, she notices the money is missing and begins to ask everyone if they saw anyone going into her purse. Someone says they saw John handling the purse. John hears this comment and runs out of the restaurant, fearing that the police will be called. This is the moment when the philosophy of justice enters the situation. The punitive approach would involve phoning the police, filing a criminal complaint against John, and hoping that he would be punished to the "fullest extent of the law." If Sally follows this approach, she would build up a case against John and begin to vilify him in her mind as an evil person who is denying her son a new pair of shoes.

A restorative approach would handle the situation differently. It would involve bringing John and Sally together through some kind of mediator, ideally someone trained in restorative justice techniques. In this mediation, both parties would be given the opportunity to speak. Because his guilt is not in doubt, the burden would be on John to accept responsibility for his action. This would require not only returning the twenty dollars but also listening to Sally explain how John's behavior had harmed her directly by denying her the chance to buy a new pair of shoes for her son. The idea behind this is to deter John from committing such harmful acts in the future by getting him to understand the impact of his actions on others.

At the same time, John would be given a chance to explain the circumstances that led him to steal the twenty dollars. Was it simply an impulsive action that he did for the thrill? Perhaps he wanted to use the money to buy a ticket to a concert. On the other hand, maybe John needed money to pay off a gambling debt or to buy medicine for a sick relative, which the family couldn't afford. Restorative justice would take into account John's circumstances and encourage a spirit of forgiveness on the part of Sally—if she feels John is indeed remorseful about his action. Moreover, if John had a genuine need for that twenty dollars, the discussion might also turn to other ways his need could be met without stealing from co-workers. In addition, in many restorative cases, the person who does the harm would be asked to perform a service for the victim. For example, in this case, the decision might entail getting John to work one of Sally's shifts and donate the wages he earned to her. This would give her time to spend with her son. Alternatively perhaps John could do some work for Sally's church or neighborhood association. The service is intended to acknowledge that harm has been done by the theft and that the best way to compensate for that harm is to do a good deed, rather than suffer a punishment.

In cases such as simple theft between two co-workers, the issues involved in restorative justice may be fairly quick to resolve. The desired outcome is that John and Sally will be able to continue to work together without any future harm taking place. Restorative justice becomes much more complicated, however, when more serious harm is involved or when the case is also prosecuted legally. Race and gender dynamics may also complicate the situation.

For example, in the case of a murder, the harm that has been done cannot be restored. A life has been lost, and this cannot be given back. A murder case that is solved will almost always end up in court, and the person who has committed the murder will face charges and likely a prison sentence. Not much can be done to alter that reality. Nevertheless, a restorative approach to murder would embrace the concepts of forgiveness and second chances. These would emerge at two key points in the process. First, if the defendant is convicted,

Restorative Justice in High Schools

Restorative justice practices can be adapted to many different settings. Montebello High School in Denver implemented a restorative justice program in 2008. Efrem Martin, a former juvenile probation officer, was hired to coordinate the effort. Within the first three months, the program addressed conflicts involving three hundred students, and suspensions went down by 30 percent. Martin said that the bulk of those three hundred would have been suspended or expelled without restorative justice. Leilani, a student who had thirty dollars stolen from her locker by a friend, was ready to fight when she found out. Instead she went to Martin and resolved the situation without physical conflict. Afterward Leilani said, "Now I know how to calm myself down."

The advent of restorative justice at the school reduced suspensions by changing the culture. Part of every agreement is an action: community service or writing a paper on an issue that relates to the conflict. Those making restitution have to check in for community service daily. This makes them accountable. "If they don't graduate from high school, the criminal justice system is waiting for them," Martin says. "I refuse to allow the criminal justice system to capture our young minds." He knows his program can't keep everyone from ending up in prison or jail, but he says, "I will die trying" to keep them out.[5]

the victim's family and friends would be encouraged to support a sentence that would give the person a second chance if he or she showed genuine remorse. This would mean opposing the death penalty or life without the possibility of parole. This differs from the approach of most victim-focused restorative practices, in which advocating for harsh sentences is seen as a recognition of victims' rights.

Once the defendant has been sentenced, a second restorative process would encourage the victim's loved ones to meet and talk with the person convicted of the crime. This would be done only after the victim's family and friends felt that they could face this person and only if he or she showed remorse and a desire to communicate honestly with them. The idea of any such restorative practice would be to create a situation in which the person convicted and the victim or survivors could ultimately find a way to live together in the same community.

PEACE CIRCLES

At the moment, restorative practices are most commonly used in local community settings to resolve domestic disputes, school and juvenile cases, and neighborhood violence. Peacemaking circles (also called restorative circles or peace circles) are among the most frequently used restorative techniques. In a peacemaking circle, a facilitator or "circle keeper" brings together all the key parties involved in a conflict or an act that created harm. The key to the peacemaking circle process is getting people to listen to one another. Many peace circles use a "speaker's piece," typically a small object with some special meaning. The person who holds the piece has the right to speak without interruption or disrespect. Traditional Apache practice used a "talking stick" for this purpose. When a speaker finishes, they pass the piece to someone else. Several organizations, including the YWCA in Madison, Wisconsin, and the Southwest Collaborative in Chicago, have used peace circles among youth in communities that the school-to-prison pipeline pervades. In such areas, organizers set up peace circles as an alternative to the punitive discipline typically dispensed by zero-tolerance school discipline policies. School authorities may call in circle keepers instead of local police when there is a conflict. In some cases, students themselves are trained as circle keepers and may use a form of peer mentoring or even peer courts to resolve the issue. In these peer-based approaches, a student who has

How Peace Circles Work

These are key concepts for peace circles promulgated by Chicago's Project Nia (*nia* is Swahili for "with purpose")

- Peace Circles are based on an assumption of positive potential: that something good can always come out of whatever situation we are in.
- No one of us has the whole picture; only by sharing all of our perspectives can we come closer to a complete picture.
- We are unlikely to tell our deepest truths unless we feel respected and safe. Circles attempt to create safe spaces.
- Circles make possible respectful and reflective dialogue even in very emotional situations.
- Circles allow people to be who they would like to be in their best inclination.
- Circles use storytelling to learn more about each other and us.
- Circles are an intentional space and need to be created intentionally.
- Circles are fundamentally democratic—allowing equal space for all participants to speak and to have voice in any decisions made.
- Circles engage all aspects of human experience—spiritual, emotional, physical, and mental.[6]

done a harmful act participates in a peace circle made up of other students—his or her peers. Circle members decide by consensus how to address the harm that has been done.

RESTORATIVE JUSTICE IN SOUTH AFRICA

Restorative practices have been used in several countries, particularly in postconflict situations. One of the most famous applications of restorative justice was the Truth and Reconciliation Commission active in South Africa in the 1990s. The commission was formed to address the legacy of the apartheid system of racial segregation, which prevailed in South Africa from 1948 to 1994. When Nelson Mandela was elected as the first Black president of South Africa in 1994, part of his mission was to reconcile the formerly disenfranchised Black majority to the white minority, which for decades had voted segregationist governments into power. During its reign, the apartheid regime carried out consistent political repression against an opposition fighting for democracy. While Nelson Mandela was the most famous individual target of this repression, the police and military imprisoned, tortured, and killed thousands of people.

Mandela's government set up the Truth and Reconciliation Commission to bring to light the human rights violations that took place during this period, as well as to set up a process to reconcile former enemies. The commission held dozens of public hearings in which victims told their stories and operatives from the apartheid police and army disclosed the acts of harm they had committed. The commission developed its own principles of restorative

Desmond Tutu on Restorative Justice

South African Nobel Peace Prize laureate Archbishop Desmond Tutu, in his book *No Future Without Forgiveness*, detailed his views on justice.

We contend that there is another kind of justice, restorative justice, which was characteristic of traditional African jurisprudence. Here the central concern is not retribution or punishment. In the spirit of *ubuntu* [traditional African humanist philosophy], the central concern is the healing of breaches, the redressing of imbalances, the restoration of broken relationships, a seeking to rehabilitate both the victim and the perpetrator, who should be given the opportunity to be reintegrated into the community he has injured by his offense. . . . Thus we would claim that justice, restorative justice, is being served when efforts are being made to work for healing, for forgiving, and for reconciliation.[7]

justice. According to its policy, if perpetrators fully disclosed all the acts they had committed and demonstrated remorse, they would be given amnesty from criminal prosecution. If they withheld information or lied, they could be sentenced to prison terms. For months on end, TV channels in South Africa covered these hearings as tales of repression, torture, and murder emerged from thousands of Black South Africans. In many instances, the sessions closed with victims and perpetrators shaking hands or embracing in a spirit of forgiveness.

While many people celebrated the South African spirit of forgiveness and the building of a "rainbow nation" where people of all colors lived harmoniously, the process didn't satisfy everyone. Many Black South Africans who had lost loved ones believed that perpetrators should have been punished with imprisonment, not given amnesty. Others argued that the amnesty should have been accompanied by a massive transfer of wealth from whites to Blacks as *true* restorative justice for the harm done by apartheid.

TRUTH, RECONCILIATION, AND MASS INCARCERATION

Considering restorative practice for the U.S. criminal justice system raises a number of important issues. First, restorative justice relies heavily on admission of guilt by those who commit crimes. They need to express remorse and be willing to carry out actions to compensate for the crime. In the present legal framework, however, admission of guilt makes a person vulnerable to prosecution and sentencing without being able to contest the evidence in the case. How would restorative justice resolve the tension between the need to avoid handing the evidence for a conviction to a prosecutor who is not sympathetic to restorative principles and the need for the people involved in the crime to communicate honestly and openly in order to fully carry out a restorative process? This would require a major transformation in the underlying principles of justice.

A second issue pertains to the kind of historical issues tackled in South Africa. How would a restorative justice process address the excesses and abuses of mass incarceration? Given the thousands of excessive sentences due to mandatory minimums, three-strikes laws, and truth-in-sentencing laws, how would those whose lives have been devastated by this process be compensated? How would their pain and deprivation be acknowledged? Who would admit guilt and take responsibility for this process that has undermined so many lives? How would the racist attitudes that underlie much of mass incarceration be confronted and addressed?

In the United States most restorative justice focuses on an individual or small groups. As a result, many people seeking an alternative have sought to extend restorative justice to include entire communities or society as a whole, through an approach called transformative justice. This would aim to address the harm caused by structural inequalities and oppression. Law professor Sheila A. Bedi explains the need: "A criminal prosecution is focused on the narrow actions of the individual alleged to have broken a law. Because a prosecution is an inherently focused, individualized inquiry, the larger cultural forces that have shaped the wrongdoer are left unaddressed. But true justice requires that we confront these cultural forces head-on. And a criminal prosecution simply can't do that."[8]

TRANSFORMATIVE JUSTICE

Though not as widely accepted as restorative justice, transformative justice builds on similar principles. It concentrates on the roots of crime and harmful actions and attempts to link the resolution of individual cases to larger issues, such as institutionalized race, gender, and class inequality. Some transformative justice practitioners, especially those who work in poor communities of color, question the validity of the idea of "restoring" justice. Many such communities don't have a past state of justice to be restored. According to this perspective, the race, class, and gender oppressions of the past and present mandate that any justice system contribute to building a new and better future free of those inequities.

A number of women's organizations dealing with issues of gender-based violence, particularly against women of color, have developed practices of transformative justice. Generation Five, a national women's organization that focuses on sexual abuse of children, has been a leader in developing the theory of transformative justice. Their well-known document *Toward Transformative Justice* stresses that "individual justice and collective liberation are equally important, mutually supportive, and fundamentally intertwined—the achievement of one is impossible without the achievement of the other."[9] The authors delve further into the meaning of restoration:

> The emphasis on restoration assumes the conditions that existed prior to an individual incident of abuse are desirable and should be restored. This ignores the common lack of rights for children, abuses of power, gender inequality, legacies of slavery and colonization, and other types of violence that pre-date and coexist with ongoing incidents of violence. As such, these models often focus on the restoration of the *status quo* and ignore the challenge of transforming the conditions of social, economic, and political injustice that are the context for, and cause of, violence.[10]

In addition to resolving conflict, transformative justice practitioners aim to use peacebuilding to develop movements that can effect broad social change. For example, in addressing the issue of violence against women of color, Incite! asks, "How can we develop an anti-violence movement that simultaneously struggles against state violence" while seeking justice at the individual level?"[11]

With regard to child sexual abuse or violence against women of color, the argument of transformative justice holds that the conditions that allow such violence to occur must be transformed in order to achieve justice in individual cases. Moreover, groups such as Generation Five and Incite! would maintain that state intervention often makes the situation worse by relying on incarceration and removing children from families and that the state may ultimately "condone and perpetuate cycles of violence" by its actions.

HOW WOULD TRANSFORMATIVE JUSTICE WORK?

To illustrate some of the parallels and differences between restorative and transformative justice, let's take a hypothetical case, of Shawna, an African American woman, who has just been released from prison after serving ten years for possession of crack cocaine. She was never a big-time dealer; she just sold enough to support her own habit. As a child, she suffered sexual abuse from an uncle, which she never revealed to anyone.

As per the typical dispensation, Shawna has been paroled to the town where her case was tried, a hundred miles from her family and her two teenage daughters. Shawna lost custody of the two girls when she went to prison, and they are now in foster care. Shawna knows no one in the town where she has been paroled, and she has to live in a homeless shelter. On her first night there, a man tried to grope her in the food line, but she slapped his hand away and called him out.

Shawna went to apply for food stamps and put her name on the list for public housing, but authorities told her that because of her drug conviction she would not be eligible. She finally found work with a housecleaning service. After she had worked there for two weeks, her parole officer paid a visit to Shawna's workplace. The parole officer searched the premises and questioned the employer at length. The next day, Shawna's employer dismissed her, saying that while he liked her as a worker, he wasn't prepared to tolerate further visits from the parole officer. Unemployed and frustrated, Shawna began spending most of her time hanging out with people from the homeless center. After a couple weeks, she finally caved into peer pressure and smoked some crack. After a week of using, she was caught shoplifting a can of beer in a convenience store. At this point, a parole violation could put her in prison for up to a year. The prosecutor also has the discretion to upgrade her charges to a felony, putting her behind bars for another decade. In the current criminal justice process, Shawna must simply hope that her parole officer and the judge are sympathetic.

A restorative justice practitioner might bring together Shawna and the convenience store owner, get Shawna to take responsibility for her action, and work out a way for her to compensate the store owner for the beer and any other harm done by the theft. In the context of mass incarceration, resolving such an issue outside the confines of the criminal justice system would benefit Shawna in the short run, keeping her on the streets and giving her another chance to find a path to success.

Transformative justice practitioners would look at her case much differently. While they would quite likely support using the restorative justice method to resolve the immediate issue with the store owner and keep Shawna out of prison, they would also mobilize around the underlying issues that are blocking Shawna's success.

They might, for example, bring together a peacemaking circle that included Shawna and other formerly incarcerated women. The circle would be a way to help Shawna and the others mobilize around the issues that affect them—the lack of jobs for people with a felony conviction, the absence of effective substance abuse treatment, intolerance of unproblematic drug use, difficulties with child custody, sexual abuse of women and children, and legal restrictions on access to state benefits. Such a group may also discuss other topics, such as how racism and gender bias affect those attending the circle. In particular, they might question the inequities in the penalties between crack cocaine and powder and work with reformers to get these laws changed. They might also discuss the workings of family services, which disproportionately deprive women of color of custody of their children. So while transformative justice practitioners would accept the idea that a restorative process would help ease the short-term pain, they would contend that in the long run systemic change that addresses the root causes of Shawna's problems is the only solution.

Perhaps the key dividing line between transformative justice and the restorative and retributive forms is the extent to which adherents believe that individuals should be held responsible for behavior that causes harm, including crime. Transformative justice advocates allocate more responsibility to structural issues such as the unfairness of the criminal justice and economic systems. On the other hand, supporters of retributive justice and most proponents of restorative practices focus on individual responsibility for making "bad decisions" and encourage people to learn how to make "better decisions" in the the future.

For retributionists, court and prison are the solution. For restorationists, the answer is to undo the specific harm and give the person who did it a chance to change. For transformationists, the priority is to change systemic injustices by mobilizing people such as Shawna who have been wronged by mass incarceration.

While there are divisions between restorative and transformative approaches, there is also a complex overlap and often useful tension between the two perspectives. Many restorative justice practitioners also work in social justice movements, while supporters of transforma-

Angela Davis on Prison Abolition

In her well-known book *Are Prisons Obsolete?*, Angela Davis gave her view on the function of prisons.

> The prison therefore functions ideologically as an abstract site into which undesirables are deposited, relieving us of the responsibility of thinking about the real issues afflicting those communities from which prisoners are drawn in such disproportionate numbers. This is the ideological work that the prison performs. It relieves us of the responsibility of seriously engaging with the problems of our society, especially those produced by racism and, increasingly, global capitalism.[12]

tive justice frequently use restorative techniques in their work. The question boils down to one of emphasis. How much time and energy does an alternative justice practitioner devote to resolving the cases of particular individuals instead of addressing the bigger picture? After all, both must grapple with the same questions. Given the complex interaction among race, gender, and justice, who should lead alternative approaches? Perhaps more important, how can the strategies that work in small, somewhat homogeneous groups be scaled up to address the needs of a system that involves millions of people?

PRISON ABOLITION

The philosophy of prison abolition draws its inspiration from the abolitionist movement to eliminate slavery in the nineteenth century. Abolitionists argue that mass incarceration, similar to slavery, is an evil, racist system that must be abolished, not slightly reformed. Hence in mobilizing around issues of mass incarceration, abolitionist organizations are highly critical of people who work solely to reform the system rather than to shut it down. For example, prison abolitionists would support campaigns to halt the building of new prisons and jails.

They would also back policies that contribute to "decarceration," measures that would free people who are currently in prison or reduce the flow of people into prison in the future. They would be less likely to be involved in campaigns to improve visiting-room facilities or expand mental-health units in prisons.

The modern theory of prison abolition emerged primarily in Europe in the 1970s. Norwegian scholar Thomas Mathiesen published an early collection of writings in 1974.[13] In the United States, the most important abolitionist writings of the period were Fay Honey Knopp and John Regier's *Instead of Prison: A Handbook for Prison Activists*.[14] These volumes emerged from the social movements of the period and linked abolishing prisons with a larger agenda of transforming society. As the social movements of the 1960s and '70s declined, however, so did support for prison abolition.

The next wave of abolitionist work emerged in the 1990s with the formation of an organization called Critical Resistance. Founded in 1997 by a collective in California, Critical Resistance stimulated extensive debates around strategies for ending mass incarceration. Members were among the first to use the term *prison-industrial complex*. Unlike most organizations dedicated to fighting mass incarceration, Critical Resistance saw the need for a broad social movement driven by common core principles and a national structure. Key members Angela Davis and Ruth Wilson Gilmore became important intellectual lights for the philosophy of prison abolition.

The main thrust of Critical Resistance's work was to emphasize the need to organize in a way that decreased the power and reach of the prison-industrial complex. The group also became known for referring to prison cells as "cages."

Abolitionists of this era articulated a vision of a society without prisons, arguing against the notion that the prison-industrial complex was a permanent fixture of society. Here's a description of this vision that was produced by the compilers of the Social Movements Wiki at Columbia University:

> As we know from the historical origins of prisons, we understand that they were not a superior form of punishment fit for all time, but rather, without taking its

complexity lightly, what made sense at a particular point in history of the eighteenth and nineteenth centuries. Slavery, lynching, and segregation are all examples of social institutions once considered to be just as much an eternal fixture in life. We need to create a new imagination that calls for a world that is completely different.[15]

The philosophy of prison abolition has influenced the actions of activists in many states and localities. In particular, organizations that focus on decarceration by campaigning to stop

An Abolitionist Rape Survivor Explains Why She Chose Not to Press Charges

As a young queer teenager from a poor family, I never considered reporting a number of rapes that I survived during those years. Looking back, I still believe I did the right thing, as I had neither the inner resources, the family support, nor the money to adequately protect myself from a legal process that could have scarred me further and escalated my drug use. I have also chosen not to press charges against my father, who was physically violent for most of my childhood. I am aware that if I did, he most likely would go to prison. My father has been a hard man to love, but I feel committed to sticking by him because he has genuinely changed during my adult years. I recognize that there has been a cycle of violence in my family that has been passed down from generation to generation, and I feel that people in my family in their own way are trying to change that without intervention from government institutions. My family is very important to me and I would not send someone to prison as a way of getting justice. . . . Justice for me meant . . . having the ability to create my own life away from the abusive people in my family. . . . Through my own ongoing healing from violence, I have developed a profound commitment to changing the roots of violence in society. I want it all to stop; from police, prison guards, men, politicians, businessmen, and armies. I have learned through my life experience that violence breeds violence and somehow we have to find a way to stop it that doesn't involve the revenge and cruelty of prisons.[16]

new jail and prison construction and close existing carceral institutions have often adopted an abolitionist perspective. For example, activists in Bloomington, Indiana, formed Decarcerate Monroe County, which mobilized against authorities' attempt to build a new county jail in 2008. In Pennsylvania a movement arose in 2011 called Decarcerate Pennsylvania, which opposed new prison building in that state. Other projects, such as Black and Pink in Boston, which advocates for the rights of LGBTQ prisoners, and the Abolitionist Law Project in Pittsburgh, have also attempted to incorporate an explicitly abolitionist view into their day-to-day work.

The spread of ideas about prison abolition has also sparked considerable debate over how people who oppose mass incarceration should focus their energy. The mission statement of Critical Resistance summarized the group's orientation this way: "Because we seek to abolish the PIC [prison-industrial complex], we cannot support any work that extends its life or scope."

The notion of not extending the life or scope of the prison-industrial complex became the focus of heated discussion among activists and academics. Key differences emerged over the role of reform in the broader process of abolition. For example, many student or university-based groups participate in education programs that bring courses, seminars, and other intellectual activities to people in prison. This prompted debate over whether taking part in such programs actually helped the prison system run more smoothly, extending its life and scope. Even if so, is it more important that doing so helps give prisoners knowledge and skills they need to become agents of social change in their communities after their release?

Another area of conflict related to the building of facilities designed to meet the special needs of certain groups of people in prison. While most abolitionists view mental health facilities and gender-responsive institutions as unnecessary "boutique jails," others involved in social justice movements argue that in situations where many people with mental illnesses face years of bad treatment in existing institutions, it is important to support efforts to improve conditions in the short term, even if it means spending more money on construction.

The question of alliances has also been a crucial area of debate stimulated by prison abolitionists. In general, abolitionists take a systemic and internationalist perspective, viewing the struggle against mass incarceration as part of the global struggle of the poor and oppressed against injustice. Many prison abolitionists would identify themselves as advocates of left-wing ideologies, such as socialism, communism, anarchism, feminism, Black nationalism, or queer liberation. They might also act in solidarity with mobilizations focused on issues such as the liberation of Palestine, global climate change, or same-sex marriage.

Few people have stated the case for prison abolition more forcefully or explained what it really means more clearly than Ruth Wilson Gilmore. Speaking just after the financial crisis of 2008, in which the government used citizens' tax money to bail out big banks failing due to their own fraudulent practices, she observed,

> The two biggest reasons that people are in prison are issues around income and issues around illness. That's the reason most people in prison are in prison. These are things we can address without putting people in cages and employing other people to watch the people in cages. So yes, we are talking about a wholesale re-structuring of society. Now some people say to me, and I'm getting old I'm in my late 50's, "this will take forever." That may be true, but anyone who has been paying the least attention to the news in the U.S. in the last week and a half, sees that things that take forever can happen overnight. The U.S. nationalized two major mortgage banks and the biggest insurance company in the world and in some way shape or form put up 700 billion dollars to bail out investment banks and Wall Street. If that can be done overnight, then a lot of things that we are talking about can also happen overnight if we had the political will. It takes clout.[17]

As the struggle to end mass incarceration advances, it is doubtless that new ideas and approaches will emerge, building on notions of restorative and transformative justice as well as abolition. In fact, these ideas are already in motion in many places throughout the United States.

Courtesy of WISDOM, Wisconsin

14

ORGANIZING TO END MASS INCARCERATION

The number of voices calling for a definitive end to the policy of mass incarceration has grown greatly in the past few years. A statement by the Vera Institute of Justice outlines recent progress:

> Today, there is bipartisan recognition at both the state and federal level that our over-reliance on incarceration is in need of recalibration. The imperative to maintain low crime rates without imposing unnecessary burdens on communities or taxpayers is pronounced. At least 29 states have taken steps to roll back mandatory sentences, with 32 bills passed in just the last five years. And at the federal level, with broad bipartisan support, Congress passed the Fair Sentencing Act in 2010, which eased the disparity in penalties for drug offenses involving crack versus powder cocaine.[1]

On May 25, 2014, even the editors of the *New York Times* summarized the case simply and unequivocally: "The American experiment in mass incarceration has been a moral, legal, social and economic disaster. It cannot end soon enough."[2]

If there really is an unprecedented chance to undo mass incarceration now, progressives' motives and the form of their appeal will affect the form that the changes take. Some believe that this is primarily a financial question. Inimai Chettiar, director of the Justice Program of the Brennan Center at New York University, expresses this viewpoint.

> No matter how righteous the cause, no matter how just the argument, criminal justice reform will not spring from moral or racial justice arguments alone. Lawmakers and advocates who seek an end to mass incarceration must demonstrate why it is in the self-interest of the powerful majority to enact our recommendations. Previous civil rights leaders knew this truth and applied it wisely. We have the opportunity to do the same and finally achieve change at the federal level and nationwide.[3]

Others, like Michelle Alexander, contend that this is about much more than finance. Alexander stated this concern in a Drug Policy Alliance forum.

> We see politicians across the spectrum raising concerns for the first time in forty years about the size of our prison state, and yet I worry that so much of the dialogue is driven by financial concerns rather than genuine concern for the communities that have been most impacted and the families that have been destroyed by aggressive anti-drug policies.[4]

In the midst of changing attitudes on mass incarceration, both theoretical debates and actions will continue. As we have seen in previous chapters, many people in various communities and organizations have fought in their own way to end mass incarceration. Some have worked in the formal political process for changes in laws and regulations. Others have used grassroots actions to tackle prison and jail expansion, deportation of immigrants, punitive school discipline policies, harsh sentencing regimes, the use of solitary confinement, and juvenile life without parole. Prisoners themselves have also resisted the impact of mass incarceration.

A key question is: how do we measure the success of these efforts? Four major factors

Table 14.1. Modes of Decarceration

Measures to Reduce Admissions

At point of contact with the system	Restorative practices to solve low-level conflict; citations instead of arrest for minor cases; diversion programs such as mental health courts and drug courts instead of incarceration; elimination or reduction of parole or probation violations, especially technical violations; reduction or elimination of arrests and criminal justice–linked processes in schools; reduction of bail amounts and increased use of release without bail; reduced use of detention in immigration cases.
Long-term prevention/ community development strategies	Inject resources into communities critically affected by mass incarceration for: education, job creation and training, psychological support services, substance abuse treatment, mental health facilities, and public housing; increase levels of welfare provision (e.g., TANF, SNAP, unemployment benefits); increase education and job training for people in prison; retrain police regarding racial/ethnic/gender sensitivity, use of force, restorative practices, and mental health crisis intervention; demilitarize police; increase police accountability; increase resources to public defenders.
Legislative Changes	Legalize or decriminalize drug possession; eliminate harsh local government ordinances aimed at survival activities (sleeping in public, jaywalking); reduce or eliminate criminal justice fines as a source of income for government; reform immigration law; reduce barriers to employment and to benefits for people with felony convictions; increase access to health care for the poor; shorten or eliminate terms of parole; reduce financial penalties/fines/restitution associated with criminal justice involvement; modify conspiracy laws; revoke asset forfeiture laws; cut back on the provision of military hardware to police; eliminate legal penalties for truancy and other school-related "misbehavior."

Measures to Increase Releases

Prison/jail/ court practices and policies	Increase use of non-bond pretrial release; create incentives for early release; increase use of community corrections (work release, work furlough); change charging practices to eliminate overcharging; enhance granting of good time to prisoners; retrain court and prison officials regarding racial/ethnic/gender sensitivity; cap prison or jail population and release people when the cap is exceeded.
Legislative changes	Reduce or eliminate harsh sentencing policies such as mandatory minimums, truth in sentencing, and three strikes; eliminate, moderate, or add flexibility to sentencing guidelines; make electronic monitoring the legal equivalent of incarceration; increase compassionate release of elderly, disabled, or extremely ill prisoners; give time off for family responsibility; mandate mass release of various categories of people incarcerated; reduce or stop allocations for prison and jail building and corrections operations and redirect resources to communities impacted by mass incarceration.

may help serve as key indicators of progress toward ending mass incarceration: reductions in the number of people incarcerated, increases in race and gender equity, reallocation of expenditures on corrections, and the effectiveness and appropriateness of the organizations involved.

REDUCING THE NUMBER OF PRISONERS

The first indication of success of any program for addressing mass incarceration will be the extent to which it reduces the prison and jail population, the process of decarceration. This population can be reduced in only two ways: putting fewer people behind bars or releasing more of those already imprisoned. To sustain change, the number of people admitted must be less than the number released. See Table 14.1 for details on some of the measures that could be used to achieve that result.

No major progress can be made against mass incarceration without putting a significant number of these decarceration measures in place. Different states and localities may choose different methods but unless the prison and jail population decreases by hundreds of thousands, mass incarceration remains a reality. To return to incarceration levels of the 1970s, which many prison reformers thought were excessive, would require a decrease in prison and jail populations of about 1.5 million.

ADDRESSING RACE AND GENDER INEQUITIES

Mass incarceration has been a highly racialized and gendered process, so a reduction in the overall number of people incarcerated doesn't guarantee that all will benefit equally from the changes. Several specific measures will be required to ensure equity in the process of change. A top priority would be to roll back the War on Drugs, which has excessively targeted African Americans. A key starting point would be to equalize totally penalties for crack and powder cocaine and retroactively grant immediate release to the thousands of people still incarcerated under the old, racially biased law. A similar approach to people who have received excessive sentences for other drug-related convictions would also have a major impact. In regard to Latinos, the most important step toward equity would be to reform immigration law and reverse policies such as Operation Streamline, which was highlighted in chapter 5. This change would make major progress toward reversing the massive rise in the incarceration of Latinos since the early 2000s.

A second crucial equity point would be to address racial profiling by police on the streets and in traffic stops. A police stop is frequently the first step to involvement in the criminal legal system, and research throughout the country has shown that people of color are the most likely targets for stops. This reform would also secure some relief for transgender and gender-uncertain people, who are also disproportionately profiled. While policing reform is crucial, Marc Mauer has highlighted racial disparities in "criminal justice processing" from arrest all the way through charging, bail, plea bargaining, trial process, and sentencing. Change in this arena needs to move beyond racial profiling in police stops to deliver meaningful gains in equity.[5]

A third equity point would be a reorientation of juvenile justice. At present, the harshest practices of juvenile justice are visited upon youth of color: overuse of school suspension, expulsion, and on-campus arrest for students; transferral of juvenile cases to adult courts; and excessive sentences in adult institutions. Reversal of these practices would be a major step toward equity.

A fourth equity point would be changes in parole laws and regulations and racially fair application of them. A disproportionate number of people on community supervision are people of color. Reducing or eliminating the use of technical violations as a ground for revoking someone's parole would help to reduce recidivism. Moreover, removing barriers so those with felony convictions can work and access state benefits (food stamps, family assistance, public housing, student grants) would enhance their chances to stay out of prison.

A fifth equity point would be reversal of the repressive local ordinances and regimes of court fines and fees that land millions of people in local jails every year. These laws criminalize daily survival activity of the homeless and unemployed, disproportionately people of color. These punitive local government policies also target the disabled and transgender people. Financial penalties often become the source of reincarceration or deepening poverty, which makes people more vulnerable to readmission into the criminal justice circuit.

A sixth equity point would be to reverse the rapid increase in incarceration of women in recent years, especially by halting the use of conspiracy charges against them.

REALLOCATING PRISON BUDGETS

Mass incarceration has cost billions of dollars over the past three decades. As people have begun to question mass incarceration more seriously, considerable attention has focused on the enormous allocations in federal, state, and local budgets for corrections and law enforcement. Many critics believe that the major argument against mass incarceration is financial. For example, the conservative group Right on Crime contends that the solution is to be "smart on crime." Former senator Newt Gingrich, a prominent member, contends that "there is an urgent need to address the astronomical growth in the prison population, with its huge costs in dollars and lost human potential. . . . The criminal-justice system is broken, and conservatives must lead the way in fixing it."[6] In Right on Crime's view, this means reducing spending on criminal justice while guaranteeing public safety. Right on Crime's recommendations typically include more systematic reentry programs, reduction in technical parole violations, more moderate sentences for people convicted of nonviolent offenses, and more community-based corrections programs. They also recommend more privatization of prisons and prisons operations in hopes of greater efficiency.

Some critics, such as scholar and longtime Critical Resistance member Ruth Wilson Gilmore, reject building a movement that includes conservatives, however. She argues that "opportunists have blown up real solidarity by promoting the delusion that it's possible to cherry-pick some people from the prison machine while constantly reinforcing the machine's centrality to all aspects of everyday life." She contends that the focus must remain on changing "the foundations on which mass incarceration has been built—structural racism and structural poverty and capitalism devouring the planet. . . . It's likely allies, *not* unlikely ones, who must form a united front if we are ever to win this freedom struggle."[7] Like Gilmore, proponents of the justice reinvestment approach don't believe that ending mass incarceration will necessarily save money. They argue that the cost of mass incarceration cannot be measured simply by the amount that federal, state, and local governments spend on corrections. They also count the damage to communities counted in lost lives and in diminished productivity. A justice-reinvestment approach would combine decarceration and alternatives to incarceration to reduce spending, and then redirect the savings into the people and communities that have been critically impacted by high incarceration rates.

To make this dream a reality, in 2002 the Council on State Governments and the Pew Center launched the Justice Reinvestment Initiative with considerable federal funding. The initiative set up programs in eleven states, combining research, policy development, implementation, and assessment. Perhaps the biggest success took place in Texas. In the Lone Star State, a combination of relaxing parole conditions and providing more access to substance abuse and reentry programs contributed to a drop in prison population at a time when experts had predicted a seventeen-thousand-bed expansion.[8] The Justice Reinvestment Initiative claimed a number of other successes.

After eight years of the Justice Reinvestment Initiative, however, a number of early supporters wrote a critique. They argued that it had veered from its original goal of reducing prison populations and reinvesting in communities. Instead, they contended, program directors had settled for reducing prison growth rather than cutting absolute numbers, and they had directed funding to law enforcement rather than communities. Here is part of the critique, published in 2010 as *Ending Mass Incarceration: Charting a New Justice Reinvestment*:

> This may be the perfect "teachable moment" to raise our collective consciousness (and conscience) and make clear how the progressive agenda cannot be achieved without dismantling the U.S. punishment system. The reasoning is clear: the combination of excessive incarceration and harsh punishment is a blunt instrument for social control that perpetuates the country's painful, historical legacy of

injustice and inequality and deprives masses of black and brown people unfairly of freedom and opportunity. It is the site of today's civil rights struggle. So while Justice Reinvestment may not be *the* answer, it could perhaps be a good instrument for righting some wrongs and setting some people free. But to do so, it needs a new orientation, and a new future.[9]

This ongoing debate highlights the differing orientations of people engaged in contesting mass incarceration. For some, slow incremental change appears to be the goal and perhaps even the limit of possibility. For others, small steps represent compromises that serve as much to sustain the system as change it.

EFFECTIVE ORGANIZATIONS

Michelle Alexander argues that "nothing short of a major social movement" can end mass incarceration. She believes that "meaningful reforms can be achieved without such a movement, but unless the public consensus supporting the current system is completely overturned, the basic structure of the . . . system will remain intact."[10] While many people accept the need for such a movement, building it is a complicated task. A key question is how to strike an effective balance between tactics and strategy. Most people wanting to end mass incarceration would agree that at least three things are required: (1) changes in laws, regulations, and policies in the criminal justice system; (2) increased education and mobilization of a wide range of communities and organizations on the issue; and (3) a reallocation of resources away from corrections.

The central issues relate to emphasis and process. Pushing for changes in laws and policies in the criminal justice arena is crucial. Blocking funding for further prison and jail expansion is important, but without eliminating the laws that were used to create mass incarceration in the first place, such as mandatory minimums and truth in sentencing, decarceration falls off the agenda. The key issue is how to achieve these legal changes and what kinds of organizations are required to do so. A range of possibilities exists. One would be to focus almost entirely on leg-

National Academy of Sciences Report

In 2014 a team of experts produced a 464-page study for the National Academy of Sciences titled *The Growth of Incarceration in the United States: Exploring Causes and Consequences*. In the concluding chapter, the authors made some recommendations.

> Based on our analysis of the evidence, we urge policy makers at the state and national levels to reconsider policies in three distinct domains: (1) sentencing policy, (2) prison policy, and (3) social policy. Doing so will require political will. Just as the expansion of the penal system was driven by changes in policy, it must be reversed through policy choices. Most fundamentally, reversing course will require state and federal policy makers to significantly reform sentencing policy. The development of new penal policies will depend, in turn, on a new public consensus that current policies have been, on balance, more harmful than effective and are inconsistent with U.S. history and notions of justice. Making this case to the public will require determined political leadership.[11]

islation and elections, relying on experts and lobbyists to advance the cause of decarceration in state legislatures and the U.S. Congress. The important targets for persuasion would be the few elected officials who propel legislative initiatives. A central focus of a social movement with this strategy would be supporting specific measures and backing candidates at all levels with a decarceration agenda. Central to such an effort would be winning the support of people all along the political spectrum, regardless of political affiliation or their positions on other issues.

ALLIANCES WITH SOCIAL MOVEMENTS

A second approach, while acknowledging the need for changes in laws and support for political candidates, would situate the struggle for change in the criminal justice system in the context of a broader movement for social justice. Demands for changes in laws and policies related to incarceration would be linked to campaigns against poverty and inequality. Outreach would build alliances with other social movements—climate justice, demilitarization, workers' rights, and racial and gender justice. This grassroots approach would be a departure from connecting with conservative officials merely because they support progress on one issue. This approach would also involve less traditional forms of organization and process, making use of network building, decision by consensus, and nonhierarchical structures. The purpose would be not only to end mass incarceration but also to build a sustainable movement for a fundamentally different type of society.

It should be noted that these approaches are not mutually exclusive. Those working primarily in legislatures or Congress would need to build links to organizations involved in other issues. Similarly, people building a broader social justice movement would sometimes need to make common cause with conservatives who back decarceration, prison closures, or other limited progressive steps. The primary consideration on either path is to choose strategies and tactics that work, choices that can never be absolutely certain ahead of time.

Regardless of approach, a social movement must confront at least three additional strategic tasks.

"Awareness Is Not Enough"

Talk and actions are not the same thing . . . there is a need to move beyond awareness and take steps to address mass incarceration in real ways . . . the rationale for and logic of punishment is unchanged. The targets of our punishment mindset also remain overwhelmingly black and poor.

—Mariame Kaba, director of Project NIA, Chicago[12]

GETTING REPRESENTATION RIGHT

The first critical issue is how to make organizations and campaign structures representative in terms of race, ethnicity, gender, and class. In particular, organizations will need to assess the extent to which they include formerly imprisoned people and their loved ones in leadership roles.

In recent years a number of organizations have emerged that argue that formerly incarcerated people and their loved ones must necessarily play a leading role in the struggle against mass incarceration. One such group, All of Us or None, which was founded in Oakland in 2005, states that their existence "is a concrete manifestation of the people affected by an evil building a movement to combat it." Organizations such as All of Us or None emphasize the important role to be played by people who remain in prison. They memorialize some of the major actions taken by organized prisoners, such as the hunger strikes in California prisons in 2011–13, initiated in the Pelican Bay security housing unit against solitary confinement.

DEFINING ALLIES

A second critical issue is how a movement chooses its allies, especially how it engages with law enforcement personnel, criminal justice officials, business, and political conservatives. During much of the era of mass incarceration, most of those involved in resistance avoided coalitions or mutual planning structures with police, prison guards, corrections officials, and the political right. For some, however, the ground has shifted. Some people argue that there has been a "convergence of agendas" between groups that formerly stood on opposite sides of the criminal justice fence. Right on Crime is one example of a group of conservatives who have changed their views. In addition, in certain cases, former law enforcement officials have come out strongly against important aspects of mass incarceration. Lastly, major corporations with long histories of conservative activism have become

Law Enforcement Against the Drug War

One of the most unusual groups to contest mass incarceration has been Law Enforcement Against Prohibition (LEAP). Made up of former drug war cops, prosecutors, judges, and others with a history of carrying out the War on Drugs, LEAP now opposes what it calls "prohibition" and instead advocates for the decriminalization and medicalization of drugs. Its principles state that adult drug abuse is a "health problem and not a law-enforcement matter" and condemn the "inordinate amount of" prosecutions of drug crimes. LEAP's executive director, Major Neill Franklin, spent thirty-four years in law enforcement, including a lengthy period as a narcotics agent.[13]

deeply involved in criminal justice reform. For example, Koch Industries, through its foundations and institutes, has given millions to sentencing reform projects and efforts to promote bipartisan unity on criminal justice.

In response to the changing terrain, many people who have spent years fighting mass incarceration fear that working too closely with nontraditional allies will create the risk of co-optation and compromise, a repackaging of mass incarceration with changes that lack substance. Appropriate alliances are crucial because the whole is often greater than the sum of its parts. As Larry Hamm, chairman of the Newark-based People's Organization for Progress, puts it, "What they're worried about now is [that] there's a potential for us to build alliances with other groups that have been economically disenfranchised in the last few decades, and that there could be an even wider societal response to the suffering that's going on in this country."[14]

OFFERING REAL ALTERNATIVES

A third key issue is to define genuine alternatives to incarceration. Some would argue that anything that keeps people out of jail or prison is an alternative. Others contend that an alternative must not only decarcerate but also embody an abandonment of the punishment paradigm, falling more in line with principles of restorative, transformative, or abolitionist notions of justice.

Electronic monitoring highlights this tension. Being on a monitor means freedom from prison or jail, but often the strict regimes of house arrest and exclusion zones lead some to conclude that electronic monitoring amounts to "virtual incarceration."

Similar ambivalence has emerged about other measures labeled "alternatives" or "diversions." For example, drug courts have been implemented as a diversion from jail in more than two thousand jurisdictions throughout the country. In drug courts, individuals facing drug charges have the option of entering a strict program of treatment instead of going to jail. Failure to follow the treatment regime results in incarceration. A number of drug courts have claimed considerable success in lowering recidivism rates.

Research by the Drug Policy Alliance and the Justice Policy Institute shows that the harshness of treatment programs makes failure a high probability, however. The Drug Policy Alliance has concluded that drug courts "provide few, if any, benefits over the incarceration model on which they seek to improve. Alternatives to incarceration for drug possession remain essential, but better alternatives must be adopted and incarceration for drug law violations should be reduced through sentencing reform."[15]

The debate over the categorization and viability of alternatives, and over gradualism versus focusing on major systemic change, will remain at the center of the struggle to end mass incarceration for quite some time. Author-activist Dan Berger raises some key concerns about prison reform as opposed to abolition.

> Even as many states move to shrink their prison populations, they have done so in ways that have left in place the deepest markings of the carceral state, such as the use of life sentences and solitary confinement, and the criminalization of immigrants. Social movements will need to confront the underlying ideologies that hold that there is an "acceptable" level of widespread imprisonment. . . . There is a risk, inherent in the sordid history of prison reform, that the current reform impulse will be bifurcated along poorly defined notions of "deservingness" that will continue to uphold the carceral logic that separates "good people" from "bad people" and which decides that no fate is too harsh for those deemed unworthy of social inclusion.[16]

In 2014 Angela Davis sounded a similar warning but also pointed to the hope of a much improved society if we are able to seize the opportunity.

> I think that this is a pivotal moment. There are openings. And I think it's very important to point out that people have been struggling over these issues for years and for decades. This is also a problematic moment. And those of us who identify as prison abolitionists, as opposed to prison reformers, make the point that oftentimes reforms create situations where mass incarceration becomes even more entrenched; and so, therefore, we have to think about what in the long run will

produce decarceration, fewer people behind bars, and hopefully, eventually, in the future, the possibility of imagining a landscape without prisons, where other means are used to address issues of harm, where social problems, such as illiteracy and poverty, do not lead vast numbers of people along a trajectory that leads to prison.[17]

STATES THAT LEAD THE WAY

While the debates about growing a social movement unfold, in several states considerable change already has taken place. Two states that have led the way in decarceration are New York and Colorado.

New York has gone furthest down the road of decarceration. From 1999 to 2012, the prison population in New York State decreased by 26 percent, and eleven prisons closed.[18] Law enforcement officials attributed this result to crime reduction by hot-spot policing and zero tolerance. Activists Judith Greene and Marc Mauer instead credit "a remarkable change in drug enforcement policy in 1999 that entailed an unprecedented curtailing of NYPD's 'war on drugs.'" They argued that these changes largely came about as the result of the work of civil society groups, such as the Correctional Association's "Drop the Rock" campaign and the Drug Policy Alliance's Real Reform coalition, which exposed the moral bankruptcy of aggressive drug prosecutions, along with work by the New York Civil Liberties Union. Eventually the public and then key officials, such as former Brooklyn district attorney Charles J. Hynes, began to change their views.[19]

Reforms to laws, such as the removal of mandatory minimum sentences, contributed to a decline in drug arrests, from 40,361 in 2008 to 29,960 in 2012. Moreover, while stop-and-frisk policy earned New York City a New Jim Crow label, the proportion of Blacks among drug arrestees actually decreased, according to figures from the state Division of Criminal Justice Services—from 42 percent of the total in 2008 to 35 percent in 2012.[20] In many cases, police issued citations rather than carrying out arrests. In other instances, instead of handing down penitentiary time, authorities channeled thousands through treatment-based diversions, such as drug courts. Relaxing conditions of parole was also part of the new approach, precipitating a huge reduction in returns to prison for technical violations. Even with all these changes, however, New York State's per capita incarceration rate in 2012 remained at 425 per 100,000, well below the then national average of 728 but about four times that of the United Kingdom and five times the rate in Sweden.

In Colorado, a statewide coalition has been the key to progress. In 1999 a few groups came together to support legislation to stop state prison expansion. Though this effort failed, the campaigners stayed together to form the Colorado Criminal Justice Reform Coalition. After over a decade of organization building, the coalition included more than a hundred affiliates throughout the state. The coalition supported successful campaigns to oppose prison and jail construction in Pueblo, Lamar, Fort Collins, and Ault. It also mobilized people in support of successful drug-policy and parole reform. In addition, the coalition prioritized education work, delivering more than 275 presentations to communities and policy makers. Its publications include a ninety-page resource guide titled *Parenting from Prison* and a reentry handbook called *Getting On After Getting Out*. It has distributed more than sixteen thousand copies of each of these publications.

Efforts by the Colorado Criminal Justice Reform Coalition contributed to a sea change in Colorado corrections. Total prison population declined by just over 7 percent from 2009 to 2012, and four prisons closed during that period. One of the key campaigns focused on the passage of Senate Bill 250, which drastically reduced sentences for drug offenses. This law complemented the 2012 referendum that legalized marijuana, providing multiple paths for people to avoid incarceration for drug charges.[21]

WHEN DOES MASS INCARCERATION END?

Marc Mauer, director of the Sentencing Project, estimated in 2014 that at the rate of decrease in the prison population from 2009 to 2012, it would take eighty-eight years to reach the per capita incarceration rates of 1980, clearly too long.[22] Mauer's scenario raises another question. Can mass incarceration be ended without a massive release of people from prisons and jails?

Even if such a mass release did take place, when could we actually pronounce mass incarceration dead? Is Mauer's reference point, 1980, the goal? Has it ended when all the harsh sentencing laws are off the books? When racial bias has been removed from our police and court practices? When a certain number of prisons and jails have been closed down? When everyone on parole or probation is employed and adequately housed?

Or is an end to mass incarceration more a spiritual or philosophical tipping point, beyond which criminal justice focuses on developing human beings and creating opportunities for communities rather than punishing criminals who are regarded as second-class citizens? Is it a moment when youth of color feel free to walk down the street without worrying about harassment or arrest and when women or transgender folks have no fear of physical or sexual violence?

For some people, mass incarceration may not end until every prison is shuttered, until the United States has become a society where even those guilty of the most harmful acts are given the opportunity for redemption and to be treated with the respect all human beings deserve.

For the moment, the United States remains a long way from an end to mass incarceration. Understanding how the system works, in particular who wins and who loses from the largest expansion of carceral facilities in human history, is an important starting point, but there is much more to be done.

NOTES

INTRODUCTION

1. Eddie Ellis, "Words Matter: Another Look at the Question of Language," Center for Nu-Leadership on Urban Solutions, New York, 2013.

1: A SNAPSHOT OF THE SYSTEM

1. Chris Hedges, "Why Mass Incarceration Defines Us as a Society," *Smithsonian*, December 2, 2012.

2. Scott Cohn, "Private Prison Industry Grows Despite Critics," *Today*, October 18, 2011.

3. Pew Research Center on the States, "One in 100: Behind Bars in America 2008," February 2008, 5.

4. International Centre for Prison Studies website, "From Highest to Lowest—Prison Population Rate," accessed July 27, 2014.

5. John Schmitt et al., *The High Budgetary Cost of Incarceration* (Washington, DC: Center for Economic Policy Research, 2010), 12; and Christian Henrichson and Ruth Delaney, *The Price of Prisons: What Incarceration Costs Taxpayers* (New York: Vera Institute of Justice, 2012).

6. Laura M. Maruschak and Erika Parks, *Probation and Parole in the United States* (Washington, DC: Department of Justice, 2011).

7. International Centre for Prison Studies, "World Prison Brief," accessed July 27, 2014, http://www.prisonstudies.org/highest-to-lowest/prison_population_rate?field_region_taxonomy_tid=All. Figures for countries other than the United States are for 2012.

8. Bureau of Justice Statistics, Annual Reports on Prisoners and Corrections, 2013, Department of Justice, Washington, DC.

9. Ibid.

10. International Centre for Prison Studies, "World Prison Brief."

11. Henrichson and Delaney, *Price of Prisons*.

12. Sentencing Project, "U.S. Felony Disenfranchisement Laws by State," Washington, DC, April 2014.

13. Joshua Rovner, "Juvenile Life Without Parole: An Overview," Sentencing Project, Washington, DC, 2014.

14. John DiIulio Jr. and William Bennett, *Body Count: Moral Poverty . . . and How to Win America's War Against Crime and Drugs* (New York: Simon & Schuster, 1996), 17.

15. Michelle Alexander, *The New Jim Crow: Mass Incarceration in the Age of Colorblindness* (New York: The New Press, 2009), 208.

16. Most official statistics on incarceration use the terms *Black*, *white*, and *Hispanic*. When referring to those figures, that terminology will be used here. Otherwise, where appropriate, I will use *African American* and *Latino/Latina*.

17. Unless otherwise specified, all figures for national and state prison populations are from annual reports in the "Prisoners" series, Bureau of Justice Statistics, Department of Justice, Washington, DC, 1980–2012.

18. National Gay and Lesbian Task Force and National Center for Transgender Equality, *Injustice at Every Turn: A Report of the National Transgender Discrimination Survey* (Washington, DC: 2011).

19. Quoted in Matt Clarke, "Celebrity Justice: Prison Lifestyles of the Rich and Famous," *Prison Legal News*, November 28, 2014.

20. Dana Ford, "Judge Orders Texas Teen Ethan Couch to Rehab for Driving Drunk, Killing 4," CNN, February 6, 2014.

21. Deanna Boyd, "Troubled Teen Is Being Treated at a State Hospital in Vernon," *Star-Telegram*, April 11, 2014.

22. Alexander, *New Jim Crow*, 99.

23. Benjamin Todd Jealous and Lateefah Simon, "The Root: We Can't Afford Not to Fix the Justice System," National Public Radio, April 7, 2011.

24. Steven D. Levitt, "The Effect of Prison Population Size on Crime Rates: Evidence from Prison Overcrowding Litigation," *Quarterly Journal of Economics* 111, no. 2 (1996): 319–51; and James Q. Wilson, "Do the Crime, Do the Time," *Los Angeles Times*, March 30, 2008.

25. Ruth Wilson Gilmore, *Golden Gulag: Prisons, Surplus, Crisis, and Opposition in Globalizing California* (Berkeley: University of California Press, 2008).

26. Loïc Wacquant, *Punishing the Poor: The Neoliberal Government of Social Insecurity* (Durham, NC: Duke University Press, 2009).

27. Tara Herivel and Paul Wright, eds., *Prison Profiteers: Who Makes Money from Mass Incarceration* (New York: The New Press, 2009).

28. Angela Y. Davis, "Masked Racism: Reflections on the Prison Industrial Complex," *Colorlines*, September 10, 1998.

29. Alexander, *New Jim Crow*, 44.

30. Davis, "Masked Racism."

31. Todd Clear and Natasha Frost, *The Punishment Imperative: The Rise and Failure of Mass Incarceration in America* (New York: New York University Press, 2013).

2: BUILDING POPULAR SUPPORT FOR GROWING THE PRISON SYSTEM

1. Martin Luther King Jr., "Letter from a Birmingham Jail," 1963.

2. Laurence M. Baskir and William A. Strauss, *Chance and Circumstance: The Draft, the War, and the Vietnam Generation* (New York: Knopf, 1978), 69.

3. Marlo Thomas, Elizabeth Mitchell, and Carl Robbins, eds., *The Right Words at the Right Time* (New York: Atria Books, 2002), 100.

4. National Advisory Commission on Criminal Justice Standards and Goals, *Task Force Report on Corrections* (Washington, DC: Government Printing Office, 1973).

5. Gallup Poll, "Death Penalty," www.gallup.com/poll/1606/death-penalty.aspx?version=print.

6. Hindelang Criminal Justice Research Center, Sourcebook of Criminal Justice Statistics, 2012, School of Criminal Justice, University at Albany, www.albany.edu/sourcebook.

7. National Advisory Commission on Criminal Justice Standards and Goals, *Task Force Report on Corrections*, 358.

8. "United Prisoners Union Bill of Rights," United Prisoners Union, 1970.

9. Ibid.

10. Cited in Kathleen Beckett and Theodore Sassoon, "The Origins of the Current Conservative Discourse on Law and Order," in *Defending Justice: An Activist's Resource Kit*, ed. Palak Shah (Somerville, MA: Political Research Associates, 2005), via Public Eye, www.publiceye.org/defendingjustice/getstarted/getstartedmain.html, 53.

11. Richard Nixon, State of the Union Address, 1970.

12. *Frontline*, "A Teacher's Guide to the War on Drugs," Public Broadcasting Service, 2009.

13. Nancy E. Marion, *A History of Federal Crime Control Initiatives, 1960–1993* (New York: Praeger, 1994).

14. Disaster Center, "U.S. Crime Rates, 1960–2013," accessed October 12, 2014, http://www.disastercenter.com/crime/uscrime.htm.

15. Bureau of Justice Statistics, Annual Reports on Prisoners, 1980–89, Department of Justice, Washington, DC.

16. Via GovTrack.us.

17. Quoted in Scott Cohn, "Private Industry Grows Despite Critics," *Today*, October 18, 2011.

18. Michelle Alexander, *The New Jim Crow: Mass Incarceration in the Age of Colorblindness* (New York: The New Press, 2009), 152

19. Ibid.

20. Naomi Murakawa, *The First Civil Right: How Liberals Built Prison in America* (New York: Oxford University Press, 2014).

21. Melissa Hickman Barlow, "Race and the Problem of Crime in *Time* and *Newsweek* Cover Stories, 1946 to 1995," *Social Justice* 25, no. 2 (Summer 1998): 155.

22. "'Welfare Queen' Becomes Issue in Reagan Campaign," *New York Times*, February 15, 2002, 51.

23. Cited in Frank Gilliam, "The 'Welfare Queen' Experiment: How Viewers React to Images of African-American Mothers on Welfare," *Nieman Reports* 53, no. 2 (1999).

24. Duchess Harris, *Black Feminist Politics from Kennedy to Clinton* (New York: Palgrave Macmillan, 2009), 123.

25. Julilly Kohler-Hausmann, "The Crime of Survival: Fraud Prosecutions, Community Surveillance, and the Original 'Welfare Queen,'" *Journal of Social History* 41, no. 2 (2007): 330.

26. Loïc Wacquant, *Punishing the Poor: The Neoliberal Government of Social Insecurity* (Durham, NC: Duke University Press, 2009), 84.

27. Prison Radio, "A Year In—More Same Than Change," January 31, 2010.

28. Kelly Welch, "Black Criminal Stereotypes and Racial Profiling," *Journal of Contemporary Criminal Justice* 23, no. 3 (2007).

29. Inside Politics, "Candidate Ads: 1988 George Bush 'Revolving Door,'" www.insidepolitics.org/ps111/candidateads.html.

30. Morgan Whitaker, "The Legacy of the Willie Horton Ad Lives On, 25 Years Later," MSNBC, October 28, 2013.

31. Cited in Eugene Borgida, Christopher M. Frederico, and John L. Sullivan, eds., *The Political Psychology of Democratic Citizenship* (New York: Oxford University Press, 2009).

32. Elayne Rapping, *Law and Justice as Seen on TV* (New York: New York University Press, 2003), 75.

33. Dennis Rome, *Black Demons: The Media's Depiction of the African American Male Criminal Stereotype* (Westport, CT: Praeger, 2004), 4.

34. Designed by John Sebelius, son of then Kansas governor Kathleen Sebelius, a description of this game can be found at the website of BoardGameGeek.

35. Tracy Huling, "Building a Prison Economy in Rural America," in *Invisible Punishment: The Collateral Consequences of Mass Imprisonment*, ed. Marc Mauer and Meda Chesney-Lind (New York: The New Press), 208–9.

3: "LOCK 'EM UP AND THROW AWAY THE KEY": THE RISE OF MASS INCARCERATION

1. Cited in Bert Useem and Peter Kimball, *States of Siege: U.S. Prison Riots, 1971–1986* (New York: Oxford University Press, 1989), 236.

2. Peter A. Mancuso, "Resentencing After the Fall of Rockefeller: The Failure of the Drug Law Reform Acts of 2004 and 2005 to Remedy the Injustices of New York's Rockefeller Drug Laws and the Compromise of 2009," *Albany Law Review* 73, no. 4 (2010): 1535–81.

3. Ashlea Surles, "An Unforgettable Mistake: William G. Milliken and Michigan's Mandatory Minimum Sentencing Program," *Michigan Journal of History* 5, no. 1 (Fall 2007): 1–21.

4. Patrick Leahy, "Bipartisan Legislation to Give Judges More Flexibility for Federal Sentences Introduced," press release, Washington, DC, March 20, 2013.

5. Paula M. Ditton and Doris James Wilson, *Truth in Sentencing in State Prisons* (Washington, DC: Bureau of Justice Statistics, Department of Justice, 1999).

6. Bureau of Justice Statistics, "Violent Crime Control and Law Enforcement Act," Department of Justice, Washington, DC, 1994.

7. Susan Turner et al., "National Evaluation of the Violent Offender Incarceration/Truth-in-Sentencing Incentive Grant Program," Department of Justice, Washington, DC, 2001.

8. Eric Lotke, Jason Colburn, and Vincent Schiraldi, "3 Strikes & You're Out: An Examination of the Impact of Strikes Laws 10 Years After Their Enactment," Justice Policy Institute, Washington, DC, 2004.

9. Information on Angelos and Jones from Erika Eichelberger, "Meet Five of the Low-Level Drug Offenders Obama Could Set Free," *Mother Jones*, April 24, 2014; information on Aaron from Cora Currier, "Obama Tells Clarence Aaron He Can Finally Go Home," *ProPublica*, December 19, 2013.

10. John Tierney, "For Lesser Crimes, Rethinking Life Behind Bars," *New York Times*, December 11, 2012.

11. Matt Taibbi, "Cruel and Unusual Punishment: The Shame of Three Strikes Laws," *Rolling Stone*, March 27, 2013.

12. "Kennedy Discusses Sentencing, Foundations of Freedom," Third Branch, September 2003.

13. Ashley Nellis, *Life Goes On: The Historic Rise in Life Sentences in America* (Washington, DC: Sentencing Project, 2013).

14. Ashley Nellis and Ryan S. King, *No Exit: The Expanding Use of Life Sentences in America* (Washington, DC: Sentencing Project, 2009).

15. Ibid.

16. Ibid.; and American Civil Liberties Union, "A Living Death: Life Without Parole for Nonviolent Offenses," New York, 2013.

17. "All states allow juveniles to be tried as adults in criminal court under certain circumstances." Office of Juvenile Justice and Delinquency Prevention, *Juvenile Justice: A Century of Change* (Washington, DC: Office of Justice Programs, Department of Justice, 1999).

18. *60 Minutes*, CBS TV, June 21, 2009.

19. Joseph Dole, "Writing from Prison," posted to Real Cost of Prisons Project, 2008.

20. Clark County [Washington] Prosecuting Attorney, "The Death Penalty in the U.S.," accessed September 14, 2014, http://www.clarkprosecutor.org/html/death/dpusa.htm.

21. Bureau of Justice Statistics, "Prisoners in 2012: Trends in Admissions and Releases 1991–2012," Department of Justice, Washington, DC, 2013.

22. Jamie Fellner, "Dispatches: Ever More US Prisoners Growing Old Behind Bars," Human Rights Watch, New York, February 9, 2015.

23. Innocence Project, "About Us," New York.

24. Ed Pilkington, "Innocent US Prisoners Exonerated in 2014 at Highest Levels in 25 Years," *The Guardian*, January 27, 2015.

25. Department of Justice, Memorandum on the Fair Sentencing Act, April 5, 2005.

26. U.S. Sentencing Commission, *Mandatory Minimum Penalties in the Federal Criminal Justice System*, special report to Congress (Washington, DC: Department of Justice, 1991).

27. Tushar Kansal, "Racial Disparity in Sentencing: A Review of the Literature," Sentencing Project, Washington, DC, 2005.

28. Legislative Analyst's Office, California, "A Primer: Three Strikes—the Impact After More Than a Decade," October 2005, www.lao .ca.gov/2005/3_strikes/3_strikes_102005.htm.

29. Nellis and King, *No Exit*, 5.

30. Nellis, *Life Goes On*, 9.

31. Amnesty International, "Death by Discrimination: The Continuing Role of Race in Capital Cases," New York, 2003.

32. Testimony of Marc Mauer, executive director, Sentencing Project, "The Impact of Mandatory Minimum Penalties in Federal Sentencing," prepared for U.S. Sentencing Commission, May 27, 2010.

4: THE WAR ON DRUGS

1. Jennifer Robinson, "Decades of Drug Use: Data from the 60s and 70s," Gallup Poll, July 2, 2002.

2. Hamilton Wright, *Report of the International Opium Commission and on the Opium Problem as Seen Within the United States and Its Possessions*, in "Opium Problem: Message from the President of the United States," doc. no. 377, 61st Cong., 2d sess. (1910), 50.

3. Katherine Beckett, *Making Crime Pay: Law and Order in Contemporary American Politics* (New York: Oxford University Press, 1999), cited in Michelle Alexander, *The New Jim Crow: Mass Incarceration in the Age of Colorblindness* (New York: The New Press, 2009), 49–54.

4. Richard Nixon, "Special Message to the Congress on Drug Abuse Prevention and Control," June 17, 1971.

5. Ibid.

6. Jimmy Carter, "Drug Abuse Message to the Congress," August 2, 1977.

7. "Nancy Reagan," National First Ladies Library, Canton, OH.

8. "Michael Jackson and the Flintstone Kids" (Just Say No campaign), YouTube, February 4, 2011.

9. Ronald J. Ostrow, "Even Casual Drug Users Should Be Shot, Gates Says," *Los Angeles Times*, September 6, 1990.

10. Jennifer Gonnerman, "Truth or D.A.R.E.: The Dubious Drug Education Program Takes New York," *Village Voice*, April 7, 1999.

11. National Drug Strategy Network, "The Debate Over D.A.R.E," May–June 1997, http://www2.potsdam.edu/alcohol/InTheNews/UnderageDrinking/20061227111716.html.

12. Glen Ford, "Last Days of 'Cracked-Up Black Runs Amok' Law," *Black Agenda Report*, May 5, 2009.

13. Peter Kraska and Louis Cubellis, "Militarizing Mayberry and Beyond: Making Sense of American Paramilitiary Policing," *Justice Quarterly* 14, no. 4 (1997): 607–29.

14. Radley Balko, "A Decade After 9/11, Police Departments Are Increasingly Militarized," *Huffington Post*, September 12, 2011.

15. Bradford Plumer, "SWAT Teams Everywhere," *Mother Jones*, January 12, 2006.

16. Brian Dolinar, "The Banality of Police Militarization: How Champaign-Urbana Acquired Its MRAP," *Truthout*, August 26, 2014.

17. "Trigger-Happy Britain? How Police Shootings Compare," Channel 4 News, BBC, January 9, 2014.

18. Marian Williams, Jefferson Holcomb, Tomislav Kovandzic, and Scott Bullock, *Policing for Profit: The Abuse of Civil Asset Forfeiture* (Arlington, VA: Institute for Justice, 2010), 18.

19. Ibid., 27.

20. Ibid., 5.

21. "From Public Enemy to Enemy of the State," *The Defenestrator*, July 6, 2008.

22. Cited in Balko, "A Decade After 9/11."

23. Ibid.; and "The Anti Drug Super Bowl XXXVI Ad Terrorists 2002," YouTube, October 30, 2013, http://adland.tv/commercials/anti-drug-terrorists-2002-30-usa.

24. Chuck Murphy and Sydney P. Freed-berg, "Three Stoplights, Seven M-16s," *St. Petersburg Times*, March 2, 2003.

25. Mark Stevenson, "El Chapo, Mexican Drug Lord, Makes Forbes' Billionaire List," *Huffington Post*, March 11, 2009.

26. Ed Vulliamy, "Mexico's War on Drugs Is One Big Lie," *The Guardian*, August 31, 2013.

27. Witness for Peace Southwest, "Drug War," 2014, http://wfpsw.org/tag/drug-war.

28. Marc Mauer and Ryan S. King, *A 25-Year Quagmire: The War on Drugs and Its Impact on American Society* (Washington, DC: Sentencing Project, 2007), 3.

29. American Civil Liberties Union, "The War on Marijuana in Black and White," New York, June 2013.

30. "Crime in the United States 2013—Arrests," in *FBI Uniform Crime Report* (Washington, DC: Department of Justice, 2014).

31. Erica Goode, "Incarceration Rates for Blacks Have Fallen Sharply, Report Shows," *New York Times*, February 27, 2013.

32. Saki Knafo, "When It Comes to Drugs, Whites Do the Crime, Blacks Do the Time," *Huffington Post*, September 17, 2013.

33. *The House I Live In*, directed by Eugene Jarecki (New York: Charlotte Street Films, 2012).

34. Ibid.

35. Kraska and Cubellis, "Militarizing Mayberry," 143.

36. William Bennett, "The Top Drug Warrior Talks Tough," *Fortune*, March 12, 1990.

37. Ronald Reagan, Remarks at the Annual Meeting of the International Association of Chiefs of Police in New Orleans, LA, September 28, 1981.

38. Jamie Fellner, "Race, Drugs, and Law Enforcement in the United States," *Stanford Law & Policy Review* 20, no. 2 (2009): 257–91; see also Alexander, *New Jim Crow*; Marc Mauer, *Race to Incarcerate* (New York: The New Press, 2006); and Loïc Wacquant, *Prisons of Poverty* (Minneapolis: University of Minnesota Press, 2009).

39. Cited in Knafo, "When It Comes to Drugs."

5: THE WAR ON IMMIGRANTS

1. Tyler Anbinder, *Nativism and Slavery: The Northern Know Nothings and the Politics of the 1850s* (New York: Oxford University Press, 1994).

2. Teacherweb.com, "Chinese Immigration in the 1800s," Student Handout 1-2A, accessed October 23, 2014.

3. Heidi Beirich, "The Anti-Immigrant Movement," Extremist Files, Southern Poverty Law Center website.

4. "The Palmer Raids," Library of Congress, Newspaper and Current Periodical Reading Room, n.d.

5. "Operation Wetback," 2013, Texas State Historical Association; and James Kilgore, "The New Operation Wetback," *Counterpunch*, August 4, 2011.

6. Human Rights Watch, "Forced Apart: Families Separated and Immigrants Harmed by United States Deportation Policy," New York, July 2007.

7. Human Rights Watch, "Presumption of Guilt: Human Rights Abuses of Post–September 11 Detainees," New York, August 2002.

8. Government Accountability Office, "Secure Border Initiative Fence Construction Costs," January 29, 2009.

9. Coalición de Derechos Humanos, "Missing Migrant Project: Introduction," accessed February 27, 2015, http://derechoshumanosaz.net /projects/arizona-recovered-bodies-project/.

10. White House, "Continuing to Strengthen Border Security," November 20, 2014.

11. Mark Grey, Michele Devlin, and Aaron Goldsmith, *Postville, U.S.A.: Surviving Diversity in Small-Town America* (Boston: GemmaMedia, 2009), 20.

12. Griselda Nevarez, "Deported Veterans Want to Return Home," *Huffington Post*, April 26, 2013.

13. Jorge Rivas, "Arizona Woman Deported After Winning Casino Jackpot," *Colorlines*, January 4, 2013.

14. Reece Jones, "Something There Is That Doesn't Love a Wall," *New York Times*, August 27, 2012.

15. Alistair Graham Robertson, Rachel Beaty, Jane Atkinson, and Bob Libal, *Operation Streamline: Costs and Consequences* (Austin, TX: Grassroots Leadership, 2012).

16. Immigration Policy Center, "Secure

Communities: A Fact Sheet," Washington, DC, November 29, 2011.

17. Silky Shah, "A Decade of Detention: The Post 9/11 Immigrant Dragnet," *SAMAR— South Asian Magazine for Action and Reflection*, no. 37 (September 11, 2011).

18. Jose Antonio Vargas, "My Life as an Undocumented Immigrant," *New York Times Magazine*, June 22, 2011.

19. Dennis J. Bernstein, "An Interview with Jose Antonio Vargas," *The Progressive*, July 20, 2014.

20. Immigration and Customs Enforcement, "ICE Total Removals" (fiscal year 2012).

21. U.S. Sentencing Commission, "Quick Facts: Illegal Reentry Offenses" (fiscal year 2012).

22. U.S. Census, 2010.

23. E. Ann Carson and William J. Sabol, *Prisoners in 2011* (Washington, DC: Bureau of Justice Statistics, Department of Justice, 2012).

24. Cody Mason, *Dollars and Detainees: The Growth of For-Profit Detention* (Washington, DC: Sentencing Project, 2012).

25. Joseph Pugliese, *State Violence and the Execution of Law: Biopolitcal Caesurae of Torture, Black Sites, Drones* (New York: Routledge, 2013), 24.

26. American Civil Liberties Union, "Warehoused and Forgotten: Immigrants Trapped in Our Shadow Private Prison System," New York, 2014.

27. Cited in Gaetano Prampolini and Annamarai Pinazzi, *The Shade of the Saguaro: Essays on the Literary Cultures of the American Southwest* (Firenze, Italy: Firenze University Press, 2013), 478.

28. Deepa Fernandes, *Targeted: National Security and the Business of Immigration* (New York: Seven Stories, 2007), 201.

29. Dream Act Now website, accessed January 31, 2015.

30. Ibid.

31. Ibid.

32. Compiled from Freedom from Fear website, including "Erica Andiola: Phoenix, AZ," accessed September 14, 2014, http:// freedomfromfearaward.com/celebrate/erika andiola.

33. Dream Defenders, "The Crisis," accessed November 17, 2014, http://dreamdefenders .org/thecrisis.

6: THE DEATH OF REHABILITATION

1. Matthew R. Derose, Alexia D. Cooper, and Howard N. Snyder, *Recidivism of Prisoners Released in 30 States in 2005: Patterns from 2005 to 2010* (Washington, DC: Bureau of Justice Statistics, Department of Justice, 2014).

2. Robert Martinson, "What Works? Questions and Answers About Prison Reform," *Public Interest*, no. 35 (Spring 1974): 22–54.

3. Ibid., 34. Martinson's argument concerning the futility of rehabilitation gained additional attention in 1980 when he jumped out the window of his ninth-floor Manhattan

apartment, punctuating the depth of his despair over the failure of rehabilitation.

4. Bruce Western, *Punishment and Inequality in America* (New York: Russell Sage Foundation, 2006), 175.

5. "Congressional Debate over Pell Grants," *Congressional Record*, 1993, p. S15748.

6. David Skorton and Glenn Altschuler, "College Behind Bars: How Educating Prisoners Pays Off," *Forbes*, May 25, 2013.

7. Richard P. Seiter and Karen R. Kadela, "Prisoner Reentry: What Works, What Does Not, and What Is Promising," *Crime & Delinquency* 49, no. 3 (2003): 360–88.

8. Jeremy Travis and Sarah Lawrence, *Beyond the Prison Gates: The State of Parole in America* (New York: Urban Institute, (2002).

9. E. Ann Carson and Daniela Golinelli, *Prisoners in 2012: Trends in Admissions and Releases, 1991–2012* (Washington, DC: Bureau of Justice Statistics, Department of Justice, 2012).

10. Derose et al., *Recidivism of Prisoners Released*.

11. Ibid.

12. Council of Advisors to Reduce Recidivism Through Employment, "A Review of the State of Illinois Professional and Occupational Licensure Policies as Related to Employment for Ex-Offenders," Safer Foundation policy paper 4, Chicago, September 2002.

13. Michelle Natividad Rodriguez and Maurice Emsellem, *65 Million Need Not Apply: The Case for Reforming Criminal Background Checks for Employment* (Oakland, CA: National Employment Law Project, 2011), 3.

14. Sentencing Project, "Felony Disenfranchisement," Washington, DC, October 24, 2014.

15. Marpessa Kupendua, "Coming Home: Revelations from Former Prisoners," *SF Bay View*, July 30, 2011.

16. Office of Justice Programs, "Crime Victims Fund," fact sheet, n.d., http://ojp.gov/ovc/pubs/crimevictimsfundfs/intro.html.

17. "Yolanda Quesada Fired from Wells Fargo for Shoplifting 40 Years Ago," *Huffington Post*, May 7, 2012.

18. "Florida Town 'Miracle Village' Is a Refuge for Sex Offenders," www.news.com.au, February 24, 2014.

19. Joan Petersilia, "Looking Back to See the Future of Prison Downsizing in America," keynote address to National Institute of Justice Conference, Arlington, VA, June 19, 2012.

20. Loïc Wacquant, "Prisoner Reentry as Myth and Ceremony," *Dialectical Anthropology* 34, no. 4 (2010): 608.

21. Susan B. Tucker and Eric Cadora, "Justice Reinvestment," Open Society Insitute Occasional Paper 3, no. 3 (2003).

7: JAIL—THE LOCAL FACE OF MASS INCARCERATION

1. All figures in table on jail populations from Bureau of Justice Statistics annual reports on jails.

2. Amanda Petteruti and Nastassia Walsh, *Jailing Communities: The Impact of Jail Expansion and Effective Public Safety Strategies* (New York: Justice Policy Institute, 2008), 13.

3. Thomas H. Cohen and Brian A. Reaves, *Pretrial Release of Felony Defendants in State Courts: State Court Processing Statistics, 1990–2004* (Washington, DC: Bureau of Justice Statistics, Department of Justice, 2007); and Thomas H. Cohen and Tracy Kyckelhahn, *Felony Defendants in Large Urban Counties* (Washington, DC: Department of Justice, 2006).

4. Pretrial Justice Institute, "Race and Bail in America," www.pretrial.org/the-problem/race -bail.

5. Bureau of Justice Statistics, "DWI Defenders Under Correctional Supervision, 1999," Department of Justice, Washington, DC, 1999.

6. Aaron Levin, "Prisons Jails Said to Need More MH Treatment," *Psychiatric News*, May 12, 2014.

7. Nicholas Kristof, "Inside a Mental Hospital Called Jail," *New York Times*, February 8, 2014.

8. David Cloud and Chelsea Davis, *Treatment Alternatives to Incarceration for People with Mental Health Needs in the Criminal Justice System: The Cost-Savings Implications* (New York: Vera Institute of Justice, 2005).

9. Christopher Petrella, "From Welfare to Cellfare," *Nation of Change*, February 24, 2012.

10. James Q. Wilson and George L. Kelling, "Broken Windows," *The Atlantic*, March 1, 1982.

11. National Law Center on Homelessness and Poverty and National Coalition for the Homeless, *Homes, Not Handcuffs: A Report on the Criminalization of Homelessness in U.S. Cities* (Washington, DC: 2009).

12. Zusha Elinson, "Homeless Lose a Longtime Last Resort: Living in a Car," *Wall Street Journal*, April 8, 2014.

13. Barbara Ehrenreich, "Author of *This Land Is Their Land*: Reports from a Divided Nation," *Salon*, August 9, 2011.

14. American Civil Liberties Union, "In for a Penny: The Rise of America's New Debtors Prisons," New York, April 2011.

15. Rebekah Diller, Alicia Bannon, and Mitali Nagrecha, "Criminal Justice Debt: A Barrier to Reentry," Brennan Center for Justice, New York University Law School, 2011.

16. Human Rights Watch, "Profiting from Probation: America's 'Offender-Funded' Probation Industry," New York, February 5, 2014.

17. Alexes Harris, "The Cruel Poverty of Monetary Sanctions," *Society Pages*, March 4, 2014.

18. Pretrial Justice Institute, "Race and Bail in America," 3; Petteruti and Walsh, *Jailing Communities*, 3.

19. Doris A. Graber, *Crime News and the Public* (New York: Praeger, 1980).

20. Federal Communications Commission, "INoC3: Television: Broadcast Televsion," 88.

21. Ibid.

22. Roopal Patel and Meghna Philip, "Criminal Justice Debt: A Toolkit for Action," Brennan Center for Justice, New York University Law School, July 10, 2012.

23. Robert Faturechi and Jack Leonard, "18 Los Angeles Sheriff's Officials Indicted, Accused of Abuse, Obstruction," *Los Angeles Times*, December 9, 2013.

24. James Austin et al., "Evaluation of the Current and Future Los Angeles County Jail Population," Report to Los Angeles County Board of Supervisors, April 10, 2012.

25. Steve Lopez, "Hard to See How Sheriff Baca Escapes Blame," *Los Angeles Times*, October 16, 2011.

26. American Civil Liberties Union, "ACLU Releases Expert's Report on Nightmarish Conditions at Men's Central Jail in Los Angeles," press release, New York, April 14, 2009.

27. Christina Villacorte, "Sheriff Lee Baca Proposes Almost $1 Billion New Jail to Replace Downtown Facility," *Los Angeles Daily News*, March 15, 2013.

28. Information on Champaign County from James Kilgore, "Reflections on the No More Jails Campaign in Champaign County (IL)," *Prison Legal News*, February 3, 2014.

29. James Ridgeway and Jean Casella, "America's Ten Worst Prisons: Tent City," *Mother Jones*, May 3, 2013.

30. Tony Ortega, "Human Plights," *Phoenix Sun-Times*, September 18, 1997.

31. Pearl Wilson, "Tent City—Sheriff Joe Arpaio's Shameful Creation," *Jon's Jail Journal* (blog), August 28, 2005.

32. Information on New Orleans from talk by Dana Kaplan at University YMCA, Champaign, IL, October 15, 2013.

8: THE SCHOOL-TO-PRISON PIPELINE

1. David L. Altheide, "Moral Panic: From Sociological Concept to Public Discourse," *Crime Media Culture* 5 (2009): 79.

2. John DiIulio Jr. and William Bennett, *Body Count: Moral Poverty . . . and How to Win America's War Against Crime and Drugs* (New York: Simon & Schuster, 1996), 112.

3. Wesley Lowery, "Education Under Arrest: Zero Tolerance Policies," *Tavis Smiley Reports*, Public Broadcasting Service, March 20, 2013.

4. Ashley Nellis, *Life Goes On: The Historic Rise in Life Sentences in America* (Washington, DC: Sentencing Project, 2013).

5. Paolo G. Annino et al., "Juvenile Life Without Parole for Non-Homicide Offenses: Florida Compared to Nation," Report for Public Interest Law Center, Florida State University, September 14, 2009.

6. Human Rights Watch and Amnesty International, *The Rest of Their Lives: Life Without Parole for Youth Offenders in the United States in 2008* (New York: Human Rights Watch, 2008).

7. Beth Schwartzapfel, "Sentenced Young:

The Story of Life Without Parole for Juvenile Offenders," *Al Jazeera America*, February 1, 2014.

8. Annette Fuentes, *Lockdown High: When the Schoolhouse Becomes a Jailhouse* (New York: Verso, 2011), 68.

9. Jacob Kang-Brown et al., *A Generation Later: What We've Learned About Zero Tolerance in Schools* (New York: Vera Institute of Justice, 2013).

10. Amanda Petteruti, *Education Under Arrest: The Case Against Police in Schools* (New York: Justice Policy Institute, 2011), 7.

11. Advancement Project, "Test, Punish, and Push Out: How 'Zero Tolerance' and High-Stakes Testing Funnel Youth into the School-to-Prison Pipeline," Washington, DC, January 2010.

12. "Echoes of the Super Predator," editorial, *New York Times*, April 13, 2014.

13. Clyde Haberman, "When Youth Violence Spread Superpredator Fear," *New York Times*, April 6, 2014.

14. Aviva Stahl, "In a Maryland Jail, Teens Charged as Adults Face Isolation and Neglect," *Solitary Watch*, June 17, 2014.

15. Schwartzapfel, "Sentenced Young."

16. Office for Civil Rights, "Data Snapshot: School Discipline," Department of Education, Washington, DC, March 2014.

17. Angel Jennings, "LA City Council Scales Back Truancy Laws," *Los Angeles Times*, February 23, 2012.

18. Joaquin Sapien, "Texas Students Thrown in Jail for Days . . . as Punishment for Missing School?," *AlterNet*, June 13, 2013.

19. Gretchen Kovach, "To Curb Truancy, Dallas Tries Electronic Monitoring," *New York Times*, May 12, 2008.

20. James Kilgore, "Tackling Debtors' Prisons: Reflecting on the Death of Eileen DiNino," *Truthout*, June 20, 2014.

21. 69 News, "Coroner Issues Ruling in Death of Woman Jailed in Child Truant Case," WFMZ-TV, August 14, 2014.

22. Kimberly Hefling and Jesse J. Holland, "Black Preschoolers More Likely to Face Suspension," Associated Press, March 21, 2014.

23. 69 News, "Coroner Issues Ruling."

24. Tunette Powell, "My Son Has Been Suspended Five Times. He's 3," *Washington Post*, July 24, 2014.

25. Lisa Wade, "Victor Rios on the Youth Control Complex," *Sociological Images*, November 10, 2010.

26. William Ecenbarger, *Kids for Cash: Two Judges, Thousands of Children, and a $2.6 Million Kickback Scheme* (New York: The New Press, 2012).

27. Nell Bernstein, *Burning Down the House: The End of Juvenile Prison* (New York: The New Press, 2014), 57.

28. Ibid., 309–10.

29. Ibid., 102.

30. Ibid.

31. Tony Fabelo et al., "Closer to Home: An Analysis of the State and Local Impact of the

Texas Juvenile Justice Reforms," Report for the Council of State Governments, January 2015.

32. Reid Wilson, "States See Marked Drop in Juvenile Prison Populations as Reforms Take Hold," *Washington Post*, January 29, 2015.

33. Maurice Chammah, "Closing Corsicana: Lessons from a Juvenile Lock-Up," *Texas Tribune*, February 12, 2014.

34. Marian Wright Edelman, "Juvenile Justice Reform: Making the 'Missouri Model' An American Model," *Huffington Post*, May 15, 2010.

35. All quotes from *Families Unlocking Futures: Solutions to the Crisis in Juvenile Justice* (Oakland, CA: Justice for Families, 2012).

36. Greg Allen, "Fla. School District Trying to Curb School-to-Prison Pipeline," *All Things Considered*, National Public Radio, November 5, 2013.

37. Los Angeles Youth Justice Coalition website, www.youth4justice.org.

38. Ibid.

39. Kang-Brown, *Generation Later*, 7

9: THE FOLKS LEFT BEHIND

1. Information on Chicago's deindustrialization from personal conversation with historian Brian Dolinar, June 17, 2014.

2. Paul Street, "Race, Prison, and Poverty: The Race to Incarcerate in the Age of Correctional Keynesianism," History Is a Weapon, 2008.

3. Patricia Atkins et al., "Responding to Manufacturing Job Loss: What Can Economic Development Policy Do?," Brookings Institution, June 29, 2011.

4. Bruce Western, *Punishment and Inequality in America* (New York: Russell Sage Foundation, 2006).

5. Peter Dreier, "Reagan's Real Legacy," *The Nation*, February 4, 2011.

6. Liz Schott and Ife Finch, "TANF Cash Benefits Continued to Lose Value in 2013," Center on Budget and Policy Priorities, Washington, DC, 2014.

7. Julilly Kohler-Hausmann, "The Crime of Survival: Fraud Prosecutions, Community Surveillance, and the Original 'Welfare Queen,'" *Journal of Social History* 41, no. 2 (2007); and James Kilgore, "Mass Incarceration: Examining and Moving Beyond the New Jim Crow," *Critical Sociology*, March 18, 2014.

8. Dorothy Roberts, "The Social and Moral Costs of Mass Incarceration in African American Communities," *Stanford Law Review* 56, no. 5 (2004): 1288.

9. David Garland, *Mass Imprisonment: Social Causes and Consequences* (New York: Sage, 2001), 2.

10. Angela Y. Davis, *Abolition Democracy: Beyond Empire, Prisons and Torture* (New York: Seven Stories, 2005), 94.

11. Andrea Strong, "We All Did the Time for My Brother's Crime," Families Against Mandatory Minimums, Washington, DC.

12. Campaign for Prison Phone Justice, "Facts," http://nationinside.org/campaign/prison-phone-justice/facts/.

13. Beth Richie, "The Social Impact of Mass Incarceration on Women," in *Invisible Punishment: The Collateral Consequences of Mass Imprisonment*, ed. Meda Chesney-Lind and Marc Mauer (New York: The New Press, 2003), 146.

14. Marc Mauer and Meda Chesney-Lind, "Introduction," in *Invisible Punishment*, 8.

15. Jeremy Travis et al., *The Growth of Incarceration in the United States: Exploring Causes and Consequences* (Washington, DC: National Academy of Sciences, 2014), 261.

16. Patricia Allard and Lynn Lu, "Reclaiming Families, Rebuilding Lives," Brennan Center for Justice, New York University Law School, August 2, 2006.

17. San Francisco Children of Incarcerated Parents Partnership, "Children of Incarcerated Parents: A Bill of Rights," San Francisco, 2010.

18. Nell Bernstein, *All Alone in the World: Children of the Incarcerated* (New York: The New Press, 2007), 150.

19. San Francisco Children of Incarcerated Parents Partnership, "Children of Incarcerated Parents."

20. Families Against Mandatory Minimums, "Family Friend Poems," http://www.familyfriendpoems.com/user/alison-henderson-313/.

21. Ibid.

22. Lisa Desjardins and Emma Lacey-Bordeaux, "Problems of Liberty and Justice on the Plains," CNN, August 10, 2012.

23. National Gay and Lesbian Task Force and National Center for Transgender Equality, *Injustice at Every Turn: A Report of the National Transgender Discrimination Survey* (Washington, DC: 2011).

24. Ibid.

25. National Network to End Domestic Violence Website, "The Violence Against Women Act (VAWA) Renewal Passes the House and Senate and Signed into Law," accessed January 31, 2015, http://nnedv.org/policy/issues/vawa.html.

26. Incite!, "Analysis: Incite!'s Dangerous Intersections," Burbank, CA.

27. Vikki Law, "Resisting Gender Violence Without Cops or Prisons," *Truthout*, December 8, 2011.

28. Roberts, "Social and Moral Costs."

29. Cited in ibid., 1287.

30. Richie, "Social Impact of Mass Incarceration on Women," 144.

10: WOMEN'S PRISONS

1. Nicole Hahn Rafter, *Partial Justice: Women in State Prisons, 1800–1935* (Boston: Northeastern University Press, 1985).

2. Andie Moss, *PREA: Implications for Women and Girls* (Washington, DC: National Institute of Corrections, 2007).

3. Sentencing Project, "Fact Sheet: Incarcerated Women," Washington, DC, December 2012.

4. Bureau of Justice Statistics, "Jail Inmates 2012," Department of Justice, Washington, DC.

5. Bureau of Justice Statistics, "Parole and Probation, 2013," Department of Justice, Washington, DC.

6. Vikki Law, *Resistance Behind Bars: The Struggle of Incarcerated Women* (Oakland: PM Press, 2013).

7. Todd D. Minton, "Jail Inmates at Midyear 2010—Statistical Tables," Bureau of Justice Statistics, Department of Justice, Washington, DC, April 2011.

8. Montana Department of Corrections, *Biennial Report 2013*, Helena, 138.

9. John Caniglia, "White Women Sent to Ohio Prisons in Record Numbers, Reports Say," *Cleveland Plain Dealer*, August 15, 2013.

10. About $1,264 in 2014 dollars. Lauren E. Glaze and Laura M. Maruschak, "Parents in Prison and Their Minor Children," Bureau of Justice Statistics, Washington, DC, August 2008, 17.

11. Sentencing Project, "Women in the Criminal Justice System: Briefing Sheets," Washington, DC, May 2007.

12. Ibid., 3.

13. Lynn M. Paltrow and Jeanne Flavin, "Pregnant Women in the United States, 1973–2005: Implications for Women's Legal Status and Public Health," *Journal of Health Politics, Policy and Law*, January 15, 2013.

14. Ibid.

15. Bob Herbert, "In America, Pregnancy and Addiction," *New York Times*, June 11, 1998.

16. Sentencing Project, "Parents in State Prison," Washington, DC, 2013.

17. Sentencing Project, "Incarcerated Women," Washington, DC, September 2013, www.sentencingproject.org/doc/publications /cc_incarcerated_women_factsheet_sep24sp.pdf.

18. Cited in American Civil Liberties Union, "The Shackling of Pregnant Women and Girls in U.S. Prisons, Jails and Youth Detention Centers," briefing paper, New York, n.d.

19. Meredith Lindsey Berg, "Pregnant Prisoners Are Losing Their Shackles," *Boston Globe*, April 18, 2014.

20. American Civil Liberties Union, "Prison Rape Elimination Act of 2003," New York.

21. Ayelet Waldman and Robin Levi, eds., *Inside This Place, Not of It: Narratives from Women's Prisons* (San Francisco: McSweeney, 2011), 43.

22. Allen J. Beck, Ramona R. Rantala, and Jessica Rexroat, "Sexual Victimization Reported by Adult Correctional Authorities, 2009–11," Bureau of Justice Statistics, Department of Justice, Washington, DC, 2012.

23. American Civil Liberties Union, "Prison Strip Search Is Sexually Abusive," New York.

24. Challen Stephens, "Averting Its Eyes, Alabama Lets Sink into Despair," AL.com, June 22, 2014.

25. American Civil Liberties Union, "Sexual Abuse in Immigrant Detention: Raquel's Story," New York, October 16, 2011.

26. Alexander L. Lee, "Nowhere to Go but Out: The Collision Between Transgender and Gender-Variant Prisoners and the Gender Binary in America's Prisons," Just Detention International, Los Angeles, 2003.

27. Jaime M. Grant et al., *Injustice at Every Turn: A Report of the National Transgender Discrmination Survey* (Washington, DC: National Gay and Lesbian Task Force and National Center for Transgender Equality, 2011).

28. Barbara Bloom, Barbara Owen, and Stephanie Covington, *Gender Responsive Strategies for Women Offenders: A Summary of Research, Practice, and Guiding Principles*, The Gender-Responsive Strategies Project: Approach and Findings (Washington, DC: National Institute of Corrections, Department of Justice, 2005).

29. Californians United for a Responsible Budget, "How 'Gender Responsive Prisons' Harm Women, Children, and Families," Oakland, 2007.

11: PRIVATE PRISONS

1. Tara Herivel and Paul Wright, eds., *Prison Profiteers: Who Makes Money from Mass Incarceration* (New York: The New Press, 2009).

2. Kentucky Office of Corrections Training, "History of Kentucky Prisons," Louisville, 1988, 3.

3. Douglas Blackmon, *Slavery by Another Name: The Re-enslavement of Black Americans from the Civil War to World War I* (New York: Anchor, 2009).

4. Ibid.

5. Bureau of Justice Assistance, "Prison Industries Enhancement Certification Program," Department of Justice, Washington, DC, 2004.

6. Quoted in Elaine J. Cohen, "When It Comes to Detention, It's About the Stories Behind the Statistics," remarks at ImagiNation: Immigration, Cathedral of Hope, Dallas, TX, posted to Grassroots Leadership blog, August 4, 2014.

7. American Civil Liberties Union, "Banking on Bondage: Private Prisons and Mass Incarceration," New York, November 2, 2011.

8. Donna Selman and Paul Leighton, *Punishment for Sale: Private Prisons, Big Business, and the Incarceration Binge* (Lanham, MD: Rowman & Littlefield, 2010), 152.

9. Ibid., 5.

10. Figures compiled from financial reports on the websites of Corrections Corporation of America and the GEO Group.

11. Forbes.com, Profile, "Damon Hininger"; Forbes.com, Profile, "George Zoley."

12. Selman and Leighton, *Punishment for Sale.*

13. Ibid.

14. Ray Downs, "Who's Getting Rich off the Prison Industrial Complex?," *Vice*, May 17, 2013.

15. Alexander T. Tabarrok, "Private Prisons Have Public Benefits," *Independent Review*, October 24, 2004.

16. "Private Prisons—the Best Investment in America," RT [Russian Television], March 20, 2012.

17. Cited in Kati Rose-Quandt, "Why There's an Even Larger Racial Disparity in Private Prisons Than in Public Ones," *Mother Jones*, January 1, 2014.

18. Julie Ebenstein, "Private Prisons Don't Save Dollars and They Don't Make Sense," American Civil Liberties Union, New York, 2013.

19. Cody Mason, *Dollars and Detainees: The Growth of For-Profit Detention* (Washington, DC: Sentencing Project, 2012).

20. Quoted in Mark Cowling, "Private Prisons Invest in Rehabilitation but Results Aren't Measured," *Casa Grande Dispatch*, May 21, 2014.

21. Michael Myser, "The Hard Sell," *CNN Money*, March 15, 2007.

22. American Civil Liberties Union, "Banking on Bondage."

23. Rachel Bloom, "Is CCA Trying to Take Over the World?," American Civil Liberties Union, New York, 2012.

24. Paul Ashton, *Gaming the System: How the Political Strategies of Private Prison Companies Promote Ineffective Incarceration Policies* (New York: Justice Policy Institute, 2011).

25. In the Public Interest, "Criminal: How Lockup Quotas and 'Low-Crime Taxes' Guarantee Profits for Private Prisons," Washington, DC, September 19, 2013.

26. Mason, *Dollars and Detainees*.

27. Ibid.

28. CBS News, "Locked Inside a Nightmare," May 9, 2000; and Mason, *Dollars and Detainees*.

29. Chris Kirkham, "GEO Group Stadium Deal Is Off; Private Prison Company Cites 'Ongoing Distraction' After Protests," *Huffington Post*, April 2, 2013.

30. Alex Friedman, "Prison Privatization: An Insider's Perspective," American Federation of State, County, and Municipal Employees, Washington, DC, March–April 2001.

31. Lee Fang, "How Private Prisons Game the Immigration System," *The Nation*, February 27, 2013.

32. Mason, *Dollars and Detainees*.

33. Priscilla Mosqueda and Forrest Wilder, "Immigrants Are Being Held in Private Texas Prisons and Are Subject to Shocking Abuse," *Business Insider*, June 10, 2014.

34. James Ridgeway and Jean Casella, "America's Ten Worst Prisons: Tent City," *Mother Jones*, May 3, 2013; and Mason, *Dollars and Detainees*.

35. American Civil Liberties Union, "Warehoused and Forgotten: Immigrants Trapped in Our Shadow Private Prison System," New York, June 2014.

36. GEO Group, "The GEO Group Awarded Contract by U.S. Immigration and Customs Enforcement for the Continued Provision of Services Under Intensive Supervision and Appearance Program," press release, Boca Raton, FL, September 10, 2014; and Mason, *Dollars and Detainees*.

12: INCARCERATION INC.

1. Christian Henrichson and Ruth Delaney, *The Price of Prisons: What Incarceration Costs Taxpayers* (New York: Vera Institute of Justice, 2012).

2. All information on construction companies from IBISWorld Industry Reports, "Prison and Jail Construction, 2013," www.ibisworld.com/industry/prison-jail-construction.html.

3. California Department of Finance, "A Performance Review: The California Department of Corrections," Sacramento, 1996; and National Association of Realtors, "USA Real Estate Median Sales Prices of Existing Homes Since 1968," Chicago, n.d.

4. Zev Yaroslovsky, "Board Clears Way for $2B Jail," Zev's Blog, May 8, 2014.

5. Sarah Lawrence and Jeremy Travis, *The New Landscape of Imprisonment: Mapping America's Prison Expansion* (New York: Urban Institute, 2004), 17.

6. Craig Harris, "New Corrections Chief Open to Expanding Private Prison Use," *Oklahoma Watch*, February 21, 2014.

7. "State Worker Salary Data Base," *Sacramento Bee*, January 22, 2015.

8. Bureau of Labor Statistics, "Occupational Employment Statistics," Department of Justice, Washington, DC, May 2013.

9. Workforce Associates, "A 21st Century Workforce for America's Correctional Profession," part one of a three-part study commissioned by the American Correctional Association, Indianapolis, May 15, 2004.

10. Ibid.

11. Bureau of Labor Statistics, "Occupational Employment Statistics."

12. Tim Kowal, "The Role of the Prison Guards Union in California's Troubled Prison System," Fair Chance Project, June 6, 2011, http://fairchanceproject.com/news/role-prison-guards-union-californias-troubled-prison-system.

13. Figures for union members compiled from the three unions' websites, July 28, 2014.

14. Ben Carrasco, "Assessing the CCPOA's Political Influence and Its Impact on Efforts to Reform the California Corrections System," Stanford Criminal Justice Working Papers, January 27, 2006.

15. Kenneth Quinnell, "AFL-CIO Delegates Condemn Mass Incarceration of People of Color," AFL-CIO Now website, September 9, 2013.

16. Bob Barker Company home page, www.bobbarker.com.

17. Dave Cook, "$9 Million and Counting: Why Prison Arcitect Underlines a Changing Tide," VG 24/7, December 5, 2013.

18. Fedmine, "Bob Barker Company, Inc.," November 17, 2013, www.fedmine.us.

19. Quoted in Aviva Shen, "States' Efforts to Privatize Prison Health Care Create 'Inhumane' Conditions," *ThinkProgress*, July 23, 2012.

20. Greg Dober, "Corizon Needs a Checkup," *Prison Legal News*, March 15, 2013.

21. Michael Myser, "The Hard Sell," *CNN Money*, March 15, 2007.

22. Andrew Welsh-Huggins, "Ohio Slaps Second Fine on Aramark for Prison Food Problems," *Daily Times*, July 30, 2014.

23. Campaign for Prison Phone Justice, www.prisonphonejustice.org.

24. Eliza Barclay, "Food as Punishment: Giving US Inmates 'The Loaf' Persists," National Public Radio, January 2, 2014.

25. Federal Communications Commission, "Second Further Notice of Proposed Rulemaking," Rates for Interstate Inmate Calling Services, October 22, 2014.

26. Meegan Leerkson, "American Securities Buys Global Tel★Link from Veritas," *Deal Pipeline*, October 31, 2011.

27. Federal Communications Commission, "Second Further Notice of Proposed Rulemaking."

28. Marilyn C. Moses and Cindy J. Smith, "Factories Behind Fences: Do Prison 'Real Work' Programs Work?," National Institute of Justice, Washington, DC, 2007.

29. Beth Schwartzapfel, "The Great American Chain Gang," *American Prospect*, May–June 2014.

30. Lisa Sundberg, "Prison Labor Drives Lufkin Factory Out of Business," *Houston Chronicle*, July 7, 2008.

31. Robert Winters, "Evaluating the Effectiveness of Prison Farm Programs," Corrections.com, September 23, 2013.

32. Unicor website, www.unicor.gov.

33. Neal Conan, "Inmates' Jobs, from Call Centers to Paint Mixing," National Public Radio, December 16, 2010.

34. Reese Ehrlich, "Prison Labor: Workin' for the Man," *Covert Action Quarterly* 54 (Fall 1995).

35. Steve Fraser and Joshua B. Freeman, "Locking Down an American Workforce," *Huffington Post*, June 20, 2012.

36. Simon McCormack, "Prison Labor Booms as Unemployment Remains High; Companies Reap Benefits," *Huffington Post*, December 10, 2012.

37. Diane Cardwell, "Private Businesses Fight Federal Prisons for Contracts," *New York Times*, March 14, 2012.

38. AFL-CIO, "The Exploitation of Prison Labor," Washington, DC, May 7, 1997.

39. Jon Swartz, "Inmates vs. Outsourcing," *USA Today*, July 6, 2004.

13: CHANGING THE MIND-SET

1. Lauren E. Glaze and Danielle Kaeble, *Correctional Populations in the United States, 2013* (Washington, DC: Bureau of Justice Statistics, Department of Justice, 2014).

2. Laura Mirsky, "Restorative Justice Practices of Native American, First Nation and Other Indigenous Peoples: Part One," International Institute of Restorative Practices, Bethlehem, PA, April 27, 2004.

3. Personal communication, August 20, 2014.

4. Marc Levin, *Restorative Justice in Texas: Past, Present and Future* (Austin: Texas Public Policy Foundation, 2005).

5. "Restorative Justice in Schools," YouTube video, October 19, 2010, www.youtube.com /watch?v=NmpGg8Dy-K4.

6. Adapted by Project Nia from Kay Pranis and Barry Stuart, "Establishing Shared Responsibility for Child Welfare Through Peacemaking Circles," in *Family Group Conferencing*, ed. Gail Buford and Joe Hudson (Piscataway, NJ: Aldine DeGruyter, 2002).

7. Desmond Tutu, *No Future Without Forgiveness* (New York: Image, 2000), 54–55.

8. Sheila Bedi, "Seeking Transformative Justice in Ferguson, Dearborn, and Beyond," *Huffington Post*, September 4, 2014.

9. Sarah Kershnar et al., *Toward Transformative Justice: A Liberatory Approach to Child Sexual Abuse and Other Forms of Intimate and Community Violence* (Oakland, CA: Generation Five, 2007).

10. Ibid.

11. Incite!, "Violence Against Women of Color: What Counts as 'Violence Against Women'?," Burbank, CA.

12. Angela Y. Davis, *Are Prisons Obsolete?* (New York: Seven Stories, 2003), 84.

13. Thomas Mathiesen, *The Politics of Abolition* (London: Martin Robertson, 1974). Mathiesen reissued his anthology with many new writings as *The Politics of Abolition Revisited* (New York: Routledge, 2014).

14. Fay Honey Knopp and John Regier, *Instead of Prison: A Handbook for Prison Activists* (Syracuse, NY: Prison Research Education Action Project, 1976; Oakland, CA: Critical Resistance, 2005).

15. Wikipedia, "Social Movement," accessed November 23, 2014.

16. Quoted in part 4, ". . . Framing Abolitionist Arguments in Terms of What We Want," in Critical Resistance, *The Abolitionist Toolkit* (2012), 8.

17. "Ruth Gilmore Interview at Critical Resistance," *The Defenestrator*, accessed October 23, 2014, www.defenestrator.org.

14: ORGANIZING TO END MASS INCARCERATION

1. Vera Institute of Justice, "Justice in Focus: Crime Bill @20," New York, 2014.

2. "End Mass Incarceration Now," editorial, *New York Times*, May 10, 2014.

3. Inimai Chettiar, "Criminal Justice Reform Is a National Economic Issue—Stop Ignoring It," *The Hill* blog, September 20, 2012.

4. Quoted in Mariame Kaba, "Prison Reform's in Vogue and Other Strange Things," *Truthout*, March 21, 2014.

5. Marc Mauer, "Racial Impact Statements as a Means of Reducing Unwanted Sentencing Disparities," *Ohio Journal of Criminal Law* 19, no. 5 (2007).

6. Newt Gingrich and Pat Nolen, "Prison Reform: A Smart Way for State to Save Money and Lives," *Washington Post*, January 7, 2011.

7. E-mail communication with the author, September 22, 2014.

8. Marshall Clement, Matthew Schwarzfeld, and Michael Thompson, *National Summit on Justice Reinvestment and Public Safety: Addressing Recidivism, Crime and Corrections Spending* (Washington, DC: Council of State Governments, 2011).

9. Judith Greene et al., *Ending Mass Incarceration: Charting a New Justice Reinvestment* (Brooklyn, NY: Justice Strategies, 2013).

10. Michelle Alexander, *The New Jim Crow: Mass Incarceration in the Age of Colorblindness* (New York: The New Press, 2009), 18

11. Jeremy Travis et al., *The Growth of Incarceration in the United States: Exploring Causes and Consequences* (Washington, DC: National Academy of Sciences, 2014).

12. Cited in "Irrational Exuberance: Mass Incarceration Is STILL an Epidemic . . . ," *Prison Culture Blog*, September 23, 2014.

13. LEAP, "LEAP Statement of Principles," accessed January 11, 2015, http://www.leap.cc/about/leap-statement-of-principles/.

14. Black Agenda Radio, August 6, 2014, http://agendareport.libsyn.com/webpage/2014/08.

15. Drug Policy Alliance, "Drug Courts Are Not the Answer: Toward a Health-Centered Approach to Drug Use," New York, 2011.

16. Dan Berger, "Social Movements and Mass Incarceration: What Is to Be Done?," *Souls: A Critical Journal of Black Politics, Culture, and Society* 15, no. 1–2 (2013): 3–18.

17. Amy Goodman and Juan González, "Angela Davis on Prison Abolition, the War on Drugs and Why Social Movements Shouldn't Wait on Obama," interview, *Democracy Now!*, March 6, 2014.

18. Marc Mauer and Nazgol Ghandnoosh, *Fewer Prisoners, Less Crime: A Tale of Three States* (Washington, DC: Sentencing Project, 2014).

19. James Kilgore, "Are We Really Witnessing the End of Mass Incarceration?," *Counterpunch*, November 2013.

20. Ibid.

21. Information on Colorado compiled from Colorado Criminal Justice Reform Coalition website, www.ccjrc.org.

22. Marc Mauer, "Can We Really Wait 88 Years to End Mass Incarceration?," *Huffington Post*, December 20, 2013.

INDEX